CAMBRIDGE UNIVERSITY PRESS
CAMBRIDGE ENGLISH Language Assessment
Part of the University of Cambridge

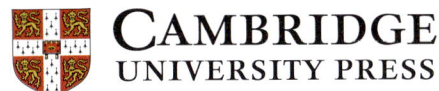

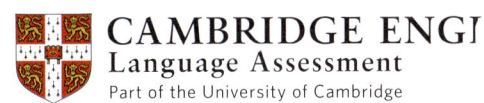

Cambridge English

EMPOWER

COMBO A STUDENT'S BOOK

B2

Adrian Doff, Craig Thaine
Herbert Puchta, Jeff Stranks, Peter Lewis-Jones

This page is intentionally left blank

Contents

STUDENT'S BOOK

Map of Student's Book	4
Unit 1 Outstanding people	7
Unit 2 Survival	19
Unit 3 Talent	31
Unit 4 Life lessons	43
Unit 5 Chance	55
Communication Plus	129
Grammar Focus	134
Vocabulary Focus	154
Audioscripts	164
Phonemic symbols and Irregular verbs	176

WORKBOOK

Map of Workbook	2
Unit 1 Outstanding people	4
Unit 2 Survival	10
Unit 3 Talent	16
Unit 4 Life lessons	22
Unit 5 Chance	28
Vox pop video	64
Audioscripts	70
Answer key	78

Contents

Lesson and objective	Grammar	Vocabulary	Pronunciation	Everyday English
Unit 1 Outstanding people				
Getting started Discuss meeting famous people				
1A Discuss people you admire	Review of tenses	Character adjectives	The letter *e*; Word stress	
1B Discuss a challenge	Questions	Trying and succeeding		
1C Explain what to do and check understanding			Rapid speech	Breaking off a conversation; Explaining and checking understanding
1D Write an article				
Review and extension More practice		WORDPOWER *make*		
Unit 2 Survival				
Getting started Discuss coping with natural disasters				
2A Discuss dangerous situations	Narrative tenses	Expressions with *get*	Sounds and spelling: *g*	
2B Give advice on avoiding danger	Future time clauses and conditionals	Animals and the environment		
2C Give and respond to compliments			Tone in question tags	Agreeing using question tags; Giving and responding to compliments
2D Write guidelines in a leaflet				
Review and extension More practice		WORDPOWER *face*		
Unit 3 Talent				
Getting started Discuss what makes something a work of art				
3A Discuss ability and achievement	Multi-word verbs	Ability and achievement		
3B Discuss sports activities and issues	Present perfect simple and continuous	Words connected with sport	Word stress	
3C Make careful suggestions			Sounds and spelling: Consonant sounds	Keeping to the topic of the conversation; Making careful suggestions
3D Write a description of data				
Review and extension More practice		WORDPOWER *up*		
Unit 4 Life lessons				
Getting started Discuss childhood experiences				
4A Discuss events that changed your life	*used to* and *would*	Cause and result		
4B Discuss and describe rules	Obligation and permission	Talking about difficulty	Sounds and spelling: *u*	
4C Describe photos			Contrastive stress	Describing photos; Expressing careful disagreement
4D Write an email to apply for work				
Review and extension More practice		WORDPOWER *as*		
Unit 5 Chance				
Getting started Discuss attitudes to risk				
5A Discuss possible future events	Future probability	Adjectives describing attitude	Sounds and spelling: *th*	
5B Prepare for a job interview	Future perfect and future continuous	The natural world		
5C Discuss advantages and disadvantages			Tone groups	Responding to an idea; Discussing advantages and disadvantages
5D Write an argument for and against an idea				
Review and extension More practice		WORDPOWER *side*		
Communication Plus p.129	**Grammar Focus p.134**		**Vocabulary Focus p.154**	

Contents

Listening and Video	Reading	Speaking	Writing
Conversation about Jocelyn Bell-Burnell	Articles: *Apple's design genius* and *The woman who reinvented children's TV*	Discussing inspiring people	
Podcast: *The 30-day challenge*	Interviews: *30-day challenge*	Asking and answering questions about challenges	
Starting a new job		Explaining a process; Checking understanding	Unit Progress Test
Conversation about technology	Article: *Tech free!*	Discussing technology	Article Organising an article
Conversation about a survival situation	Article: *Lost at sea*	Telling a survival story	
Interview: *The Tiger*	Leaflet: *How to survive … an animal attack*	Giving advice; Asking questions	
Taking photos		Giving compliments and responding	Unit Progress Test
Talking about getting lost	Leaflet with guidelines for hiking	Discussing the natural environment	Guidelines Organising guidelines in a leaflet
Conversation: learning experiences	Text about learning: *Learning to learn*	Talking about something you have put a lot of effort into	
Radio programme: *The Sports Gene*	Article: *Born to be the best?*; Two articles about US baseball players	Discussing sport and ways to improve performance	
Making wedding plans		Planning a party	Unit Progress Test
Interviews about sports	Article: *A nation of armchair athletes?*	Talking about popular sports	Article describing data Describing data
Interview: *Psychology of money*; Two monologues: *Life-changing events*	Two texts about winning the lottery	Talking about how your life has changed	
Two monologues: training for a job	Article: *Training to be the best*	Discuss experiences of training and rules	
Presenting photos		Discussing photos; Disagreeing carefully	Unit Progress Test
Three monologues: living in different places	Webpage about being an international student 'buddy'	Discussing living in a different country	Job application Giving a positive impression
Monologue: *What are your chances?*	Quiz: *Are you an optimist or a pessimist?*; Article: *Why we think we're going to have a long and happy life.*	Discussing possible future events	
Conversation: talking about work	Quiz: *The unknown continent*; Article: *Cooking in Antarctica*	Role play: a job interview	
Money problems		Explaining and responding to ideas for a café	Unit Progress Test
News reports: extreme weather	Essay about climate change	Giving opinions on climate change	For and against essay Arguing for and against an idea

Audioscripts p.164   **Phonemic symbols and Irregular verbs** p.176

This page is intentionally left blank

UNIT 1
Outstanding people

CAN DO OBJECTIVES
- Discuss people you admire
- Discuss a challenge
- Explain what to do and check understanding
- Write an article

GETTING STARTED

a Look at the picture and answer the questions.
1 Who do you think the man and the woman are? Where are they?
2 What are the people behind them doing?
3 What do you think the man and the woman have just said to each other? What's going to happen next?

b Discuss the questions.
1 On what occasions do you normally take photos? When was the last time you took a 'selfie'?
2 If you could take a 'selfie' with a famous person, who would you choose and why?
3 What role do you think celebrities and famous people play in modern society? How important is it that they should:
  – be good role models? – inspire other people?

7

1A She is an inspiring woman

Learn to discuss people you admire
- **G** Review of tenses
- **V** Character adjectives

1 READING

a 💬 What kinds of people do you admire most? Why?

b 💬 Look at photos a and b. What do you think these people have done that make other people admire them?

c Read *Apple's design genius* and *The woman who reinvented children's TV* quickly and check your answers.

d Read the texts again and answer the questions. Write JI (Jony Ive), JC (Joan Ganz Cooney) or B (both).

Who … ?
1. had training in their area of work
2. carried out some research
3. set up their own company
4. was one of the first people in their role
5. initially found the work challenging
6. was interested in other people's learning
7. believes the things we use should be beautiful
8. has won prizes for their work

e 💬 Who do you think is more inspiring, Jony Ive or Joan Ganz Cooney? Why?

Apple's design genius

I've always loved great design. Ever since I can remember, I've been fascinated by the shape and look of objects. In my opinion, Apple Inc. is the number one company in the world for product design.

In the time that ¹**you're reading** this article, around 750 iPhones and 300 iPads will be sold internationally. These iconic devices generate millions of pounds a day for Apple, and the man behind their iconic look is known as a 'design genius'. In 2013, *Time Magazine* listed him as one of the 100 most influential people in the world, but can you name him?

If you said Steve Jobs, you'd be wrong, although it was Jobs who first recognised this man's talent. His name is Jony Ive.

Born in London, Jony Ive studied industrial design at Newcastle Polytechnic. After graduating, ²**he helped** set up the London design agency Tangerine. In 1992, while ³**he was working** at Tangerine, he accepted a job offer from Apple.

His first years in the job were tough and the design work wasn't very interesting. The company was also struggling to make money. However, when Steve Jobs returned to Apple in 1997 and saw the design work that Ive ⁴**had produced**, he immediately recognised Ive's ability and promoted him. Ive's first success in his new role was the design of the original, colourful iMac in 1998, which was quickly followed by the first iPod in 2001. Thanks to Ive's simple, elegant designs, Apple became one of the most successful companies in the world. Since then, ⁵**he has been** responsible for the iPhone, iPad and Apple Watch. Ive's design involves not only the way these products look but also the way they work. ⁶**He believes** devices have to be both beautiful and practical.

Jony Ive's key contribution to Apple is now being recognised and he has received numerous awards. There is no doubt that Steve Jobs was a larger-than-life ideas man and businessman who created a hugely successful company. However, without Jony Ive's design talent, Apple may not have become such a huge success.

So what have I learnt from Jony Ive? That the best designs are often the simplest.

a

8

THE WOMAN WHO REINVENTED CHILDREN'S TV

I've always felt passionate about television's ability to entertain and educate. I grew up watching what I consider to be a master class in how you can combine these two aspects of television: *Sesame Street*. This is the programme that brought us Big Bird, Elmo, Cookie Monster and friends. They're all the invention of a woman I consider a genius: Joan Ganz Cooney.

In the mid-1960s, Ganz Cooney was working as a producer of television documentary programmes in America. She realised television could play an important role in the education of pre-school children. She researched this idea and, in 1967, she wrote an outline for *Sesame Street*.

Ganz Cooney presented her ideas to the TV channel she was working for at the time. However, the channel rejected her proposal, saying that they thought she didn't have the right experience to produce a TV programme for children. As a result, she set up Children's Television Workshop with a colleague, and two years later they had managed to raise eight million dollars to finance production. Even so, many people working in the television industry questioned her ability to manage such a project. This was during the 1960s, when the industry was largely controlled by men.

At first, Ganz Cooney didn't want to fight to keep her role as the director of the production company and the producer of the programme. However, her husband and a colleague encouraged her to do so, because they knew the project would fail without her involvement. This meant she became one of the first female television executives in America.

In 1969, two years after her initial research, *Sesame Street* went on air, and today it's still going strong. However, Joan Ganz Cooney didn't stop there. She continued to take an interest in early childhood education, and in 2007, she set up a centre to help improve children's digital literacy. I really admire the way she has quietly got on with helping young children. She's not a household name like Big Bird, but she's had a huge impact on the education of millions of children around the world.

Sesame Street Facts
- more than 120 million viewers worldwide
- shown in more than 140 different countries
- now has a production budget of around $17 million a year

UNIT 1

2 GRAMMAR Review of tenses

a Match the verbs 1–6 in bold in *Apple's design genius* with the tenses below.

☐ present simple
☐ past simple
☐ present continuous
☐ past continuous
☐ present perfect
☐ past perfect

b Complete the sentences with the tenses in 2a.
We use the:
1 _____ to refer to an event that takes place at a specific time in the past.
2 _____ to refer to a temporary event in progress in the present.
3 _____ to refer to a state or action that began in the past and has continued until now.
4 _____ to refer to something that's generally true.
5 _____ to refer to an action that was in progress in the past when something else happened.
6 _____ to refer to a past action that occurred before another past action.

c Underline examples of the six tenses in the second text.

d ▶ Now go to Grammar Focus 1A on p.134

e Read the text about Nikola Tesla and circle the correct words.

f ▶1.3 Listen and check your answers.

Nikola Tesla

Not many people ¹*have heard / heard* of Nikola Tesla, who ²*played / was playing* a key role in creating the alternating current (AC) supply of electricity we ³*are having / have* in our homes today. Early in his career, Tesla ⁴*has worked / worked* with Thomas Edison. He ⁵*had emigrated / has emigrated* to the USA from Europe in 1884. While Tesla ⁶*was working / had worked* for Edison, they had an argument over payment for an invention, so Tesla ⁷*was deciding / decided* to work independently. It was then that he developed a motor that could produce an alternating current. Throughout his life, Tesla continued to conduct experiments and ⁸*helped / was helping* develop X-ray radiography and wireless communication. There is no doubt that he ⁹*has had / had had* a large impact on modern technology. Many of the gadgets that we ¹⁰*are enjoying / enjoy* today would not have been possible without Nikola Tesla.

UNIT 1

3 LISTENING

a ▶1.4 Listen to two colleagues, Amelia and Chloe, talking about a female scientist, Jocelyn Bell-Burnell. Tick (✓) the correct sentences.
1 She's always been famous. ☐
2 She isn't very well known. ☐
3 She made an amazing discovery. ☐
4 She created a new mathematical theory. ☐

b ▶1.4 Listen again. Are the sentences true or false?
1 Amelia's reading a non-fiction book about planets and stars.
2 Jocelyn Bell-Burnell discovered a particular kind of star.
3 She won a Nobel Prize for her discovery.
4 She did badly when studying science at high school.
5 Life wasn't easy for her when she made her discovery.
6 The press didn't treat Jocelyn Bell-Burnell seriously.
7 Amelia has been inspired by Jocelyn Bell-Burnell.

c 💬 Discuss the questions.
1 Could Jocelyn Bell-Burnell's story have happened in your country? Do you know any similar examples?
2 How popular is science in your country? Is it popular with both men and women?
3 Is it important what gender a scientist is? Why do you think it was important in the case of Jocelyn Bell-Burnell?

4 VOCABULARY
Character adjectives

a Underline the five adjectives that describe people's character in sentences 1–4. Which two adjectives have a similar meaning and what's the difference between them?
1 She's a respected physicist.
2 She is an inspiring woman.
3 She was really determined, but in a quiet way.
4 Well, you've always been motivated, that's for sure. And stubborn.

b ▶1.5 **Pronunciation** Listen to the pronunciation of the letter *e* in these words. Which two sounds are the same? What are the other two sounds?

r**e**sp**e**cted   d**e**t**e**rmined

c ▶1.6 Look at the words in the box and decide how the underlined letter *e* is pronounced. Add the words to the table, then listen and check. Practise saying the words.

sl<u>e</u>pt   r<u>e</u>vise   h<u>e</u>lpful   s<u>e</u>rve   d<u>e</u>sire
pr<u>e</u>fer   id<u>e</u>ntity   univ<u>e</u>rsity   wom<u>e</u>n

sound 1 /ɪ/	sound 2 /e/	sound 3 /ɜː/

d Complete the sentences with the character adjectives in 4a.
1 Once Dan gets an idea in his head nothing will change his mind. He's the most _____ person I know and it's really annoying.
2 I'm not the sort of person who gives up easily – I'm very _____ when I want to achieve something.
3 He's worked hard and has done some very interesting research. He's a highly _____ chemist who's known around the world.
4 Doing a PhD is hard work so you have to be quite _____ if you want to do one.
5 In my last year of high school we had a really _____ biology teacher. Her lessons were so interesting that we all worked very hard for her.

e ▶ Now go to Vocabulary Focus on p.154

5 SPEAKING

a Think of an inspiring person, who has influenced you in some way. It can be someone you know or it can be someone famous. Make notes about the person. Use the questions to help you.
• What is this person's background?
• What important things has this person done in their life?
• Why are they inspiring?
• How have they changed or influenced your life?

b 💬 Tell other students about your person. Ask questions.

> My cousin Vera is an athlete. She trains really hard every day – she's really determined.

> How does she stay motivated?

1B Are you finding it difficult?

Learn to discuss a challenge
G Questions
V Trying and succeeding

The 30-day challenge

1 SPEAKING and LISTENING

a 💬 Look at photos a–c and read *The 30-day challenge*. Then discuss the questions.
1 What are the people in the photos doing? Have you ever taken up similar activities? If so, how successful were you?
2 Why do you think doing something for 30 days gives you a better chance of succeeding?

b ▶1.10 Listen to a podcast about the 30-day challenge. Tick the main point that Alison makes.
1 The 30-day challenge is a good way to give up bad habits.
2 It's difficult for the brain to adapt to new habits.
3 If you try something new for 30 days, you're more likely to keep to it afterwards.

c ▶1.10 Alison made some notes at the seminar. Complete her notes with one or two words in each gap. Listen again and check.

Seminar notes
- It takes the brain 30 days to adapt to a new ¹_____.
- 30 days isn't a ²_____ time, so it's fun to do something new.
- Also a chance to try something ³_____ – not just giving up bad habits.
- Two ways to do it:
  1 do something that doesn't get in the way of your ⁴_____
  2 take time out to do something you've always ⁵_____ do
- You need to make an ⁶_____ !

Have you ever started a new hobby, but given up after only a couple of weeks? Or started a course and stopped after the first few lessons? Most of us have tried to learn something new, but very few of us ever really get any good at it – it's just too difficult to continue doing something new.

But now there's some good news: did you know that if you can keep up your new hobby for just 30 days, you have a much better chance of succeeding? And you may learn something new about yourself too.

d What examples of 30-day challenges did you hear? Use words from both boxes for each challenge.

Cycle everywhere, even if it rains.

| ~~cycle~~ drink climb get up eat paint write |

| rise poem coffee new picture mountains ~~everywhere~~ |

e What do you think of the ideas Alison talks about? Make notes.

f 💬 Compare your ideas.

11

UNIT 1

2 VOCABULARY
Trying and succeeding

a ▶ 1.11 Complete the sentences with the words and phrases in the box. Listen and check your answers.

> give up   have a go at   keep it up   keep to
> make an effort   manage to   successfully
> try out   work out

1 Often if we try something new, we _____ after about a week or two because our brain hasn't adapted.
2 So if you _____ do something new for a month, you'll probably _____ it.
3 Maybe you wouldn't want to _____ for your whole life, but it might be fun to do it just for 30 days.
4 If you're successful it's great, but if it doesn't _____, it doesn't matter too much.
5 It's not just about giving up bad habits. The idea is really that you _____ something new.
6 Or you can take time out and _____ something you've always wanted to do.
7 Obviously to do something like that you need to _____.
8 They're all about half-way through and they've done it _____ so far.

b Match words and phrases from 2a with the meanings.

1 succeed _____, _____
2 stop trying _____
3 not stop trying _____, _____
4 try hard _____
5 try to see if it works _____, _____

c Complete the sentences below about 30-day challenges. Use the words and phrases in 2a and your own ideas. There is more than one possible answer.

1 He tried giving up coffee for 30 days. It wasn't easy, but he …
2 You've got up at 5.30 every day for three weeks now. You've only got one week to go, so …
3 30-day challenges sound fun. I want to do something different, so I think I'll …

d 💬 Work in small groups. Tell the group about a time when you:
- found something difficult but didn't give up
- made a real effort to succeed
- had a go at something unusual
- did something which worked out successfully
- tried to do something which didn't work out

3 READING

a Look at challenges 1–3. Who do you think will find it easy and who will find it difficult?

b Read the interviews and check your ideas.

30-DAY CHALLENGE

Challenge 1: Farah decided not to eat meat.

What made you decide to become vegetarian, Farah?
Well, for quite a long time now I've been trying to eat less meat, partly for health reasons. I think vegetables are better for you.
1 _____
Yes, but I always thought I'd miss meat too much. The idea of being a vegetarian for 30 days was really good, because I could give it a try and then see how I feel.
2 _____
No, I feel really good. Actually, I don't miss meat at all, so I think I'll easily manage the 30 days and I might try carrying on longer. I certainly think I'm a bit healthier than I used to be.

Challenge 2: Mona decided to draw something every day.

Mona, why did you decide to draw something every day?
Well, I've never been very good at drawing, but I've always thought I'd like to start drawing things around me. It's one of those things that you think about doing, but you never get round to.
3 _____
All kinds of things. At the start I drew objects around me at home. Then I went out in my lunch break and started drawing things outdoors, like yesterday I drew a duck in the park – that was really difficult!

So do you feel it has been worthwhile?
Oh yes, definitely. I'm still not very good at drawing, but it's been lots of fun and it's very relaxing.

UNIT 1

c Complete the interviews with the missing questions.

a And who do you practise with? Or are you just working alone?
b But didn't you ever think of being vegetarian before?
c And how do you feel? Are you finding it difficult?
d And do you think you'll carry on after the 30 days?
e What have you drawn pictures of so far?

d ▶ 1.12 Listen and check your answers.

Challenge 3: Steve decided to learn Italian.

Steve, what language did you decide to learn?
Well, I thought I'd choose a language that isn't too different from English, so I decided to try Italian.

Isn't it difficult to keep going with it?
Yes, it is. I've had to be very strict with myself. I'm using a book with a CD, so I usually try to cover one lesson a night.
4 _____
Well, there's an Italian restaurant just round the corner and I'm friends with the owner, so I go there and I chat to him. That's one reason I chose Italian.
5 _____
Maybe, or I might try a different language every month. I'm thinking of trying Japanese next.

4 GRAMMAR Questions

a Read the rules about questions. Find examples of each type of question in the interviews and 3c.

1 In questions, we usually put the auxiliary verb before the subject. If there is no auxiliary verb, we add *do* or *did*.
Are you making dinner? **Have you** eaten?
What **did you** eat?
2 If the question word (*who, what* or *which*) is the subject, we keep normal word order.
Who spoke to you? **What happened** next?
3 If a question has a preposition, it can come at the end:
You were talking to someone. → *Who were you talking* **to**?
4 To ask an opinion, we often ask questions starting with a phrase like *Do you think … ?*
Is it a good idea? → **Do you think** *it's a good idea?*

b Compare examples a and b.

a Did you see her at the party?   b Didn't you see her at the party?
Which example … ?
1 is a neutral question (= maybe she was there, maybe not)
2 expresses surprise (= I'm sure she was there)

c Compare examples c and d.

c Which colour do you want?   d What colour do you want?
Which example … ?
1 asks about an open choice (there may be lots of colours to choose from)
2 asks about a limited range (e.g. black, red or green)

d ▶ Now go to Grammar Focus 1B on p.134

e 💬 Work in pairs. You are going to role-play two of the interviews in 3b and continue with your own questions.

1 Choose one of the interviews.
Student A: Interview Student B. Add your own questions.
Student B: Answer Student A's questions using your own ideas.
2 Choose a second interview. This time Student B interviews Student A.

5 SPEAKING

a Work in pairs.

1 Write a short poem every day
2 Get up at dawn
3 Go running

1 Write down three challenges you might do in the next three months.
2 Look at your partner's challenges. Write some questions to ask about each one. Ask about:
• reasons for doing the challenge
• details of what he/she plans to do
• how he/she feels about it

Are you planning to … ?
Do you think it will be … ?
How are you going to… ?

b 💬 Interview your partner about their three challenges. Do you think he/she will be successful?

1C Everyday English
Don't touch the sandwiches!

Learn to explain what to do and check understanding
- **S** Breaking off a conversation
- **P** Rapid speech

1 LISTENING

a Discuss the questions.
1. In your country, how do students manage financially? Do they … ?
   - rely on their parents
   - get a part-time job
   - use student loans
2. What do you think is the best way? Why?
3. If you had to do a part-time job to earn some money as a student, what job would you choose and why?

b Look at the photo of Tessa and Becky from Part 1. Who do you think they are?
1. tourists visiting a famous building
2. college students doing a course
3. journalists who have just done an interview

c ▶1.15 Watch or listen to Part 1 and check your ideas.

d ▶1.15 Watch or listen again. Answer the questions.
1. Are Becky and Tessa friends? How do you know?
2. Why does Becky have to go?

e ▶1.16 Watch or listen to Part 2. Are these sentences true or false?
1. Becky and Tom are married.
2. Becky is free this evening.
3. Becky is in a hurry.

2 CONVERSATION SKILLS
Breaking off a conversation

a ▶1.17 Look at these ways to break off a conversation and say goodbye.
1. I really must go now.
2. I must run.
3. I've got no time to talk now.
4. I'll see you tomorrow.

Listen to the speaker. Which words does she not use in 1–4?

b Look at some more ways to break off a conversation. Which words has the speaker not included?
1. Must be off now.
2. Talk to you later.
3. Can't talk just now.
4. Nice talking to you.

3 PRONUNCIATION Rapid speech

a ▶1.18 In rapid speech we often leave out sounds. Listen to the phrases below. Which sound is left out? Is it a consonant sound or a vowel sound?
1. must go
2. must run
3. got to go
4. can't talk

b Read the conversation. Put B's replies in order. Is more than one order possible?
- **A** So how was your holiday?
- **B** Got to go. / Sorry. / Can't talk now. / It was great.
- **A** OK, well, have a nice evening.
- **B** Bye. / See you tomorrow. / Yeah, thanks. / Must be off now.

c Work in pairs. Have short conversations.
Student A: Tell Student B about what you did last weekend. Continue until he/she stops you.
Student B: You're in a hurry. Use expressions in 2b and 3b to break off the conversation.

Then swap roles.

14

4 LISTENING

a ▶1.19 Watch or listen to Part 3. What happens to Becky? Choose the correct answer.
1 Becky meets Sam and learns how to make coffee.
2 Becky learns how to handle food and meets a café customer.

b ▶1.19 Watch or listen again. Answer the questions.
1 Sam explains two things to Becky. What are they?
2 What does Phil do in the café?
3 Why do they call him 'JK'?
4 Who is Emma?

c 💬 Discuss the questions with other students. Give reasons for your answers.
1 Do you think the others like Phil coming to the café?
2 Do you think Becky will be good at her new job?

d ▶1.20 Watch or listen to Part 4. Which of these topics do Tom and Becky mention?

| coffee   food   Becky's new job   the reason Tom is here |
| Phil's book   their wedding plans |

e ▶1.20 Watch or listen again. What do Tom and Becky say about each topic?

Becky and Sam

Becky and Emma   Phil

5 USEFUL LANGUAGE
Explaining and checking understanding

a Look at the expressions Sam uses to explain what to do. Put the words in italics in the correct order.
1 *most / thing / is, / the / important* don't touch the food.
2 *to / always / remember* use these tongs.
3 *is, / remember / thing / to / another* the tables are all numbered.

b ▶1.21 Listen and check your answers.

c Why does Sam use these expressions?
1 because he needs time to think
2 because he's not sure
3 to emphasise important points

d Look at these ways to check that someone has understood an explanation. Complete the questions with the endings in the box.

| the idea?   got that?   clear?   I mean? |

1 Is that …
2 Do you understand what …
3 Have you …
4 Do you get …

e ▶1.22 **Pronunciation** Listen to each question in 5d said in two ways. Which way sounds … ?
• friendly and polite
• unfriendly and not so polite

To sound friendly, does the speaker's voice go up (↗) or down (↘) at the end?

f Practise asking the questions in 5d in a friendly and polite way.

g Here are some other things Sam could explain to Becky. Imagine what he could say using language in 5a and 5d. What could Becky say to show she has understood?
1 how to clear and arrange a table when a customer leaves
2 what to do with the coffee machine at closing time
3 what to do if customers leave something behind

h 💬 Practise the conversation in 5g. Swap roles.

6 SPEAKING

a Choose a process you are familiar with or something you know how to do. It could be:
• something connected with a sport or a hobby
• how to use a machine or an electronic device
• how to make or cook something.

b You are going to explain the process to your partner. Prepare what you will say. Think how to emphasise the important points and check that your partner understands. Use expressions from 5a and 5d.

c 💬 Work in pairs. Take turns to explain the process to your partner and ask each other questions to check understanding.

Unit Progress Test

CHECK YOUR PROGRESS

You can now do the Unit Progress Test.

UNIT 1

15

1D Skills for Writing
I really missed my phone all day

Learn to write an article
W Organising an article

1 SPEAKING and LISTENING

a 💬 Discuss the questions.
1 In your daily life, how much do you depend on technology?
2 What aspects of technology make your daily life easier?

b 💬 Look at the survey results below and discuss the questions.
1 Do you think people you know would agree with these results?
2 Do you agree with the results? Is there anything else you would like to add to the list?

MODERN LIFE IS RUBBISH!
A survey in the UK revealed the things that British people hate most about modern life. Here are the top five:

1 self-service check-outs
2 sales calls
3 selfies
4 slow internet connection
5 mobile phone battery life

c ▶1.23 Listen to Gitta and Derek talking about technology. Are they describing positive or negative experiences? Do they talk about the same device?

d ▶1.23 Listen again. What's the speaker's relationship with the other person in the story? What made the experience positive or negative? Why?

e 💬 Discuss the questions.
1 Do you agree with Gitta's reaction to her boss? Why / Why not?
2 Do you know people like Derek? Do you think they should try to change? Why / Why not?

f Work on your own. Think about the questions below and make notes.
- When has technology created a problem for you?
- When has technology helped you solve a problem of some kind?

g 💬 Discuss your experiences in 1f.

2 READING

a Read *Tech free!* Are any of the things in the survey mentioned?

b Read the text again. Are the sentences true or false?
1 Before the experiment, Sam was a bit worried by the idea.
2 Sam was annoyed that he had to chat to someone in the bank.
3 The bank teller was clearly surprised that Sam wanted to withdraw money.
4 Sam saved time by not using the self-service check-out at the supermarket.
5 Sam was able to work better when he wrote by hand.
6 As the day progressed, Sam thought less about using his phone.
7 Sam learnt something about the way we depend on technology.

c 💬 How would you feel if you had to live without using technology for one day? Discuss what you would enjoy and not enjoy.

3 WRITING SKILLS Organising an article

a How does Sam organise his article? Choose the correct summary. He …
1 explains his attitude towards technology, describes his day, requests readers to do the same thing
2 explains his level of dependency on technology, describes his day, finishes with an evaluation of the experience
3 explains his feelings about technology, describes his day, finishes by promising to repeat the experience

b How does Sam get the reader's attention at the beginning of the article?

UNIT 1

TECH FREE!
by Sam Winton

Home | Blog | Follow me

¹Have you ever wondered what it would be like to give up technology? I'm a TV journalist and I spend a lot of my working life in front of a computer or a TV. I decided to conduct my own private experiment: I would spend a day trying to manage without technological devices. What a scary thought!

²The first thing I usually do every day is reach for my smartphone to check the time and read any messages or emails. But I'd locked it away in a drawer the night before. Already I was feeling very cut off from the world, and it was only … actually, I had no idea what time it was!

³After breakfast, I needed to get some cash. Inevitably, this meant a trip to the bank because cash points are technological devices. I had to queue, but I had a very nice conversation with a woman whilst I was waiting. Not surprisingly, the bank teller thought I was a bit strange withdrawing money this way. I think she thought I was a robber!

⁴Then it was on to the supermarket. You may be wondering what's technological about that. Well, I had to make sure I avoided the self-service check-out and joined the queue for a normal one – with a real person. Naturally, it took longer, but I had a great chat with the guy who served me, and he told me about a new club that is opening up nearby. Would I have found out about that if I'd gone to the self-service check-out? No.

⁵Afterwards, I came home to have a go at writing a news story by hand. Strangely, I found it easier to concentrate on my writing. But my hand and fingers got really sore! And I have to confess – by this stage, I was having to make a real effort not to get my phone out and check my messages. I was starting to wonder what my friends were doing. Maybe they were making plans to go to that new club, and I would never know!

⁶All in all, I wouldn't say I could live without technology. Predictably, I really missed my phone all day. The worst part was not being able to check updates in the news or from my friends. I felt very out of touch. However, I kept to my promise of a tech-free day and I did have more face-to-face interaction. Undoubtedly, it made me realise just how addicted to technology we all are.

c Complete the tasks below.
1 In paragraphs 2–5, underline the linking word or phrase that sequences the events in Sam's day. The first one has been done for you.
2 In paragraph 6, what linking phrase shows that Sam is going to summarise his experience?

d Look at the example sentence from the article. The adverb *Inevitably* shows the writer's attitude. Find five other comment adverbs in the article.

Inevitably, this meant a trip to the bank because cash points are technological devices.

e Add the adverbs in the box to the sentences. (Sometimes there is more than one possible answer.)

amazingly   naturally   inevitably
(not) surprisingly

1 Why do some websites always ask you to change passwords? Having created a password for my bank account, I was asked to change it two weeks later.
2 I usually hate anything to do with technology. I quite like using the self-service check-out at the local supermarket.
3 I always expect IT products to be very expensive. The tablet I bought last week cost very little.
4 I find it very difficult to install new software. I've downloaded the latest version of a program and my computer has frozen.

f Which piece of advice is not correct for writing an article? Why?
1 Begin the article with a question to get the reader's attention.
2 Use direct questions to connect with the reader of your article.
3 Think about how you can structure the main part of the article. You can use a sequence of events or you could compare and contrast ideas.
4 Use linking words to guide the reader.
5 Be as objective as possible.
6 Use comment adverbs to show your opinions.
7 Summarise your experience or ideas and evaluate them.

4 WRITING

a Imagine you had to live for a week without a technological device you use in your daily life. Choose a device from the survey, the article or use your own ideas. Make notes about what the experience might be like.

b 💬 Discuss your notes.

c Write an article about your experience. Organise your article to follow the structure in 3a. Use the linking phrases and adverbs from 3c–e to help you.

d Swap articles with another student. Does the article follow the advice in 3f? Is the article interesting to read? Why? What could make it more interesting?

17

UNIT 1
Review and extension

1 GRAMMAR

a Write verbs in the gaps in the correct tense.

My wife Anna and I first ^{1}_____ (meet) at a party while I ^{2}_____ (live) in London in the 1970s. When I ^{3}_____ (arrive) most people ^{4}_____ (already/leave). I ^{5}_____ (notice) Anna immediately. She ^{6}_____ (wear) a blue dress and she ^{7}_____ (chat) with a group of people on the balcony. I ^{8}_____ (go) up to her and we ^{9}_____ (start) talking. We both ^{10}_____ (feel) as if we ^{11}_____ (know) each other all our lives. Now we ^{12}_____ (be) both in our 70s. We ^{13}_____ (know) each other for 44 years.

b Read an interview with a famous actor about his life. Correct the mistakes in the questions.

1 *Where you grew up?*
  In San Diego, in California. I left when I was 18.
2 *Did not you like living in San Diego?*
  Yes, but there were more opportunities in San Francisco.
3 *How long for did you stay there?*
  About eight years. Then I moved to New York.
4 *What did make you decide to move?*
  I got an offer to act at the Apollo Theater in New York.
5 *Do you think was it a good decision?*
  Oh yes. It was a chance to work with some great people.
6 *With who did you work?*
  Oh, lots of good actors – Terence Newby, for example.

2 VOCABULARY

a Add an adjective to complete each gap.

1 The students are all keen to learn English. They're very m_____.
2 All Sophie's family and friends have warned her about marrying Fred but she's going to anyway. She's so s_____.
3 Everyone agrees the new president is a good leader. She's highly r_____.
4 My brother used to be very shy, but he's become much more s_____ since he left home.
5 I've always loved acting more than anything else. I'm p_____ about it.
6 Five thousand people came to hear him talk. He's a very i_____ speaker.
7 Try not to criticise his work. He can be very s_____ about it.
8 Just because they're rich they think they're better than everyone else. I hate a_____ people like that.

b Choose the correct answers.

1 I ^{1}*had / took* a go at running a café, but it didn't work ^{2}*up / out*. I didn't manage ^{3}*to make / in making* enough money so I had to sell it.
2 He's really ^{4}*doing / making* an effort to lose weight. He's on a diet and he's ^{5}*kept / held* it up for six weeks now. But I don't know if he'll ^{6}*stay / keep* to it for much longer.
3 There's only one way to find out if you can do something ^{7}*successful / successfully*, and that's to try it ^{8}*on / out*!

3 WORDPOWER *make*

a Match the remarks with the pictures.

a 'I can't make up my mind.'
b 'It really makes a difference to the room.'
c 'I can't make out what it is.'
d 'We'll have to make the best of it.'
e 'This is to make up for last night.'
f 'That doesn't make sense.'
g 'It wants to make friends with us.'

b ▶1.24 Listen to the conversations and check your answers.

c Add a word or phrase from exercise a after *make* in these sentences.

1 What was that? I can't make _____ what you're saying.
2 Why don't you drive faster? We need to make _____ lost time, or we'll be late.
3 So do you want to come with us? You need to make _____.
4 When the sun shines, it makes _____ to the way I feel.
5 I didn't buy any more food. You'll just have to make _____ of it.
6 He gave a long explanation but it didn't make _____ to me. I still don't understand.
7 Don't sit in front of the computer all day. You should go out and make _____ with people.

d 💬 What kind of person are you? Discuss these questions.

1 If you upset a friend, how would you make up for it? Would you buy a present, buy flowers, apologise …?
2 When you buy clothes, do you make up your mind quickly or do you need a long time to decide?
3 You have to spend the night at an airport. Would you stay there and make the best of it, or would you pay money for a hotel?
4 You see a dog in the street. Would you try to make friends with it or would you keep out of its way?

🔄 REVIEW YOUR PROGRESS

How well did you do in this unit? Write 3, 2 or 1 for each objective.
3 = very well   2 = well   1 = not so well

I CAN …

discuss people I admire	☐
discuss a challenge	☐
explain what to do and check understanding	☐
write an article	☐

CAN DO OBJECTIVES

- Discuss dangerous situations
- Give advice on avoiding danger
- Give and respond to compliments
- Write guidelines in a leaflet

UNIT 2
Survival

GETTING STARTED

a Look at the picture and answer the questions.
1 What do you think has happened here?
2 Who are the people in the picture?
3 What's the man on the phone saying?

b Discuss the questions.
1 What do you think are the worst kinds of natural disasters? Why?
2 Think of a natural disaster that has happened in your country. How effective was the response of the emergency services? How well did people cope?
3 Why do you think some people cope better with challenging situations than others?

2A It was getting late and I was lost

Learn to discuss dangerous situations
G Narrative tenses
V Expressions with *get*

1 LISTENING

a Look at pictures a–d. What would you be most afraid of in each situation?

b ▶1.25 Listen to someone talking about their holiday. Which of the pictures is being described? Where was the holiday?

c ▶1.25 Listen again. Number events a–h in the order that they happened.

a bought a new surfboard
b lost the board
c waved to a life-guard
d swam against the current
e fell off the surfboard
f learnt to surf with instructors
g went surfing alone
h was rescued

2 VOCABULARY Expressions with *get*

a Match expressions 1–10 in bold with meanings a–j.

1 ☐ I can't wait to **get away**.
2 ☐ I've always wanted to learn how to surf and I'll finally **get to** do it.
3 ☐ I **couldn't get over** just how strong they are.
4 ☐ Actually, I **got into** a bit of **trouble** once.
5 ☐ I tried to **get hold of** it.
6 ☐ It **got swept away** by the wave.
7 ☐ I soon realised that I **wasn't getting anywhere**.
8 ☐ I **got the feeling** I was being pulled out to sea.
9 ☐ So I waved to **get someone's attention**.
10 ☐ I had a bad experience, but I soon **got over** it.

a make no progress
b go in a different direction in a powerful way
c have the chance to do something
d go somewhere else
e be very surprised by something
f find myself in difficulty
g take it in my hand
h recover from something negative that happened
i make someone notice
j have the sensation that

b Complete the sentences with the correct form of the phrases in 2a. Write one word in each gap.

1 She ran out on the road to _____ the policeman's _____.
2 They were exhausted and hungry, but after some food and sleep they soon _____ _____ the experience.
3 When he saw the same tree for the third time, he began to _____ _____ _____ that he was lost.
4 He went on a course about surviving in the woods and _____ _____ put into practice his fire-making skills.
5 They decided to ski off the main trail where the snow was fresh, but it was also quite dangerous and they soon _____ _____ _____.
6 The boat was sinking, but we all managed to _____ _____ _____ a life-jacket.
7 She was crossing the river, but the current was strong and she _____ _____ _____ by the water.
8 They had been walking for hours, but they'd only walked about two kilometres. They felt like they weren't _____ _____.
9 They were in such a rush to _____ _____ to the mountains, they left without taking sensible walking boots.
10 When they were in the water, they _____ _____ _____ how high the waves were.

c ▶ Now go to Vocabulary Focus on p.155

20

UNIT 2

3 READING

a Read the article *Lost at sea* and answer the questions.
 1 How long was Robert Hewitt in the water?
 2 What problems did he have to overcome?

b Can you remember what these numbers refer to? Write sentences about each number. Then read the text again and check your answers.
 1 200-metre
 2 seven kilometres
 3 fourth day
 4 three hours
 5 half a kilometre
 6 third day

c 💬 Answer the questions.
 1 What do you think most helped Robert to survive?
 2 Do you think that Robert made the right decision on day one not to try to swim for shore? Give reasons.
 3 What was the biggest challenge Robert had to overcome?
 4 What would you have done in Robert's situation?

REAL DIVING

Stories   Articles   Diving in NZ   Shop

LOST AT SEA

How long could you survive at sea? One day? Two? And when would you start to lose hope?

When Robert Hewitt came to the surface, he ¹**realised** straight away that something was wrong. He ²**'d been diving** for sea urchins and crayfish off the coast of New Zealand with a friend, and ³**had decided** to make the 200-metre swim back to shore alone. But instead, strong underwater currents had taken him more than half a kilometre out to sea.

Lying on his back in the middle of the ocean, Robert told himself not to panic. He was a strong swimmer and he ⁴**was wearing** his thick wet suit. 'I'm not going to die. Someone will come,' he told himself. But three hours passed and still no one had come for him. Robert would soon have to make a tough decision.

He was now a long way from the coast and the tide was taking him further out, but he decided not to try to swim for shore. He felt it was better to save his energy and hold on to his brightly coloured equipment. But the decision was not an easy one. 'I just closed my eyes and said, "You've made the right decision. You've made the right decision" until that's all I heard,' he remembers.

As night approached, Robert established a pattern to help him survive in the water. To stay warm, he kept himself moving and took short naps of less than a minute at a time. Every few hours, he called out to his loved ones: 'Just yelling out their names would pick me up and then I would keep going for the next hour and the next hour and the next.'

When he woke the next morning, he couldn't believe he was still alive. Using his bright equipment, he tried to signal to planes that flew overhead. But as each plane turned away, his spirits dropped. He managed to drink water from his oxygen tank to keep himself alive, but as day turned to night again he started to imagine things.

Robert woke on the third day to a beautiful blue sky. Now seven kilometres off the coast, Robert decided he had to swim for it. But the sun was so strong and Robert quickly ran out of strength. Hope turned to disappointment yet again: 'I felt disappointed in myself. I thought I was a lot fitter. I thought I would be able to do it.' Robert then started to think he might not survive.

On the fourth day, the lack of food and water was really starting to affect him. Half unconscious, and with strange visions going through his head, he thought he saw a boat coming towards him with two of his friends in. Another vision, surely.

But no – 'They put me in the boat and I said something like "Oh, how's it going, what are you guys doing here?"' Then he asked them the question that he'd asked in all his visions: 'Can I have some water?' As they handed him the water and he felt it touch his lips, he knew. This was not a vision. He'd been found! After four days and three nights alone at sea, Robert had been found! Sunburnt, hungry and exhausted, but alive …

GLOSSARY

sea urchin

crayfish

21

UNIT 2

4 GRAMMAR Narrative tenses

a Look at the verbs in bold in *Lost at sea* and match them with the uses a–d.

- a a completed action that takes place before the main events in the story
- b a background action in progress at the same time as the main events in the story happened
- c a continuous activity that happens before the main events in the story and explains why the main events happen
- d a completed action that tells you what happens at a specific time in the story

b ▶1.29 **Pronunciation** Listen to the three sentences. Underline the stressed verb in each sentence. How do we pronounce the words *had been*? Listen again and repeat.

He *had been* diving for seafood.
He *had been* swimming in the sea
He *had been* wearing a wet suit.

c ▶ Now go to Grammar Focus 2A on p.136

d Work in pairs. Student A: Read about Eric Le Marque. Student B: Read about Ricky Megee. Answer the questions about your text.
  1 Where does the text take place?
  2 Does the person survive?

e Underline the correct verbs in your text.

f You are going to tell your partner about your story. Make notes.

g 💬 Tell your partner your survival story. Use correct verb forms.

5 SPEAKING

a Think of a dangerous situation that you or someone you know was in, or it could be something you know about from a book or film. Make notes about the questions.
  - Where and when did it take place?
  - Who was involved?
  - What was the scene or background to the story?
  - What were the main events?
  - How did you / the person feel?
  - What was the outcome?

b 💬 Tell each other your story. Use different narrative tenses and expressions with *get*. Ask questions.

Student A: ERIC LEMARQUE

It was getting late and Eric LeMarque decided to have one final run on his snowboard. As he [1]*'d gone / was going* down the mountain, he [2]*came / was coming* across some thick fog and headed in the wrong direction. All of a sudden he was completely lost. All he had with him was his snowboard, some bubble gum and an MP3 player. Eventually, he [3]*remembered / 'd remembered* something he [4]*was seeing / 'd seen* in a movie about using an MP3 player as a compass. This meant he was able to get an idea of where he was and head in the right direction, up the mountain. Eric was missing for a week. During that time, he fell in a river, almost went down a waterfall and had to walk through snow that was four and a half metres deep! On the eighth day he was seen by a helicopter that [5]*had searched / had been searching* for him. He was completely exhausted but alive.

Student B: RICKY MEGEE

A farmer couldn't believe what he saw when he came across a stranger living on his farm. The man, Ricky Megee, [1]*lived / had been living* off the land in the Australian bush for two months. Ricky [2]*had been driving / had driven* near the border of Western Australia and Northern Territory. He [3]*stopped / had stopped* to help some people whose car had broken down and offered one of them a lift to a nearby town. Unfortunately, the passenger turned out to be a robber, who stole Ricky's car. Ricky was now completely lost in the bush. He [4]*ate / had eaten* insects, snakes and frogs and eventually managed to find a dam to provide him with water. He built a small shelter there and waited, hoping to be rescued. 71 days after being left, Ricky was found by the farmer. He [5]*'d lost / was losing* more than 50 kg in weight during his time in the bush.

2B If it runs towards you, don't run away

Learn to give advice on avoiding danger
- **G** Future time clauses and conditionals
- **V** Animals and the environment

1 READING

a 💬 Think of three wild places you know of.
- Would you be scared to go for a walk there?
- What dangers could you face?
- What would you do to get out of danger?

b 💬 Look at pictures a–e and answer the questions.
1 Which of the animals do you think are the most and least dangerous?
2 How good do you think your chances are of surviving an attack by these animals?

c Read the text and check your answers.

d Read the text again. Tick (✓) the correct sentences.
1 Some animals are less dangerous than people think.
2 If you go walking, you can't avoid meeting dangerous animals.
3 Not many animals attack without reason.
4 Having a weapon may help you survive an attack.
5 Most animals have a part of their body which is vulnerable.
6 It's better to run away than to try to fight.

e Do you think the text is … ?
a a serious survival guide for travellers
b part of a scientific book about animals
c an article written mainly for interest and amusement

How to survive ...
an animal attack

YOU'RE WALKING IN A FOREST WHEN SUDDENLY A WILD ANIMAL APPEARS FROM NOWHERE AND IT DOES NOT LOOK FRIENDLY. WHAT DO YOU DO?

The first important point is that there's not usually much you can do, except hope it goes away again. With luck, you may never have to defend yourself against a wild animal, but it doesn't hurt to know what to do if an escaped leopard attacks you in your back garden, or if you're going for a country walk and you suddenly meet a family of wolves.

BE AWARE
The first thing is to know which animals are really dangerous. Many people are scared of animals that are in fact harmless, and not scared enough of animals that could kill you. Most animals won't attack people unless you do something to make them angry. Bears, for example, will usually move away as soon as they hear you and they'll only fight if they think you're attacking them or their young. Wolves won't normally attack unless they are very hungry, and then only if they're in a group. Tarantulas are horrible and hairy, but they aren't actually dangerous at all – you can let them walk over you. On the other hand, tigers and crocodiles are serious killers who will be happy to eat you for breakfast.

BE PREPARED
It's a good idea to take a stick, a knife or a pepper spray when you go for a walk in the wild in case you meet a dangerous animal. Have it in a place where you can easily find it. It may mean the difference between life and death.

KNOW YOUR ENEMY
If you ever find yourself face to face with a large and dangerous animal, you'll want to know their strong and weak points. Common weak points are:
- the nose
- the eyes
- the neck.

People have sometimes survived by punching sharks, large cats, and crocodiles on the nose, and pushing your thumbs into their eyes will also work well, as long as you press hard enough. Otherwise, you might just make them angry!
You can also try to get a psychological advantage. Provided you seem bigger and more dangerous than the animal, it will probably leave you alone, so make a lot of noise and try to make yourself look bigger.

WHAT NEXT?
If scaring them doesn't work, then you have two options: running or fighting. Remember that most animals are better at running and fighting than humans, so don't expect things to end well. But if you decide to fight, fight back with everything you have. Often during animal attacks people give up before the fight has even started. If you have any sharp objects or weapons, then use them. Hit the animal's weak points, keep shouting and make sudden movements. Good luck!

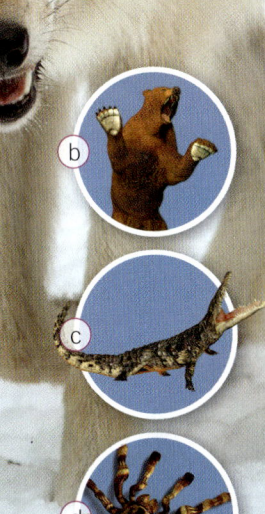

23

UNIT 2

f Look at the ideas below for surviving attacks by three different animals. For each animal, decide which ideas are the best.

g ▶ **Communication 2B** Now go to p.131 to check your answers.

1 A wolf
a hit it on the nose with a stick
b look it straight in the eyes
c run away immediately

2 A shark
a swim away quickly
b swim towards it
c hit it in the eye if it bites you

3 A bear
a run straight uphill as fast as you can
b lie down and 'play dead'
c hit the trees with sticks if you think bears are nearby

2 GRAMMAR Future time clauses and conditionals

a Look at the words and phrases in bold in sentences 1–5 and answer questions a–e.

1 They'll only fight **if** they think you're attacking them.
2 They won't attack people **unless** they're trapped or provoked.
3 Bears, for example, will usually move away **as soon as** they hear you.
4 **Provided** you stay absolutely still, the bear will lose interest and go away.
5 **As long as** you don't panic, it will probably swim away.

a Which two words or phrases have a similar meaning to *if*?
b What does sentence 2 mean?
   1 A bear will only attack you if it's trapped or provoked.
   2 A bear will attack you anyway, even if it isn't trapped.
c What does sentence 3 mean?
   1 When bears hear you they will wait, then move away slowly.
   2 When bears hear you they will move away immediately.
d Look at these examples:
   If you stay still, the bear will go away
   (= something good will happen).
   If you move, the bear will attack you
   (= something bad will happen).
   In which example could we use *as long as* or *provided* instead of *if*?
e What tense is used after the words and phrases in bold? What tense is used in the other part of the sentence?

b Find one more example in *How to survive an animal attack* of each of these words and phrases:
1 as long as
2 unless
3 provided

c ▶ Now go to Grammar Focus 2B on p.136

d Complete the sentences. There is more than one possible answer. Compare with other students.
1 Sharks won't attack you unless …
2 Wolves will only attack if …
3 Tarantulas won't bite you provided …
4 If you hit a crocodile on the nose …

24

UNIT 2

3 LISTENING and VOCABULARY Animals and the environment

a 💬 *The Tiger* by John Vaillant tells the true story of a hunter and a Siberian tiger. Use the words in the box to guess what happened.

| tiger   mattress   attacked |
| hut   forest   wounded   shot |
| killed   boots |

b ▶1.34 Listen to an interview about the book. Was the story similar to yours?

c ▶1.34 Which of these questions *doesn't* Miles answer? Listen again and check.
1 Is a Siberian tiger bigger than other tigers?
2 How far can it jump?
3 Have many people been killed by Siberian tigers?
4 Can tigers plan ahead?

d ▶1.35 Listen to the second part of the interview. Tick (✓) the things Miles talks about.
1 his own feelings about the tiger
2 life in Siberia
3 the relationship between humans and tigers
4 tigers as an endangered species
5 how to survive a tiger attack

e 💬 Do you think Miles would agree with statements 1–5? Write *Yes* or *No*. Then explain why.
1 It's a good thing they killed the tiger.
2 The tiger was just behaving naturally.
3 Tigers have always caused problems for people in Siberia.
4 In some ways, humans are more dangerous than tigers.
5 We should hunt more tigers to keep them under control.

f Which of the words in the box can we use to talk about … ?
1 animals   2 places

| at risk   creature   endangered   environment   extinct |
| habitats   hunt   natural   protected   rare   species |

g ▶1.36 Complete the sentences with the words in 3f. Then listen and check your answers.
1 … in eastern Siberia, one of the wildest and most _____ _____ on Earth.
2 Imagine a _____ that is as active as a cat and has the weight of an industrial refrigerator.
3 Humans and tigers _____ the same animals and share the same _____.
4 Tigers are _____ because of humans.
5 Tigers have become extremely _____.
6 There are 40 million humans but only 500 tigers, so they really are an _____ _____, and although they're _____, they could easily become _____ in a few decades.

4 SPEAKING

a A visitor is coming to stay in your country. Make notes about:
- endangered species and where you can see them
- dangerous animals or other creatures (e.g. birds, fish, insects)
- other possible risks or dangers (e.g. diseases, dangerous places, travel, weather)

b Imagine what you could tell the visitor and what advice you could give. How could you use the words in the box?

| if   as soon as   in case   unless   as long as   provided |

c 💬 Work in pairs. Student A, talk about your country. Student B, you are the visitor. Ask Student A questions. Then change roles.

> Take malaria tablets in case you get bitten by a mosquito.

> Be careful of dogs if you go jogging.

2C Everyday English
What a great shot!

Learn to give and respond to compliments
- **S** Giving compliments and responding
- **P** Agreeing using question tags

1 LISTENING

a Discuss the questions.
1. Do you like taking photos? Why / Why not?
2. In your opinion, what makes a good photo?
3. Do you think you are good at taking photos? Why / Why not?

b Look at photo a and answer the questions.
1. What is Becky doing?
2. Why do you think she needs Tessa to help?

c ▶1.37 Watch or listen to Part 1. Check your answers.

d ▶1.37 Are the sentences true or false? Watch or listen again to check.
1. Becky asks Tessa to help her check the height of the tripod.
2. Becky is happy with the shots she takes.
3. Tessa wonders if it's necessary to use a lot of equipment.
4. Tessa wants to take a photo of a small animal.

2 CONVERSATION SKILLS Agreeing using question tags

a ▶1.37 Watch or listen again. How does Tessa respond to Becky's comment 'It's quite difficult'?

b Choose the correct word.
1. We can use statements with question tags to *agree / disagree* with someone.
2. Using a different adjective in the answer is more *interesting / friendly*.

c Complete B's answers with the correct verb forms.
1. **A** I think she's a lovely person.
   B Yes, she's very charming, _____ she?
2. **A** Their instructions weren't very clear.
   B No, they weren't helpful, _____ they?

d Complete the rule.

> If the sentence is positive, we use a _____ tag. If the sentence is negative, we use a _____ tag.

e Complete B's replies. Use an adjective from the box in the first gap and the correct verb form in the second gap.

| welcoming | soaking | breathtaking | worried |

1. **A** Your clothes are all wet.
   B Yes, they're _____, _____ they?
2. **A** The scenery there is exceptional.
   B Yes, it's _____, _____ it?
3. **A** They weren't a very friendly group of people.
   B No, they weren't _____ at all, _____ they?
4. **A** He looks a bit anxious.
   B Yes, he does look _____, _____ he?

3 PRONUNCIATION Tone in question tags

a ▶1.38 Listen to the examples. Does the tone go up (↗) or down (↘) on the question tag? What's the difference in meaning?
1. No, it isn't very quick, is it?
2. No, they weren't helpful, were they?
3. Yes, you need to make things easy, don't you?

b Practise saying the exchanges in 2e. Try to use the correct tone in the reply.

c Discuss people and things you and other students know – for example, a person, a café, a film or a car. Use the adjectives below and question tags to agree.
- amusing – funny
- cheerful – happy
- interesting – fascinating
- frightening – terrifying
- exhausting – tiring

> That photo is really striking.
>
> Yes, it's stunning, isn't it?

26

UNIT 2

4 LISTENING

a Look at photo b of Becky and Tessa. Which approach to taking photographs would you prefer? Why?

b Look at the two photos of flowers. Which do you like best? Why?

Becky's photo

Tessa's photo

c ▶1.39 Watch or listen to Part 2. What are Becky and Tessa's opinions of their own photos?

d ▶1.39 Watch or listen to Part 2 again. Answer the questions.
1 How did Tessa start taking photos?
2 What do Becky and Tessa have trouble deciding?
3 What does Becky think about her photo of a squirrel? What does Tessa think?
4 Where do they go for coffee?

5 USEFUL LANGUAGE
Giving compliments and responding

a ▶1.40 Listen and complete the conversation.
BECKY _____ a _____ shot!
TESSA It's all _____.
BECKY You _____ just _____ to get a really good shot. The light is amazing.
TESSA Thanks. Guess it's _____ bad.

b Answer the questions about the conversation.
1 Do Becky's compliments sound excited?
2 Is Tessa's response grateful or neutral?

c Look at the bold words in compliments 1–4. Match them to the words and phrases in a–d.
1 That's a **lovely** picture!   a talented / skilled
2 You're so **good** at taking photos. b excellent / amazing / beautiful / striking
3 I **love** the way you caught the light. c were able to / succeeded in
4 You really **managed to** get it just right. d really like / am impressed by

d Which of these responses are grateful and which are neutral?

    Do you think so?   It's OK, I guess.

    Thanks, I'm glad you like it.   I'm really pleased you like it.

e 💬 Work in pairs. Imagine you have both finished writing an essay and have read each other's essay. Use the ideas below to have a short conversation. Take turns to be A and B.

A	B
Tell your partner how easy/difficult it was to write the essay.	Agree with A using a question tag.
Say you've read your partner's essay and compliment him/her.	Respond gratefully.

6 SPEAKING

a Work alone. What compliments can you give to your classmates? Think about:
- things they do or make as hobbies
- their jobs
- things they have done in your English classes
- the clothes they are wearing.

b 💬 Talk to different students in your class. Give compliments and respond.

    That's a really nice sweater you're wearing.   Thanks, It's not bad, is it?

🔄 **Unit Progress Test**

CHECK YOUR PROGRESS

You can now do the Unit Progress Test.

27

2D Skills for Writing
Make sure you know where you are going

Learn to write guidelines in a leaflet
W Organising guidelines in a leaflet

1 SPEAKING and LISTENING

a 💬 Discuss the questions.
1 When was the last time you went to some kind of natural environment?
2 What did you do there?
3 How did you prepare for your trip?

b ▶1.41 Listen to Luiza talking about an experience she had in Canada. Answer the questions.
1 Which natural environment does she talk about?
2 Near the beginning she says *I got in trouble*. What was the trouble?

c ▶1.41 Listen again and answer the questions.
1 Why did Luiza get lost?
2 How did she decide which way to go?
3 What helped her find the clearing?

d 💬 At the end, Luiza says: *I suddenly had this strange feeling I was not alone.* What do you think happened next? Discuss your ideas.

e ▶1.42 Listen to the continuation of Luiza's story. Were your ideas correct?

f ▶1.42 Listen again. Are the sentences true or false?
1 Luiza knew what to do.
2 She felt calm and wasn't afraid.
3 The helicopter saw Luiza the first time it flew over.
4 Luiza was surprised to find out she was close to the main track.

g 💬 What would you have done in Luiza's situation?

2 READING

a 💬 Think about Luiza's experience. Imagine you are going hiking in a forest. What do you need to remember in order to be safe?

b Read the leaflet *Be wise and survive*. Were your ideas similar? Put headings in spaces a–c in the leaflet. There is one extra heading.
1 In the forest   3 Identifying useful plants
2 If you get lost   4 Preparation

c Read the leaflet again. What should you … ?
1 take with you when you go hiking
2 not do when you are hiking
3 do about food and drink if you are lost
4 do if you are lost: move around or stay in one place

desert

beach

forest

mountains

Be wise and SURVIVE!

We all enjoy being in the great outdoors. There are lots of amazing environments, but some of them can be quite challenging, even dangerous, and it's important that you think about safety. Here are some simple guidelines to help you stay safe.

A _____

1. Get a map of the area and make sure you know where you are going.
2. Check the weather forecast.
3. Wear clothes and shoes that are suitable for the conditions. If you think the weather may change suddenly, take extra clothing.
4. If you are going on a longer walk, take some emergency food with you.

B _____

5. Provided you follow the signs, you shouldn't get into trouble.
6. Never take shortcuts unless you're absolutely sure where they go.
7. Allow plenty of time to get to your destination or get back before it gets dark.

C _____

8. As soon as you realise you're lost, stop, keep calm and plan what you will do next.
9. Don't eat all your food at once. Have a little at a time.
10. Try to find a source of water you can drink from like a river or a stream. Being able to drink is more important than being able to eat.
11. Don't keep moving around. Find somewhere that is dry and get plenty of rest. It's easier for rescuers to find you if you stay in one place.
12. Always try to stay warm. You can cover yourself with dry plants.
13. If you need to keep moving, make sure you use rocks or pieces of wood as signs that show rescuers where you are going.
14. As long as you tell yourself you'll survive, you probably will!

UNIT 2

3 WRITING SKILLS
Organising guidelines in a leaflet

a Notice these verb forms used in the leaflet.
1. **Check** the weather forecast. – positive imperative
2. **Don't eat** all your food at once – negative imperative
3. **Never take** shortcuts … – frequency adverb + imperative
4. **If** you **think** the weather may change suddenly, **take** extra clothing. – if + present tense + imperative

Find one more example of each verb form in the leaflet.

b Choose the correct answers.
1. What's the function of the verb forms in 3a?
   a to give advice
   b to make indirect suggestions
2. Why are those forms used?
   a to make the information clear and direct
   b to show hikers they have a strong obligation

c Correct the incorrect sentences.
1. Not eat any plants you don't recognise.
2. Never leave the main group of people you are hiking with.
3. If you will hear a rescue team, make lots of noise.
4. Always carries a pocket knife.
5. As soon as it starts getting dark, stop and think about what to do next.
6. If you have a map, take it with you.

4 WRITING

a 💬 Choose one of the situations in the box and make notes on advice you could include in a leaflet.

camping in a forest   backpacking in a foreign country
swimming in the sea   hiking in the mountains

b Write a leaflet for the situation you chose above. Remember to:
- use headings
- include the different imperative forms in 3a
- make the information clear and direct.

c Swap leaflets with another student. Does the leaflet include headings and different imperative forms? Is the information clear and direct? What improvements could be made?

d Give your leaflet to other students. Read other leaflets and decide which leaflet you think is the clearest and the most useful.

UNIT 2
Review and extension

1 GRAMMAR

a Complete the text with the verbs in brackets. Use the past simple, past continuous, past perfect or past perfect continuous forms.

The first time I [1]_____ (try) scuba diving [2]_____ (be) when I [3]_____ (live) in Cairns in North Queensland, Australia. I [4]_____ (travel) around the world and I [5]_____ (decide) to stop and work for a few months. I [6]_____ (be) on a gap year between finishing university and beginning work. Years before, someone [7]_____ (tell) me the best way to see the Coral Reef [8]_____ (be) by scuba diving. The diving I [9]_____ (do) on the Great Barrier Reef [10]_____ (be) fantastic. As I [11]_____ (dive) I [12]_____ (see) spectacular marine life.

b Make sentences by matching the halves. Put the linking expression in brackets in the correct place.

1 ☐ you won't find it difficult to learn to ski
2 ☐ you won't make much progress
3 ☐ you'll make steady progress
4 ☐ you won't be able to control your skis
5 ☐ you'll stay warm
6 ☐ you'll start making progress after a week

a	you can move your toes in your boots	(unless)
b	you're generally fit and healthy	(if)
c	you keep moving	(provided)
d	you choose an easy ski slope	(as long as)
e	you're patient with yourself	(provided)
f	you're prepared to fall down a lot at first	(unless)

2 VOCABULARY

a Correct the errors in the sentences.
1 I dropped my hat in the sea and it got swept by a wave away.
2 She couldn't get it over how hot it was.
3 He got trouble for being late.
4 I got feeling they didn't like guests.
5 She's now getting over it the shock of losing her job last week.
6 They're planning to get out to the countryside this weekend.

b Complete the words.
1 In North America, red wolves are considered an e _ _ _ _ _ _ _ _ _ s _ _ _ _ _ _ _.
2 In the UK, large blue butterflies are a _ r _ _ _ _ and are p _ _ _ _ _ _ _ _.
3 The New Zealand moa bird has been e _ _ _ _ _ _ _ for about six hundred years.
4 It's possible to find many Chinese alligators in zoos and research centres, but there are fewer living in their n _ _ _ _ _ _ h _ _ _ _ _ _ _.
5 In Australia, just over 20 per cent of the native plants are considered r _ _ _ and need to be conserved.

3 WORDPOWER face

a Match the examples 1–8 with the definitions a–h.
1 ☐ Although he said he enjoys the taste of the raw fish, he still **made a face**.
2 ☐ She **faced a difficult choice** between the two jobs she was offered.
3 ☐ Her **face fell** when I told her the painting was worthless.
4 ☐ I've been studying all day and I **can't face** doing my homework now.
5 ☐ It's not good news, but I feel I need to **say it to his face**.
6 ☐ We just have to **face the fact** that we haven't got enough money to buy a house.
7 ☐ I tripped on a loose brick and fell **flat on my face**.
8 ☐ I could tell my boss wasn't happy about the outcome. Now I have to talk to her and **face the music**.

a to be disappointed
b to accept another person's criticism or displeasure
c to accept an unpleasant situation
d to show from your expression that you don't like something
e to fall over badly and feel a bit embarrassed
f to make a difficult decision
g to say something directly to someone
h to not want to do something unpleasant

b In which of the expressions 1–8 is *face* used as a noun and in which as a verb?

c Which one of the following nouns doesn't collocate with *face*?
1 a problem   2 the truth   3 a difficult decision
4 the facts   5 a success   6 reality

d Add words to the gaps.
1 When did you last fall _____ on your face?
2 What was the last _____ choice you had to face?
3 What happened the last time you saw someone's face _____?
4 What's something difficult you've had to say _____ someone's face?
5 What can't you face _____ after class?
6 When was the last time you had to face _____ music?

e 💬 Ask and answer the questions in 3d.

REVIEW YOUR PROGRESS

How well did you do in this unit? Write 3, 2 or 1 for each objective.
3 = very well   2 = well   1 = not so well

I CAN ...

discuss dangerous situations	☐
give advice on avoiding danger	☐
give and respond to compliments	☐
write guidelines in a leaflet	☐

CAN DO OBJECTIVES

- Discuss ability and achievement
- Discuss sports activities and issues
- Make careful suggestions
- Write a description of data

UNIT 3
Talent

GETTING STARTED

a Look at the picture and answer the questions.
1 What are the people doing?
2 Why do you think three people are needed for the job?
3 What could the man on the left be thinking?

b Discuss the questions.
1 What makes something a work of art?
2 Do famous artists have natural talent? Or is their success due to luck, hard work or something else? Why do you think so?

31

3A I'm not very good in the morning

Learn to discuss ability and achievement
G Multi-word verbs
V Ability and achievement

1 LISTENING

a Think about how to learn something new. Do you agree or disagree with sentences 1–5? Why?
1 My teacher will get angry if I make mistakes.
2 Children learn faster than adults.
3 I must practise every day in order to make progress.
4 If something seems very easy, I must be doing it wrong.
5 Long practice sessions are best.

b ▶1.43 Listen to an experienced teacher talking about the same sentences. Are his ideas similar to yours? Do you agree with his ideas?

2 READING

a Discuss the questions.
1 How long does it take to learn something well?
2 What's the best time of day to learn something new?
3 How important is memory when we learn something new?

b Read *Learning to learn*. Match texts a–c with the questions in 2a.

c Read questions 1–6 from people who have to learn something. Use information in the texts to answer the questions.
1 I have to learn a lot of historical dates for an exam. What's a good way to do this?
2 I want to join a beginners' kickboxing class. Is it better to join the morning or afternoon class?
3 I know I have a natural talent for tennis. Do I need to practise hard to do well?
4 If I study first thing in the morning after my brain has rested, I'm sure I'll learn more. Do you agree?
5 I have to find out about the way car engines work, but the book I'm reading is really boring. Should I just stick with it?
6 I don't just want to be a good computer programmer – I want to be a brilliant one. What can I do to achieve that?

d Discuss the questions.
1 What information in the texts surprised you?
2 What information made sense to you?
3 Have you had any experience of the ideas discussed in the text?
4 Do you think you'll change your learning practice as a result of the information?

LEARNING TO LEARN

a

IT'S ALL ABOUT RHYTHM
Bodies and brains need time to warm up

'Early bird' or 'night owl', we all have different body clocks and rhythms. However, research is beginning to show that we're all quite similar in the way our minds and bodies behave at different times of the day. Understanding these rhythms helps us work out when's the best time to learn.

If learning means having to use your brain, the morning is the best time.

But not first thing. Our bodies and brains need time to warm up and our body temperature rises slowly from the moment we wake up. Between ten in the morning and midday, most people are at their best in terms of their ability to concentrate and learn.

If we want to learn something physical, then it pays to wait until the afternoon.

Between 2 pm and 6 pm our muscle strength is at its peak and our hand–eye coordination is very efficient. This means the afternoon is probably better for learning new sports or perhaps a new dance step.

32

3 VOCABULARY
Ability and achievement

a Look at the adjectives in bold and answer questions 1–4.

And when you look at all the people who are **outstanding** at what they do …
… they seem so much more **talented** …
…that's what it takes to become really **skilled**.
Those who became **exceptional** practised about two thousand hours more …
… in order to learn something and become very **successful** at doing it, all you'll need is about 10,000 hours!
Without a doubt, there are people who are **brilliant** at certain things …
All the musicians in the study had the **potential** to become world famous

1 Which two adjectives describe a good level of ability?
2 Which adjective describes a good level of achievement?
3 Which three adjectives describe a very high level of ability or achievement?
4 Look at the noun in bold in the last sentence. Are the musicians world famous now or are they likely to be in the future?

b Write the noun forms of the adjectives.
1 skilled _____
2 talented _____
3 brilliant _____
4 able _____

c Complete the sentences with the words in the box.

| at   for   to (x2) |

1 He's very talented _____ playing the guitar.
2 He has lots of potential _____ succeed in his career.
3 She's got a real talent _____ drawing.
4 She definitely has the ability _____ become a brilliant actor.

d Think of an example of someone who:
1 is skilled at some kind of sport or art
2 has a talent for some kind of musical instrument
3 is famous and you think is brilliant
4 you think is exceptional in their field
5 is the most successful person you know.

e 💬 Tell each other about your answers in 3d. Give reasons for your opinions.

GIVE ME STRENGTH
A new word suggests a picture

Isn't it strange how we can remember the words of a much loved poem that we learnt at primary school more than twenty years ago, but we can't remember where we left our keys about ten minutes ago? More than 130 years ago this problem caught the attention of the German psychologist Herman Ebbinghaus and he came up with a theory: the strength of memory.

Ebbinghaus believed that if we find new information interesting, then it'll probably be more meaningful to us. This makes the information easier to learn and also helps the strength of memory. It also helps if we associate the new information with something else. For example, a new word we learn might make us think of a picture. This association can also build memory strength.

Using associations to help us remember what we learn is known as 'mnemonics'. For example, some people are able to remember a long sequence of numbers because the shape of all those numbers reminds them of a specific physical shape such as a guitar. Mnemonic techniques are often used by competitors in the World Memory Championships held each year in London.

Popular spelling mnemonics:
BECAUSE
   Big **E**lephants **C**an't **A**lways **U**se **S**mall **E**xits
HERE or HEAR?
   We h**ear** with our **ear**.

A QUESTION OF TALENT?
"All you'll need is about 10,000 hours!"

We've all had the experience of trying to learn something new only to find out that we're not very good at it. We look around at other people we're learning with and they seem so much more talented and are doing so much better. It seems to come naturally to them. And when you look at all the people who are outstanding at what they do – the really famous people who are superstars – all you see is natural ability. The conclusion seems obvious: talented people must be born that way.

Without a doubt, there are people who are brilliant at certain things – they have a talent for kicking a football around a field, or they pick up a violin and immediately make music. However, there's also a lot to be said for practice. Psychologist K. Anders Ericsson studied students at Berlin's Academy of Music. He found that even though all the musicians in the study had the potential to become world famous, only some of them actually did. What made the difference? The answer is simple: time. Those who became exceptional were more competitive and practised about two thousand hours more than those who only did well. So, according to Ericsson, that's what it takes to become really skilled. It turns out that practice really does make perfect, and in order to learn something and become very successful at doing it, all you'll need is about 10,000 hours!

UNIT 3

4 LISTENING

a ▶1.44 Listen to Seamus, Fiona and Henry talk about their learning experiences. Answer the questions.
 1 Who talks about … ?
  a the best time to learn
  b learning hours
  c the strength of memory
 2 Do the speakers think the learning ideas they talk about work for them?

b ▶1.44 Listen again and make notes about the things they talk about.
 1 Seamus
  a copying comics
  b friends
  c graphic design
 2 Fiona
  a chemistry
  b system for remembering symbols
  c colleagues' attitudes
 3 Henry
  a tour preparation
  b daily learning routine
  c results

c 💬 Whose ideas do you think make more sense? Why?

5 GRAMMAR Multi-word verbs

a What is the meaning of the multi-word verbs in bold? Which multi-word verb is most similar to the verb on its own?
 1 All of my friends **were** also really **into** comic books, but none of them tried to **come up with** their own stories.
 2 … so we decided to **try** it **out**

b ▶ Now go to Grammar Focus 3A on p.138

6 SPEAKING

a Think of something you've done that you have put a lot of effort into. For example:
 • your job
 • a free-time activity
 • study of some kind
 • playing a musical instrument
 • learning a language

Make notes about these questions:
 1 What special skills or talent do you need?
 2 What level of ability do you think you have achieved?
 3 How have you learnt new information necessary for this activity?
 4 Do you need to remember a lot of things to do this well?
 5 How much time have you put into it?

b 💬 Work in small groups. Tell each other about your activity. Ask questions.

c 💬 Who in your group do you think has put in the most effort? Who has been successful?

3B There are lots of good runners in Kenya

Learn to discuss sports activities and issues
- G Present perfect simple and continuous
- V Words connected with sport

1 READING

a Look at the pictures. What sports do they show? How many of the people do you recognise?

b 💬 What do you think makes a successful athlete or sportsperson? Choose the five things in the box you think are most important. Are there any you think are unimportant?

| attitude   general level of fitness   luck |
| desire for money   genetic make-up |
| support from the community   technique |
| parents   training and practice |

c 💬 Compare your ideas with other students.

d Read the text *Born to be the best* about professionals in four sports. In what way are they all similar?

e Read the text again and answer the questions about each sport.
1 What sport is it?
2 Who is given as an example?
3 What unusual features are mentioned?
4 What is the result?

f Which of the things in 1b are mentioned in the text? Do you think this is important for all sports activities or only for top professional players?

Born to be THE BEST

CHAMPION SKIER
Champion cross-country skier Eero Mäntyranta had an unusual gene which made him produce too many red blood cells. Cross-country skiers cover long distances and their red blood cells have to send oxygen to their muscles. Mäntyranta had about 65% more red blood cells than the normal adult male and that's why he performed so well. In the 1960, 1964, and 1968 Winter Olympic Games, he won a total of seven medals. In 1964, he beat his closest competitor in the fifteen-kilometre race by forty seconds.

RECORD HIGH JUMP
On the seventh high jump of his life, Donald Thomas cleared 2.22 m. The next year, after only eight months of training, Thomas won the world championships. How did he achieve this victory? Not from training. He had unusually long legs and an exceptionally long Achilles tendon, which acted as a kind of spring, shooting him high into the air when he jumped.

THE WORLD'S BEST RUNNERS
Why do so many of the world's best distance runners come from Kenya and Ethiopia? Because a runner needs not just to be thin, but also to have thin legs and ankles. Runners from the Kalenjin tribe, in Kenya – where most of the country's best athletes come from – are thin in exactly this way. Compared to Europeans, Kalenjins are shorter but have longer legs, and their lower legs are half a kilo lighter.

BASEBALL PRO
Professional baseball players have, as a group, remarkable eyesight. A typical baseball professional can see at seven metres what the rest of us can see at four metres. This means that, however much they trained, only a tiny proportion of the population would be able to do what professional baseball players can do naturally: see a ball that is travelling towards them at 150 km an hour.

UNIT 3

2 VOCABULARY
Words connected with sport

a Find words in the texts which have a similar meaning to the words in italics.

1. Eero Mäntyranta was a cross-country skier *who often won competitions*.
2. He *did so well* because he had more red blood cells than most skiers.
3. He easily beat the closest *person competing with him*.
4. Before the world high jump *competition*, Thomas only had eight months of *practice*.
5. Thomas achieved a great *win*.
6. Most of Kenya's best *sportspeople* are from the Kalenjin tribe.
7. Baseball players *who play for a living* have very good eyesight.

b ▶ Now go to Vocabulary Focus on p.156

3 LISTENING

a ▶1.48 The texts in 1d are from a book called *The Sports Gene*. Listen to the first part of a programme in which people discuss the book. Answer the questions.

1. What do we know about Barbara McCallum?
2. What does she think of the ideas in the book?

b ▶1.48 Answer the questions. Then listen again and check.

1. What is the main message of the book?
    a The best athletes are often genetically different from most other people.
    b There is a particular gene which makes you a good athlete.
    c Being a good athlete is mainly a question of luck.
2. Which of these factors does Barbara say are important in Kenyans' success in running?
    a They start running at an early age.
    b Many people have long legs.
    c Children learn to run in bare feet.
    d They train for hours every day.

c ▶1.49 Listen to the second part of the programme and answer the questions.

1. What do we know about Marta Fedorova?
2. What does she think of the ideas in the book?

d ▶1.49 💬 Listen again and discuss the questions.

1. What does Marta notice about the people she has played against?
2. What conclusion does she reach from that?
3. In what way does she say sporting events like the Olympics are 'unfair'?
4. Do you agree with her conclusion? Why / Why not?

UNIT 3

4 GRAMMAR
Present perfect simple and continuous

a Match sentences 1–4 with the uses of the present perfect simple and continuous (a–d).
1 ☐ You**'ve been playing** tennis since you were a child.
2 ☐ I**'ve** also **read** the book.
3 ☐ I**'ve been thinking** a lot about this recently.
4 ☐ I**'ve lived** in Kenya myself.

> a to talk about a recent completed action, e.g. *I've lost my glasses*.
> b to talk about an activity that started in the past and is still continuing, e.g. *We've been waiting since this morning*.
> c to talk about an experience at some unspecified time in your life, e.g. *He's climbed Mount Everest*.
> d to talk about a recent activity which continued for a while (which may or may not still be continuing), e.g. *I've been reading a lot of good books lately*.

b ▶ Now go to Grammar Focus 3B on p.138

c Add a sentence using the present perfect simple or continuous.
1 I don't think I could play squash any more. I …
   I haven't played it for years.
2 She's really fit. She …
3 Of course I can play chess. I …
4 Why don't you buy a new pair of skis? You …

d Think about a sport (or other free time activity) that you have been doing for some time. Make notes about questions 1–4.
1 How good are you at it?
2 How long have you been doing it? Why did you start?
3 What are the main reasons you've become good at it (or haven't!)? Is it more to do with … ?
   • your genetic make-up and natural ability
   • developing technique and practising
   • support from other people
4 Do you think any of the things you have read or heard in this lesson are relevant to the activity you've been doing?

e 💬 Tell other students about your activity.

5 READING and SPEAKING

a Read about two famous US baseball players and answer the questions.
1 How are they similar?
2 How are they different?

b Think about the questions.
If 'sport isn't as fair as we like to think', should players be allowed to find ways to improve their performance? Which of these ways do you think are acceptable? Why?
• training hard
• having an operation (e.g. replacing arm muscles, improving eyesight)
• taking legal substances to enhance their performance (e.g. energy drinks)
• taking illegal substances to enhance their performance (e.g. drugs)

c 💬 Compare your ideas. Do you agree?

CASE STUDY: TOMMY JOHN

Tommy John is one of the best-loved figures in American baseball. In 1974, after an injury to his arm, he was the first player ever to have an operation to replace the muscles of his right arm with artificial ones. After his operation, he went on to win 164 games, more than he did before science helped to improve his performance. His 'bionic arm' enabled him to win at least 20 games a season. He had one of the longest careers in baseball history, retiring at the age of 46, and is regarded by the public as a sporting hero. Since then, at least a third of major-league baseball players have had the same operation, now known as 'Tommy John surgery'.

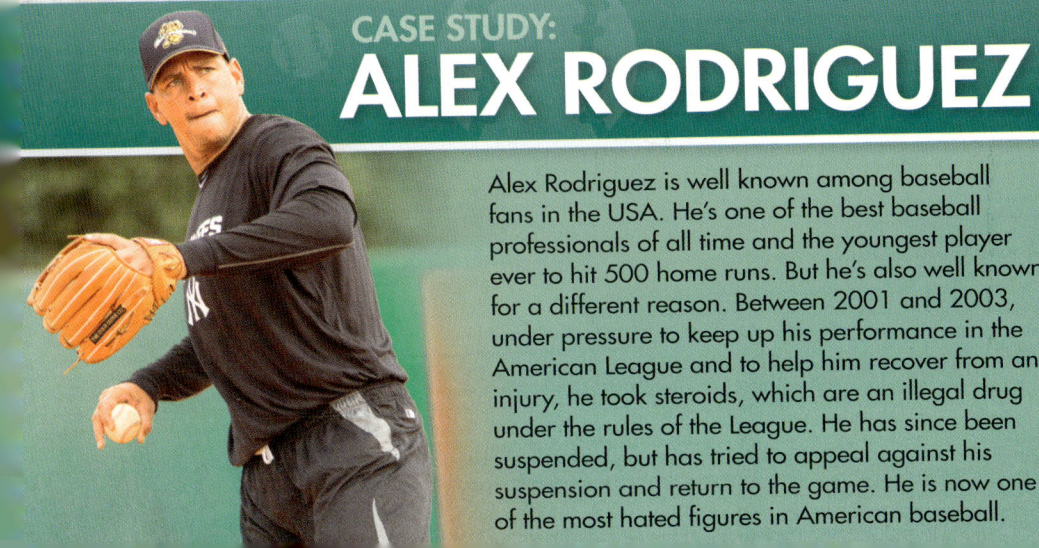

CASE STUDY: ALEX RODRIGUEZ

Alex Rodriguez is well known among baseball fans in the USA. He's one of the best baseball professionals of all time and the youngest player ever to hit 500 home runs. But he's also well known for a different reason. Between 2001 and 2003, under pressure to keep up his performance in the American League and to help him recover from an injury, he took steroids, which are an illegal drug under the rules of the League. He has since been suspended, but has tried to appeal against his suspension and return to the game. He is now one of the most hated figures in American baseball.

37

3C Everyday English
Who should we invite?

Learn to make careful suggestions
- **S** Keeping to the topic of the conversation
- **P** Consonant sounds

1 LISTENING

a Discuss the questions.
1 What kind of events do people usually celebrate?
2 Do you prefer small or big celebrations? Why?

b Look at photo a and answer the questions.
1 Where do you think Becky and Tom have been?
2 What do you think has happened?

c ▶1.51 Watch or listen to Part 1 and check your ideas in 1b.

d ▶1.51 Watch or listen again. Tick (✓) the topics that Becky and Tom talk about.

photographs Becky has taken	Tom's colleagues
dinner	Becky's café job	Tom's promotion
Becky's classmate, Tessa	

e ▶1.51 Watch or listen again. What do they say about the topics?

f ▶1.52 Watch or listen to Part 2. What wedding plans do Becky and Tom talk about?

g ▶1.52 Watch or listen to Part 2 again and answer the questions.
1 What's the first decision they have to make?
2 Who seems more focused on wedding plans? Why do you think so?

2 CONVERSATION SKILLS Keeping to the topic of the conversation

a Read this conversation from Part 2. How does Becky return to the original topic of the conversation? Underline the expression she uses.

BECKY So when are you going to tell your parents about your promotion?
TOM At the weekend, I think. We're seeing them on Saturday, remember?
BECKY Oh yes. Anyway, as I was saying – about Tessa …
TOM Tessa, yes, your classmate …

b Join words from A and B to make expressions.

A	B
as I	were saying …
to go/get	back to …
just	was saying …
as we	getting/going back to …

c We can put two of these words before the expressions in 2b. Which words are they?

so   actually   oh   anyway

d Work in pairs. Have short conversations. You need to agree on an English language study plan and organise what to study, how much to study, when, etc.

Student A: Explain your ideas for your study plans. Make sure you keep to the topic of the conversation.
Student B: Answer your partner's questions about the study plans, but keep trying to change the topic of conversation to something else.

Swap roles.

I think we should start with vocabulary.

Why don't we go to the café first?

As I was saying, we should start with …

38

UNIT 3

3 PRONUNCIATION
Sounds and spelling: Consonant sounds

a Look at the examples from Parts 1 and 2. Underline words that begin with the sounds in the box.

| /b/ | /f/ | /g/ | /k/ | /p/ | /v/ |

1 I've gradually got better …
2 … guests, a venue for the reception, the cake.
3 But don't you agree that she'd be perfect …
4 We'll need a photographer.

b ▶1.53 Listen to these two words. Which begins with a voiced sound? Which begins with an unvoiced sound?

better   people

Do you use your lips differently in the /b/ and /p/ sounds?

c ▶1.54 Listen to six words. Which word do you hear in each pair?

1 bill   3 van   5 lap
  pill   fan   lab
2 goat   4 leave   6 bag
  coat   leaf   back

d 💬 Work in pairs. Take turns saying one word from each pair. Which word does your partner say?

4 LISTENING

a ▶1.55 Watch or listen to Part 3. What is the main topic of Becky and Tom's conversation?
1 food for the wedding   3 the guests they'll invite
2 their wedding clothes

b ▶1.55 Watch or listen again. What do they say about the topics below? Make notes.
1 Aunt Clare   4 Regent's Lodge
2 Uncle Fred   5 after they get married
3 Tom's colleagues

5 USEFUL LANGUAGE
Making careful suggestions

a ▶1.56 Becky and Tom make careful suggestions to each other. Can you remember the missing words?

BECKY   We ____ ____ invite them to the evening reception.
TOM   But don't you agree that it'd ____ ____ not to invite them?

Listen and check.

b Why do Becky and Tom make careful suggestions? Choose the best answer.
1 They feel the subject-matter is a bit sensitive and they don't want to offend each other.
2 The wedding won't happen for a few months, so it doesn't feel real to them.

c Look at these examples of careful suggestions. Match the examples to the correct uses below.
a Don't you think it's a good idea to … ?
b How does it sound if we/I … ?
c Another idea might be to …
d I think maybe we should …
e I thought maybe we could …

1 Putting forward an idea carefully
2 Asking the other person to give their point of view

d Correct the careful suggestions.
1 Another idea might to be booking a DJ for the reception.
2 Don't you think a good idea to invite more people?
3 Maybe I thought we could get married at home.
4 How does it sound we only have a small cake?

e ▶ Communication 3C Student A: Go to p.131. Student B: Go to p.130.

6 SPEAKING

a You are going to have a class party. Work alone and think of ideas for the party.
• when
• where
• party theme and music
• food and drinks

b 💬 Discuss your ideas and make careful suggestions. Make sure everyone keeps to the topic of the conversation.

We could always do it at college.

Another idea might be to rent a hall.

Unit Progress Test

CHECK YOUR PROGRESS

You can now do the Unit Progress Test.

3D Skills for Writing
It doesn't matter what sport people choose

Learn to write a description of data
W Describing data

1 SPEAKING and LISTENING

a Discuss the questions.
1 What's the most unusual sport you've ever seen or heard of? Have you tried it?
2 What do you think are the most popular sports in your country to participate in? Why do you think they are popular?
3 How do you think new sports become popular?

b Look at photos 1–3. What are the names of the sports? Which of these sports have you tried? Which would you like to try?

c ▶1.57 Marco talks to three people at a sports complex: Lizzie, Barry and Patricia. Listen and match the speakers to the sports in the photos.

d ▶1.57 Listen again and make notes for each speaker:
1 reasons for choosing their sport
2 experience of the sport
3 future plans

e Are any of these sports popular in your country? Why / Why not?

2 READING

a Look at the bar chart. Are the sentences true or false?
1 The data only shows information about people who take part in sports.
2 The data doesn't give information about children's sport participation.
3 The data shows every year between 2005 and 2013.
4 Most of the sports have more participation in 2012/2013 than in 2005/2006.

Once-a-week sport participation – top five UK sports. 18 years and over.

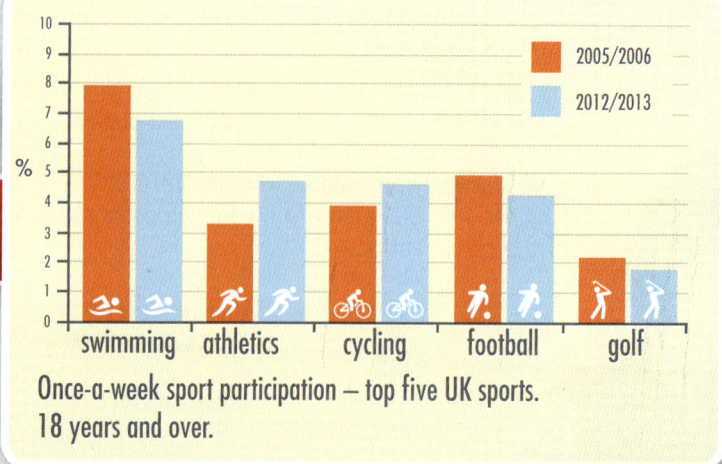

b Read the article *A nation of armchair athletes*. Does the article give the same information as the bar chart?

c Read the article again and answer the questions.
1 Does the writer think the major sporting event encouraged people to take part in sports?
2 Does the information represent only five sports?
3 What piece of information did the writer not expect?
4 What possible reason does the writer give for the increased interest in cycling?
5 What change does the writer mention in the final paragraph?

3 WRITING SKILLS
Describing data

a Match the summaries with the paragraphs (a–e) in the article. Which paragraph … ?
1 ☐ states the main conclusion you can draw from the data
2 ☐ adds extra information not shown in the data
3 ☐ interprets the data in more detail
4 ☐ outlines the issue that the article and the data is about
5 ☐ explains what the bar chart is about

40

b Look at paragraph d in the article again and complete the table.

	Adjective	Noun
there is a/an	1_____	increase
	obvious	2_____
	3_____ / 4_____	decrease
	Verb	Adverb
the number(s)/ size	has/have increased	5_____ / 6_____
	7_____	significantly

c Notice *This* in paragraph d in the text. Answer the questions.
  1 Does it refer back or forward to other information in the paragraph?
  2 How is information organised in the paragraph?
    a data followed by a comment
    b a comment followed by data

d Use the data about a British city to write sentences. Use language from 3b.
  1 People playing tennis: 2014 = 18%; now = 22%
  2 Number of football teams: 1 year ago = 53; now = 39
  3 Gym memberships: 2014 = 21%; now = 33%
  4 Number of volleyball teams: 2 years ago = 26; now = 23

4 WRITING

a Look at the bar chart and read the notes below. What does the information show?

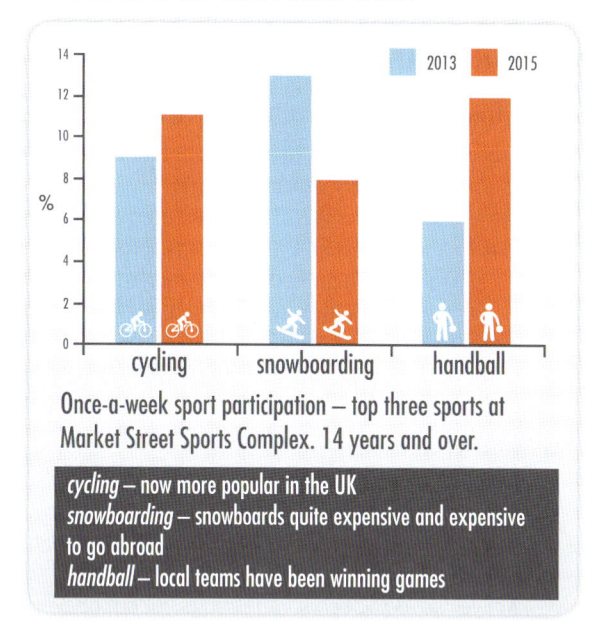

Once-a-week sport participation – top three sports at Market Street Sports Complex. 14 years and over.

cycling – now more popular in the UK
snowboarding – snowboards quite expensive and expensive to go abroad
handball – local teams have been winning games

b Work in pairs. Plan an article about the data and notes in 4a. Then write your article.

c Swap your article with another pair. Does the article use language from 3b correctly? Does it include verbs and nouns? Does it have the same organisation as 3a? Was it easy to understand?

A nation of armchair athletes?

a There's no doubt that international sporting events are good for sport. There's always huge interest in them and people are glued to their TV sets watching different events. Of course, this is all about watching sports, but does it also mean that people get off the sofa and actually take part in sports?

b The bar chart looks at the five most popular sports in the UK in terms of people participating – not just sitting around and watching them on TV. One point to note is that all these sports include a range of activities. So, for example, 'swimming' also includes the sports of diving, water polo and deep water diving, while 'football' includes five-a-side games as well as full teams. The results in the graph show percentages of people who actively participate in that sport at least once a week.

c The blue and the red columns make a direct comparison between the year from October 2005 to October 2006 and a similar period in 2012/2013, just after a major sporting event. As you can see, the statistics show there has been no sudden increase in British people getting actively involved in sport.

d In fact, most surprising of all, there's a significant decrease in the number of people getting involved in swimming, the number one sport in the UK. You can see that there has also been an obvious change in the number of people wanting to go out and kick a football. There's a slight decrease in the number of people playing golf although participation hasn't decreased significantly. The most noticeable increase in sport participation can be seen in athletics. Perhaps this is because athletics features regularly at international sporting events. It also requires very little equipment initially, so can be a low-cost sport. Interest in cycling has also increased slightly. *This* might be because cycling includes BMX and cross-country, which makes this a very varied sport. Cycling enthusiasts have reported that interest in different kinds of cycling has increased noticeably in recent years.

e It's important to remember that the information in the table only focuses on the five most popular sports in the UK. Recent reports show that British people are becoming interested in a wide range of sports and are taking up activities like snowboarding and handball. It doesn't really matter what sport people choose to get involved in – the key thing is that they get out of their armchairs and take part.

41

UNIT 3
Review and extension

1 GRAMMAR

a Put the words in italics in the correct order.
1 I didn't know Spanish before I went to Mexico but I managed to *up / pick / it* very quickly.
2 I'm just as good as you. There's no need to *me / down / look / on* just because I didn't go to university.
3 It's still raining. This weather is starting to *get / down / me*.
4 I don't believe she was ever married to a film star. I think she *it / up / making / is*.
5 She's very creative. She keeps *up / with / coming* new ideas.
6 I don't know how to do this task. I just can't *out / figure / it*.

b Choose the correct verb tenses in these conversations.
1 **A** Come in. Sorry the flat is such a mess.
  B What have you [1]*done / been doing*? There are things all over the floor.
  A I've [2]*sorted / been sorting* things out but I haven't quite [3]*finished / been finishing* yet.
2 **A** How are things? I haven't [4]*seen / been seeing* you for ages. What have you [5]*done / been doing*?
  B Oh, nothing much. I've got exams next month so I've [6]*studied / been studying* most of the time.

c Think of things you could say in answer to these questions using the present perfect simple or continuous.
- What have you been doing these days?
- How's your family?
- You're looking fit. Have you been doing a lot of sport?
- So what's new?

d 💬 Have conversations, starting with the questions in 1c.

2 VOCABULARY

a Rewrite the sentences, using the word in brackets, so that they keep the same meaning.
1 We're looking for someone who can lead a team of researchers. (ability)
2 She can design things very well. (skilled)
3 The members of the band all play music extremely well. (outstanding)
4 He could become a very good politician. (potential)
5 He's better than most goalkeepers. (exceptional)
6 My sister can cook very well. (brilliant)

b Give a different form of the words in italics to complete the definitions
1 Someone who *trains* sportsmen is a *trainer*.
2 A person who *competes* in a sport is a _____ .
3 The sporting activity that *athletes* do is called _____ .
4 Someone who does sport as a *profession* is a _____ sportsperson.
5 If you *perform* well, you give a good _____ .
6 A team that wins a *victory* is _____ .

3 WORDPOWER *up*

a Match the comments with the pictures. Where are the people and why are they saying this?

1 ☐ '**Drink up**. We need to go.'
2 ☐ 'Could you **speak up**? We can't hear you.'
3 ☐ 'I've **used up** the shampoo. Is there any more?'
4 ☐ 'Let me see the bill. I think they've **added** it **up** wrongly.'

b Adding *up* often gives an extra meaning to a verb. In which examples in 1a does *up* mean … ?
 a to the end   b together   c louder

c What does *it* mean in each example below?

| a suggestion | a language | a glass | a word |

1 You dropped it so I think you should **clear** it **up**.
2 I don't know. I'll have to **look** it **up**.
3 It was easy. I **picked** it **up** in about six months.
4 Why don't you **bring** it **up** at the meeting?

d ▶1.58 Listen and check your answers. What was the problem in each case?

e Here are some more multi-word verbs with *up*. Match the two parts of the sentences.

1 Walk more slowly! I can't   **look up to** him.
2 He's a good father. His children really   **turned up**.
3 We invited 50 people, but only a few   **put up with** it.
4 He's so rude. I don't know why people   **keep up with** you.

f Match the multi-word verbs in 3e with these meanings.
 a tolerate   c appear or arrive
 b go at the same speed   d admire or respect

g 💬 Work in pairs. Choose two of the multi-word verbs in 3a, c or e. Think of a situation and write a short conversation which includes both verbs.

h 💬 Act out your conversation. Can other students guess your situation?

🔄 REVIEW YOUR PROGRESS

How well did you do in this unit? Write 3, 2 or 1 for each objective.
3 = very well   2 = well   1 = not so well

I CAN …

discuss ability and achievement	☐
discuss sports activities and issues	☐
make careful suggestions	☐
write a description of data	☐

42

CAN DO OBJECTIVES

- Discuss events that changed your life
- Discuss and describe rules
- Describe photos
- Write an email to apply for work

UNIT 4
Life lessons

GETTING STARTED

a Look at the picture and answer the questions.
1. Where are these people? What are they doing?
2. What is the girl thinking?
3. Why do you think they're doing this?

b Discuss the questions.
1. Is it important to help children prepare for what might happen to them later in life. Why?
2. Which of your childhood experiences have had an impact on your adult life?
3. In general, how far do you think experiences in childhood influence the choices you make in your life?

43

4A She's happier now than she used to be

Learn to discuss events that changed your life

G *used to* and *would*
V Cause and result

1 SPEAKING

a 💬 Imagine you suddenly became very rich, either by winning or inheriting money. How would you spend the money if you had … ?
   a $10,000   b $100,000   c $1,000,000

b 💬 Read the headlines a–c.
   1 What do you think happened to these people?
   2 Do you know anyone (either people you know or people you have read about) who has won or inherited money? What did they do with the money?

a £1.8 MILLION LOTTERY WIN WRECKED MY LIFE

b 'HOW I SPENT MY PRIZE MONEY'
Nigerian Idol Season III winner, Moses Obi

c HOMELESS BROTHERS INHERIT $7 BILLION
Zsolt Pelardi: 'Maybe we can finally have a normal life'

2 READING

a Read the first part of two texts about people who won the lottery. What do you think the people did? Which person do you think spent the money most wisely?

b The words in the boxes give an outline of each story.

Sharon Tirabassi:
wild shopping   huge house   family   friends
electric bike   happier   kids   pay day   family values

Ihsan Khan:
taxi driver   dream   number   Mercedes   mansions
mayor   earthquake   school   satisfied   parliament

Find words in the boxes which mean:
1 the day when you get money from your job
2 large luxury houses
3 a sudden movement of the earth
4 the people who make the laws of the country
5 children
6 pleased that you have got what you wanted
7 the leader of the city government
8 traditional principles of being honest and decent

c 💬 What do you think each person's story is?

HOW TO SPEND A $10 MILLION LOTTERY WIN IN LESS THAN THREE YEARS

Nine years after winning $10.5 million in the lottery, Sharon Tirabassi is back catching the bus to her part-time job. She's working to support her kids in their rented house in northeast Hamilton, USA. Tirabassi, one of this city's biggest lotto winners, has gone from being super rich to living from week to week.

LOTTO WINNER TAKES HOME FORTUNE TO PAKISTAN

People who win the lottery usually spend their money on things they've always wanted: a dream holiday or a beautiful house. But Ihsan Khan had a different idea. He kept his money and brought it back to Battagram, the town in Pakistan where he grew up.

d ▶ **Communication 4A** Student A: Read the story of Sharon Tirabassi on p.129 and answer the questions. Student B: Read the story of Ihsan Khan on p.130 and answer the questions.

e 💬 Work in the same pairs. Take turns to tell your stories and include the keywords in 2b. Ask questions about your partner's story to check anything you don't understand.

f 💬 Discuss the questions.
1 What sensible decisions do you think Sharon and Ihsan made? What poor decisions did they make?
2 Why do you think they made these decisions?
3 Which moral or 'message' comes out of these stories for you? Write it down and compare your idea with other students.

> Be careful what you wish for!
>
> Believe in your dreams.
>
> If you have lots of money, don't go to Las Vegas!

3 GRAMMAR
used to and *would*

a Look at sentences a–c and complete the rules with the words in the box.
   a Ihsan Khan **used to** work as a taxi driver and security guard in the USA.
   b He **used to** think he could use his money to fix everything.
   c She **would** regularly go on shopping trips where she **would** buy anything she fancied.

---
now   past   used to (x2)   would (x2)

We use *used to* and *would* to talk about things in the ¹_____ which are no longer true ²_____.
To talk about states, thoughts and feelings in the past, we can only use ³_____, not ⁴_____.
To talk about habits and repeated actions, we can use either ⁵_____ or ⁶_____.

b Find and underline other examples of *used to* and *would* in the texts.

c Look at the sentences and answer the questions.
   a Today, the Tirabassi family **don't** live in a huge house **any more**.
   b He used to think he could use his money to fix everything, but he **no longer** believes that.
1 What do the words in bold mean?
   (a) things are the same as before
   (b) things are different now
2 Rewrite sentence a with *no longer* and sentence b with *not any more*. How does the word order change?

d ▶ Now go to Grammar Focus 4A on p.140

4 LISTENING

a You are going to listen to an interview with Monica Sharpe, a researcher into the psychology of money. How do you think she will answer these questions?
1 Does winning lots of money make you behave badly?
2 Does having lots of money make you happy?
3 Does buying things make you happy?

b ▶ 2.5 Listen and check your answers.

c ▶ 2.5 Tick (✓) the points Monica makes. Listen again and check.
1 Most people who get a lot of money spend it all quickly.
2 We enjoy hearing stories about people who won the lottery and then lost all their money.
3 Suddenly having lots of money usually has a negative effect on you.
4 Most people feel much happier just after they win money.
5 In the long term, being rich doesn't always make you happier.
6 It's better to spend money on things you can own, like houses and cars.

d 💬 Which of the points in 4c do you agree with? Can you think of examples from people you know or have heard about?

UNIT 4

5 VOCABULARY Cause and result

a ▶2.6 Underline the correct expressions in bold. Then listen and check your answers.

1 Of course people like to believe that winning money leads **into / to** disaster.
2 The idea that winning a lot of money **causes / is caused by** misery is actually a myth.
3 Suddenly having a lot of money is just as likely to have a positive effect **on / to** you as a negative effect.
4 They measured how happy people are as a result **from / of** winning the lottery.
5 Getting richer doesn't actually **effect / affect** how happy you are.
6 But spending money on experiences usually results **in / on** longer-term happiness.

b Answer the questions about the expressions in 5a.

1 Which expressions have a similar meaning to 'causes'?
2 Which expression has a similar meaning to 'caused by'?
3 What is the difference between *affect* and *effect*?
4 Look at sentences 4 and 6. In which sentence is *result* a verb and in which is it a noun?

c Complete the sentences with the words in the box.

| affect   effect   cause   lead   result (x2) |

1 He's much friendlier than he used to be. Getting married has had a positive _____ on him.
2 Having no money at all can often _____ to problems in a relationship.
3 I hear John and Barbara have split up. I hope it won't _____ our friendship with them.
4 It's well known that smoking can _____ cancer.
5 Hundreds of villagers' lives were saved as a _____ of Ihsan Khan's help.
6 Be careful! Borrowing large amounts of money can _____ in serious financial problems.

d Think about an important event in your own life, and another event that happened as a result. Write three sentences about it using expressions in 5a.

e 💬 Read your sentences to each other and ask questions.

6 LISTENING

a Look at the information about Alphonso and Dragana. How do you think their lives have changed? Think about:

lifestyle   attitude to life   daily routine   work   money   leisure

HOME   BLOG   BODY & MIND   RELATIONSHIPS

LIFE-CHANGING EVENTS

Sometimes a single big event can change your life. Two people tell us their stories.

Dragana went to study abroad for a year.

Alphonso and Carmen have just had their first baby.

b ▶2.7 Listen to Alphonso and Dragana. Which of the topics in 6a do they talk about?

c ▶2.7 Are the sentences true or false? Correct the false sentences. Listen again and check.

Alphonso
1 They both used to work.
2 They didn't have much money.
3 The baby hasn't changed his attitude to life much.

Dragana
4 She's from a big city in Croatia.
5 She didn't enjoy being in Berlin.
6 The experience has changed her attitude to other cultures.

7 SPEAKING

a Think about yourself now and how you have changed in the last 10 years. Make notes on some of these topics:

- work
- free time
- attitude to life
- daily routine
- family and relationships
- money

b 💬 Tell each other how you think you have changed using *used to / would*.

46

4B We weren't allowed to talk in class

Learn to discuss and describe rules
- **G** Obligation and permission
- **V** Talking about difficulty

1 SPEAKING

a 💬 Look at photos a–d. What kind of training do you think is needed for these jobs? Which training would be the hardest?

b Read what these people say about training. Do you agree with their opinions?

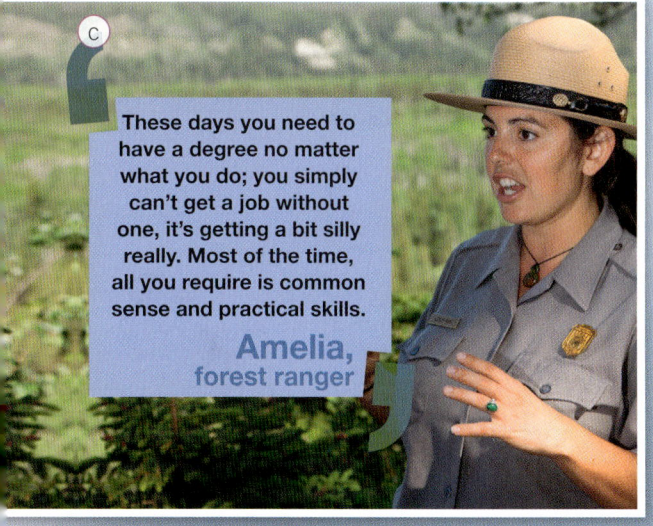

2 GRAMMAR 1 Modality review

a Underline all the modal verbs or phrases (e.g. *can*, *have to*) in the quotes.

b Complete the rules with the correct modal verb or phrase in 2a.

1. We use _____, _____ and _____ when we talk about something that's necessary.
2. We use _____ to talk about something that isn't necessary.
3. We use _____ when we talk about something that's possible.
4. We use _____ to talk about something that's not possible.

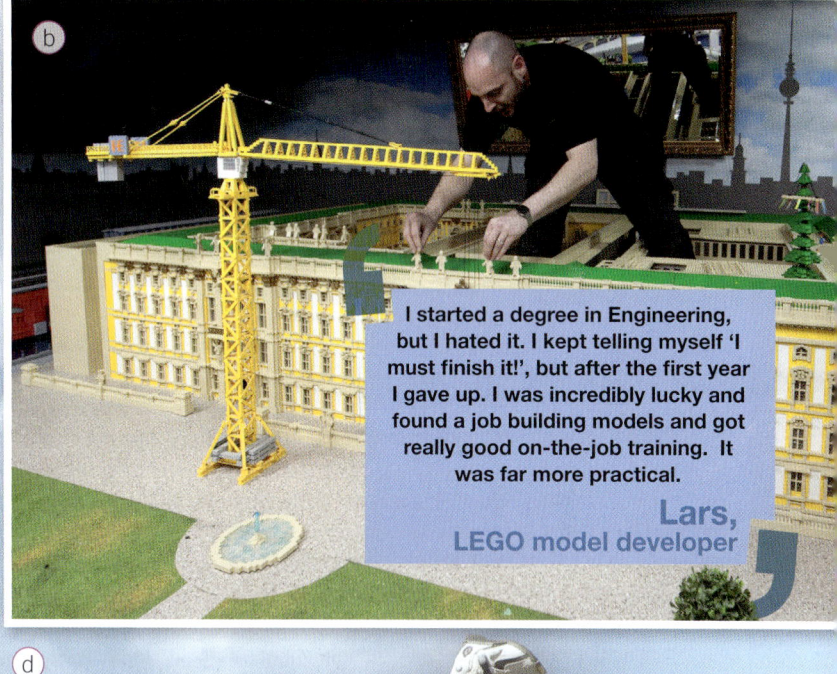

a "You can do all the studying you like, but until you've done the actual job, you don't know what it really involves."
— **Sheela**, pilot

b "I started a degree in Engineering, but I hated it. I kept telling myself 'I must finish it!', but after the first year I gave up. I was incredibly lucky and found a job building models and got really good on-the-job training. It was far more practical."
— **Lars**, LEGO model developer

c "These days you need to have a degree no matter what you do; you simply can't get a job without one, it's getting a bit silly really. Most of the time, all you require is common sense and practical skills."
— **Amelia**, forest ranger

d "You don't have to have a university degree to get a good job these days – it's as much about training and practice."
— **Tony**, stuntman

47

UNIT 4

3 READING

a 💬 Look at photos a–d and answer the questions.
1 What jobs are shown in the photos?
2 What kind of training might you need for this work?

b Read the texts. Were your ideas correct?

c Read the texts again. Who do you think would say this, someone at the Peking Opera School (P) or someone doing Swiss Guard training (S)?
1 The easiest class was learning how to act.
2 I feel part of an on-going history.
3 I had no problems being accepted as I'm very tall.
4 I often feel exhausted.
5 I can't remember the words of that song.
6 My parents didn't have to pay for my training – I did later on.
7 I get asked some very silly questions.
8 This sword is very uncomfortable to wear.

d 💬 Which of the two kinds of training seems harder to you? Which one would you choose to do? Why?

4 VOCABULARY Talking about difficulty

a All the adjectives in bold, except for one, describe something that is *very* difficult. Which adjective is not as strong as the others?

The training was **punishing**.
Discipline was very **strict**.
Teachers could be quite **tough**.
He described his time at school as '**arduous**'.
It's not likely to be quite as **gruelling** as Jackie Chan's training.
Those lucky enough to be selected go through **rigorous** training.
Sometimes they might need to use force to resolve a **tricky** situation.

TRAINING TO BE THE BEST

∽ Becoming Jackie Chan ∽

How do you get to be the next Jackie Chan? Most people think you should find a martial arts master and learn all their secrets. Jackie Chan's training was in a Peking Opera School in Hong Kong. These schools used to train people for traditional Chinese theatre and apart from the acrobatics and martial arts, students also learnt speech, song and dance.

The training was **punishing**. Students would rise at 5 am and train for at least ten hours. Discipline was very **strict** and teachers could be quite **tough**.

Jackie Chan, who did his training in the 1960s, described his time at school as '**arduous**'. Students had to repeat exercises again and again until they got them right. At the same time, they would need to learn traditional character roles used in Chinese theatre.

Students were sent to Peking Opera Schools when they were children. They would stay at the school and were given food and accommodation as well as training. This meant that they built up a debt that they had to repay once they began performing in Chinese theatre. They were forced to sign a contract agreeing to this.

During the 1960s, interest in traditional Chinese theatre declined and the schools closed down. Today there are still academies in China that offer a mixture of the study of and training in Peking opera. However, it's not likely to be quite as **gruelling** as Jackie Chan's training.

∽ The voice is a weapon ∽

Imagine getting up each day and going to work back in the sixteenth century. That's probably what it feels like for guards around the Vatican City, the people who are dressed in the amazing uniforms from the Renaissance that you can see in the pictures.

These people are part of a 500-year-old tradition. All the guards are Swiss and they are there to protect the Vatican and the Pope. They're the oldest military unit that still exists today and is still active.

Getting into the Swiss Guards isn't easy. You need to be a Swiss male between the ages of 19 and 30 and you need to be at least 1.74 metres tall. You also have to have completed basic military training with the Swiss Army and have some kind of professional qualification like a degree or diploma.

Those selected go through **rigorous** training. They start by learning about the history of the Swiss Guards and how to recognise key people around the Vatican. At the same time, there is weapons training. Vatican Swiss Guards have to learn to handle old-fashioned weapons such as swords.

However, Swiss Guards also learn that the very first weapon they should use is their voice. Guards often have to deal with difficult tourists who want to explore parts of the Vatican not open to the public, so their training involves lessons in both Italian and English. Of course, sometimes they might need to use force to resolve a **tricky** situation, so they are trained in self-defence, a mixture of karate and judo developed specially for the Guards.

In this day and age, it's difficult to think of a job where you learn languages, martial arts and how to use a sword. It's no easy task, but in order to wear one of the most striking uniforms in the world, that's what the Swiss Guards have to do.

48

b Which adjective in 4a means … ?
1 something is so hard you have to push yourself almost to the point of hurting yourself
2 something is very difficult because the training is very thorough and detailed
3 something is difficult because there are rules that must be obeyed

c Ask and answer the questions. Give extra details.
1 Imagine you have to run a marathon. Would it be tough or punishing for you?
2 Can you remember a teacher you had at school who was very strict?
3 What's a job that requires rigorous training?
4 Have you ever been in a tricky situation? What happened?

d ▶ Now go to Vocabulary Focus 4B on p.157

5 LISTENING

a ▶2.10 Listen to Miranda, who trained at a drama school, and Fred, who trained at a football academy. Which sentence describes their experience best?
1 They both enjoyed the training, but felt they missed a part of growing up.
2 They weren't sure about the training, but they know they'll do well anyway.
3 They weren't sure about the selection process, but they feel they did well during the training.

b ▶2.10 Listen again. Are the sentences true or false?
Miranda
1 During the audition process she had to perform scenes from plays twice.
2 She was confident she would get into drama school.
3 All her tutors were tough.
4 The school was flexible when she wasn't sure if she wanted to continue training.
Fred
5 His parents were unsure whether he should join the academy.
6 They knew they would have to sacrifice a lot of time to help Fred.
7 He was surprised to find that he enjoyed analysing football matches.
8 He felt disappointed for his friend, Jack.

c Do you think the kind of sacrifice that Miranda and Fred made was worth it? Why / Why not?

6 GRAMMAR
Obligation and permission

a Look at the words and phrases in bold in sentences 1–6. Which show obligation (O) and which show permission (P)?
1 I **was supposed to** prepare a song as well, but they forgot to let me know.
2 … there was a workshop for a day where they **made** us work on new scenes from plays …
3 … in her class we **weren't allowed to** talk or use our voices in any way.
4 … they could see this was a pretty unique opportunity, so they **let** me do it.
5 … we **were allowed to** see the games for free.
6 … there were some boys who **were forced to** give it all up …

b ▶ Now go to Grammar Focus 4B on p.140

7 SPEAKING

a Think of a time (at school, university or work) when you had to do some training and follow rules. Make notes about the questions.
What was the situation?
Who made the rules?
Were some of the rules very strict?
Were there some rules you didn't follow?
How did you feel about the experience?

b Discuss your experiences. What similarities and differences were there?

4C Everyday English
Thank you, you've saved my life

Learn to describe photos
- P Contrastive stress
- S Expressing careful disagreement

1 LISTENING

a Discuss the questions.
1 How do you feel about showing your work to other people? Do you … ?
   a always show other people what you've done
   b only show your work if you think it's good
   c never show your work unless you really have to
2 How do you feel about people commenting on it or criticising it?

b Look at photo a from Part 1. Where do you think Becky and Tessa are? Who are they talking to?

c ▶2.13 Watch or listen to Part 1 and check your ideas.

d ▶2.13 Answer the questions. Watch or listen again and check.
1 Whose photos are they?
2 What does the tutor especially like?
3 What's the topic for the next assignment?

2 USEFUL LANGUAGE Describing photos

a Which of the expressions below could describe the photos? Write *1*, *2*, *n* (*neither*) or *b* (*both*).

1 ☐ And here's a <u>close-up</u> of some leaves.
2 ☐ We tried to get a <u>closer shot</u> with this photo.
3 ☐ Here's <u>a more distant shot</u> of the tree.
4 ☐ And this is the same tree, but <u>from further away</u>.
5 ☐ Here's another shot of the tree, but <u>from a different angle</u>.
6 ☐ As you can see, there are mountains <u>in the background</u>.
7 ☐ That's my car <u>in the foreground</u>.
8 ☐ This one's a bit <u>out of focus</u>!

b ▶2.13 Which underlined expressions in 2a did Becky use? Watch or listen again and check.

c ▶ Communication 4C Student A: Go to p.129. Student B: Go to p.131.

d Work in pairs (one student from A and B in each pair). Take turns to show your photos to your partner and discuss them. Ask questions about your partner's photos.

e Discuss the photos. In what ways are the photos similar? In what ways are they different?

3 LISTENING

a ▶2.14 Watch or listen to Part 2. Answer the questions.
1 What are Becky and Tessa talking about?
2 Where is Becky going next?

b Who thinks these things, Becky (B) or Tessa (T)?
1 Bridges are an interesting topic.
2 The theoretical part of the course is boring.
3 She is missing information for the essay.

50

UNIT 4

4 CONVERSATION SKILLS
Expressing careful disagreement

a ▶2.15 Look at the exchange between Tessa and Becky. Then listen to what they actually say. What is the difference?

TESSA Yes, bridges. So boring.
BECKY I don't agree. They're not at all boring.

b Why does Becky use careful ways to disagree?

c The sentences below are replies to what another person said. What do you think each speaker is talking about? Match the replies with the topics in the box.

| a football match   a film   bank managers |
| a restaurant meal   a party |

1 <u>Really, did you think so? I thought</u> he played quite well.
2 <u>I'm not sure about that.</u> It doesn't seem that expensive.
3 <u>I know what you mean, but on the other hand</u> it's a very responsible job.
4 <u>Oh, I don't know.</u> I think it could be quite good fun.
5 <u>Maybe you're right,</u> but I enjoyed some bits of it.

d ▶2.16 Listen to the conversations and check your answers.

e 💬 How could you disagree with the comments below? Prepare replies using <u>underlined</u> expressions from 4c. Then take turns to reply.
1 I love Café Roma. It's a great atmosphere.
2 I'd never want to have a cat. All they do is sit around and sleep.
3 I don't know why people play golf. It's such a boring sport.

5 PRONUNCIATION Contrastive stress

a ▶2.15 Listen again to Becky's reply and answer the questions below.
TESSA Yes, bridges. So boring.
BECKY Oh, I don't know. **It's not that boring**.

1 Underline the word which has the strongest stress in the **bold** sentence.
2 Does the sentence mean … ?
   a They're not all boring.
   b They're not as boring as you think they are.
   c They're not as boring as other kinds of architechture.

b 💬 Reply to the comments below using *not that*.
1 I thought that was a really interesting lecture.

> Oh, I don't know. …

2 I find photography a very difficult subject.
3 Look at that bridge. It's so unusual.
4 I thought the questions in the exam were incredibly easy.

c ▶2.17 Listen and check. Were your replies similar?

6 LISTENING

a ▶2.18 Watch or listen to Part 3. Which of these is the best summary of what happens?
1 Becky gives Tessa a coffee and some books she found in the library. Then they talk about the wedding. Then Tessa notices Phil and asks who he is.
2 Becky gives Tessa her lecture notes, then they talk about the wedding. Then Tessa meets Phil and they talk about his book.

b 💬 Are the sentences true or false? Discuss the false sentences – what actually happens?
1 Becky gives Tessa her lecture notes and some photos.
2 Tessa is grateful to Becky for her help.
3 Becky wants Tessa to be their wedding photographer.
4 Tessa refuses because she thinks she's not good enough.
5 Phil finishes typing and saves what he's written.
6 Phil asks who Tessa is.
7 Tessa wants to read Phil's novel.

7 SPEAKING

a ▶ **Communication 4C** Student A: Go to p.130.
Student B: Go to p.129.

b Present an opinion on one of the topics to the rest of the class. Do they agree with you?

Unit Progress Test
CHECK YOUR PROGRESS
You can now do the Unit Progress Test.

51

4D Skills for Writing
I'm good at communicating with people

Learn to write an email to apply for work
W Giving a positive impression

1 SPEAKING and LISTENING

a If you go to live in a different country, do you think it's important to … ?
- learn the local language
- make friends with local people
- go somewhere beautiful with a good climate

Why do you think these things are important or not important?

Katowice, Poland

Nick from England

Jean from France

Muscat, Oman

Toronto, Canada

Eva from Colombia

b ▶2.19 Listen to three people talking about living in the places in the photos. Which topics do they mention?

meeting people   the climate   food and drink
the culture of the country   speaking the language

c ▶2.19 Listen again. Answer these questions about each speaker.
1. What did they like?
2. What did they find difficult?
3. How was it different from their own country?

d Which speakers make these points? How did their own experience support these opinions?
1. It's important to learn the local language.
2. Beautiful cities aren't always the best places to live.
3. The weather influences the way people live.
4. Foreigners often don't make an effort to get to know the local culture.
5. Living abroad can be worthwhile even if you don't always have a good time.

e The speakers say that meeting local people is important when you live in a different country. Think of three ways you could meet local people. Which is your most interesting idea? Why?

2 READING

a Read the leaflet about becoming an international student 'buddy' in London. Answer the questions.
1. What is a 'buddy' and what does he/she do?
2. What are the advantages of becoming a buddy?
3. What kind of person are they looking for?

BE A BUDDY FOR THE INTERNATIONAL STUDENTS' CLUB

Are you curious about other cultures? Are you eager to get to know and meet new people from all over the world?
Volunteer to offer assistance and friendship to international students as a 'buddy' at your university or college.

Responsibilities
After an international student has been assigned to you, you will show them around during the first weeks of their stay. You'll give them an insight into the student life in your area and generally help them out.

What we offer you
- free membership and benefits of belonging to the International Students Club
- free training courses which will look great on your CV (a certificate of participation awarded)
- the opportunity to get a wide range of cross-cultural experience

52

UNIT 4

b Paulo wrote an email applying to be a buddy and saying why he is suitable. Which of the reasons below do you think he should use?

> he understands the needs of foreign students
> he loves living in London   he's outgoing and sociable
> he's interested in other cultures
> he speaks several languages
> he has plenty of free time   he knows London well

Read the email and check your answers.

3 WRITING SKILLS
Giving a positive impression

a Paulo uses phrases in his email which give a positive impression. Underline the phrases which have these meanings.

1 I *speak* English *well*.
2 I *like being with other people*.
3 I *have no problem talking to people*.
4 I *am able to* understand the needs of students.
5 I *know* the city *well*.
6 I *have always been interested* in learning about other countries.
7 I would be *willing* to give up my free time.
8 I could *help* your programme.

b Paulo writes *I am sure this would help me …* instead of *I think …* in order to sound more confident. Find four more expressions like this in the email.

c What is the advantage of using the expressions in 3a and 3b when applying for a job? Which answer is not correct?

1 They make the writer sound positive and enthusiastic.
2 They make the email more interesting to read.
3 They give the impression that the writer could do the job well.

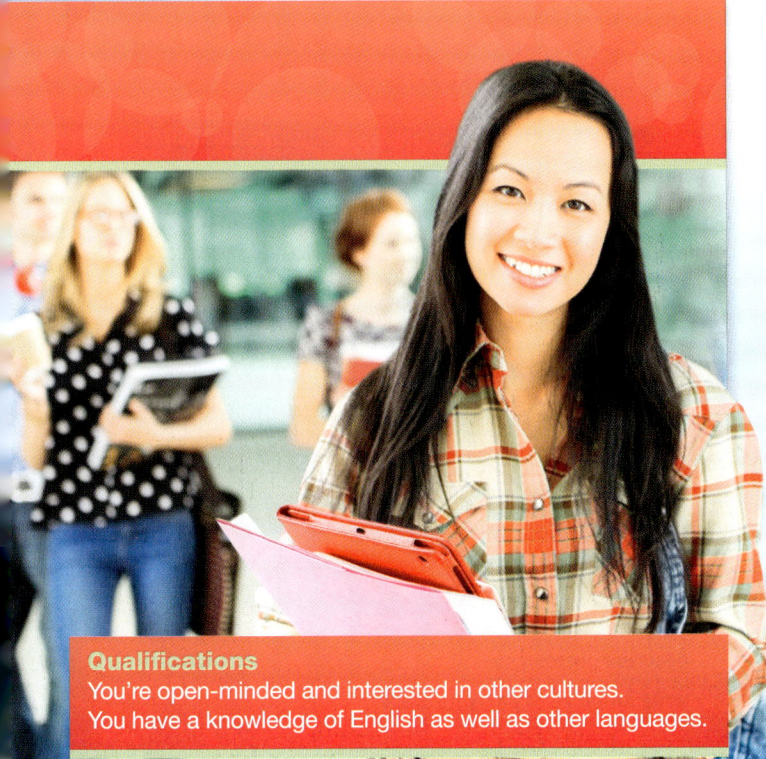

Dear Sir/Madam,

¹I saw the information about international student buddies on your website and I am writing to apply for the role.

²I am a Brazilian student at Birkbeck College, London, where I am studying international law. I am fluent in English, Spanish, French, and Portuguese, which would help me to communicate with students from different countries. I am also very sociable and good at communicating with people, which I am sure would help me to establish a good relationship with new students.

³As a foreign student in London myself, I am in an excellent position to understand the needs of students coming from other countries. I have a thorough knowledge of the city and the student life here. I am confident that I would be able to help students to feel at home and find their way around.

⁴I have always been very keen on learning about other cultures and my own circle of friends in London is completely international. I strongly believe we should encourage people from different cultures to come together to help promote intercultural understanding.

⁵I would be more than happy to give up my free time to work as an international student buddy and I'm certain I could make a valuable contribution to your programme.

I look forward to hearing from you.

Yours faithfully,
Paulo Figueiredo

4 WRITING

a Plan an email applying to do voluntary work. Choose one of these situations. Make a list of reasons why you would be suitable.

- A website is advertising for volunteers to work in an international summer camp and organise activities for teenagers.
- A voluntary organisation wants helpers to make contact with English-speaking families living in your country and help them to adapt to your culture.
- A large secondary school in your area wants volunteers to give talks to pupils about different jobs and to help them decide on a future career.

b Write the email. Include:
- an opening sentence, explaining why you are writing
- two or three paragraphs, explaining why you are suitable
- phrases from 3a and 3b
- a final sentence to conclude the email.

c Work in pairs. Look at your partner's email. Does it … ?
- make it clear why he/she is suitable
- have a clear structure
- use expressions from 3a and 3b to give a positive impression

d Swap your email with other students. Would they choose you as a volunteer?

Qualifications
You're open-minded and interested in other cultures.
You have a knowledge of English as well as other languages.

UNIT 4
Review and extension

1 GRAMMAR

a Use the words in brackets to rewrite the sentences. Make sure the meaning doesn't change.
1. I was a nurse but now I work for a drug company. (used to)
2. I don't do shift work now. (no longer)
3. When I was a nurse I sometimes slept in, but now I always get up early. (would)
4. I no longer take my lunch to work because there's a cafeteria at the drug company. (any more)
5. I don't wear a uniform in my new job so I can now wear my own clothes. (used to)
6. I don't have to deal with difficult patients now. (no longer)
7. I'm much happier than I was before. (used to)

b Correct five obligation and permission expressions in the text.

I went to a very strict primary school when I was a child. I wasn't allowed to do about two hours homework every night which meant there was little time to play with my friends. But often my parents told me just to study for an hour and wrote a note for the teacher excusing me from homework. In class we weren't let to talk to each other when we were working on a task because teachers didn't like noisy classrooms. However, we allowed to put up our hand and ask our teacher a question as she felt it was good to help students. We weren't allowed to do some kind of physical exercise every day after lunch, but that made us very tired in the afternoon. One good thing is that they supposed us learn a musical instrument and I learnt to play the clarinet, which I still enjoy doing.

2 VOCABULARY

a Complete the sentences with a preposition followed by your own idea.
1. Tiredness is usually caused _____ …
2. A sunny day always has a positive effect _____ …
3. Too much exercise can result _____ …
4. Visiting a foreign country can lead _____ …
5. As a result _____ learning English, I …

b 💬 Work in pairs. Compare your ideas. Ask your partner why they completed the sentences in that way.

c Which word in the box collocates best with the nouns?

| rigorous | tough | punishing | strict | arduous | tricky |

1. _____ training programme / schedule
2. _____ laws / parents
3. _____ plastic / teachers
4. _____ journey / task
5. _____ testing / training
6. _____ situation / question

d 💬 Discuss three examples from 2c that you have experience of.

3 WORDPOWER as

a Replace the underlined words with *as* expressions in the box.

as a whole   as far as restaurants are concerned
as for   as a matter of fact   as far as I'm concerned
as far as I know   as if   as follows

1. I'm glad you're happy. But speaking of Alan, it's impossible to please him.
2. All students in the class are improving their speaking.
3. I'm not English. To tell you the truth, I'm from Denmark.
4. My list of complaints are below: 1) There was no hot water …
5. It felt like we had always lived there.
6. In my opinion, the cost of food here is very high.
7. Thinking about restaurants, there are some excellent ones in our neighbourhood.
8. From what I've seen and from what people tell me, she's usually on time.

b Add a word to the gaps in 1–8 and then match to a–h.
1. ☐ The key reasons for our success are as _____
2. ☐ As far as I _____
3. ☐ I'm fit and well. As _____
4. ☐ As far as I _____
5. ☐ The team as _____
6. ☐ She's not boring. As _____
7. ☐ It looks as _____
8. ☐ As far as sport is _____

a … whole played very well.
b … they make the best coffee in town.
c … concerned, I go running twice a week.
d … matter of fact, she's a really interesting person.
e … my husband, he's got the flu.
f … football is more about the money than the sport.
g … 1. We trained very hard …
h … it's going to be a sunny day.

c Complete the sentences with your own ideas.
1. As far as I'm concerned …
2. As far as I know …
3. It looks as if …
4. Our class as a whole …
5. As far as English is concerned …

d 💬 Tell another student your sentences and ask questions.

REVIEW YOUR PROGRESS

How well did you do in this unit? Write 3, 2 or 1 for each objective.
3 = very well   2 = well   1 = not so well

I CAN …

discuss events that changed my life	☐
discuss and describe rules	☐
describe photos	☐
write an email to apply for work	☐

CAN DO OBJECTIVES

- Discuss possible future events
- Prepare for a job interview
- Discuss advantages and disadvantages
- Write an argument for and against an idea

UNIT 5
Chance

GETTING STARTED

a Look at the picture and answer the questions.
1 What kind of place do you think this is? Why do you think so?
2 Why is it an unusual place to jump?
3 What could the man be thinking?
4 Imagine you're on the beach below. What could you be thinking?

b Discuss the questions.
1 Why do you think some people like doing extreme and dangerous things?
2 Do you think they do these things in spite of the risk or because of the risk?

5A You could live to be a hundred

Learn to discuss possible future events

G Future probability
V Adjectives describing attitude

1 READING

a Read the quiz and answer the questions.

Are you an optimist or a pessimist?
Test yourself!

As you read each question, try to imagine yourself in each situation. Think of how you would react (be honest!) and then choose a) or b).

1 You bought a book, but you left it on the bus on the way home. Do you think you will get it back?
a) Yes, probably – I'll call the bus station.
b) Not very likely – someone probably took it.

2 You want to buy a shirt/dress that you've seen in a shop. You find they've just sold the last one. Do you think:
a) Oh well, I can probably find something similar.
b) Why am I always so unlucky?

3 You get an 'A' in an exam. Do you think:
a) Wow, I'm really good!
b) I was lucky with the questions.

4 You're crossing the road. A driver gets annoyed and shouts at you. Do you think:
a) He/She must be having a difficult day.
b) People are so rude!

5 You're trying to figure out a problem with your computer. Do you think:
a) There must be some simple solution to this.
b) I just don't understand computers. I give up.

6 You start a new fitness programme and you're really tired the next day. Do you think:
a) Wow, I worked hard yesterday – it'll be easier next time.
b) Wow, I must be really unfit!

7 A friend you haven't seen for months says 'You're looking good.' Do you think:
a) Yes, he's right. Nice of him to notice.
b) Does he really mean it or is he just being nice?

b Work in pairs. Compare your answers to the quiz. Did you have mostly a or mostly b answers?

c ▶ Communication 5A Now go to p.131.

d Read the article *Why we think we're going to have a long and happy life* quickly. Choose the correct words to complete the summary.
Most people are naturally *optimistic / pessimistic* and this is generally *an advantage / a disadvantage* for the human race, because it helps us to be *realistic about the future / more successful*.

WHY WE THINK WE'RE GOING TO HAVE A LONG AND HAPPY LIFE

Researchers have found that people all over the world share an important characteristic: optimism. Sue Reynolds explains what it's all about.

WE'RE ALL ABOVE AVERAGE!
Try asking a 20-year-old these questions:
- What kind of career will you have?
- How long do you think you'll live?

Most people think they'll be able to earn above-average salaries, but only some of the population can be in that top half. Most young men in Europe will say they expect to live well into their 80s, but the average life expectancy for European men is 75. Most people will give an answer that is unrealistic because nearly everyone believes they will be better than the average. Obviously, they can't all be right.

Most people are also optimistic about their own strengths and abilities. Ask people 'How well do you get on with other people?' or 'How intelligent are the people in your family?' and they'll usually say they're above average. Again, they can't all be right. We can't all be better than everyone else, but that's what we think.

LOOKING ON THE BRIGHT SIDE
There is a reason for this. Research has shown that, on the whole, we are optimistic by nature and have a positive view of ourselves. In fact, we are much more optimistic than realistic and frequently imagine things will turn out better than they actually do. Most people don't expect their marriages to end in divorce, they don't expect to lose their jobs or to be diagnosed with a life-threatening disease. Furthermore, when things do go wrong, they are often quick to find something positive in all the gloom. Many people who fail exams, for example, are quite sure they were just unlucky with the questions and they'll do better next time. Or people who have had a serious illness often say that it was really positive, because it made them appreciate life more. We really are very good at 'looking on the bright side'.

Even if our optimism is unrealistic and leads us to take risks, without it we might all still be living in caves …

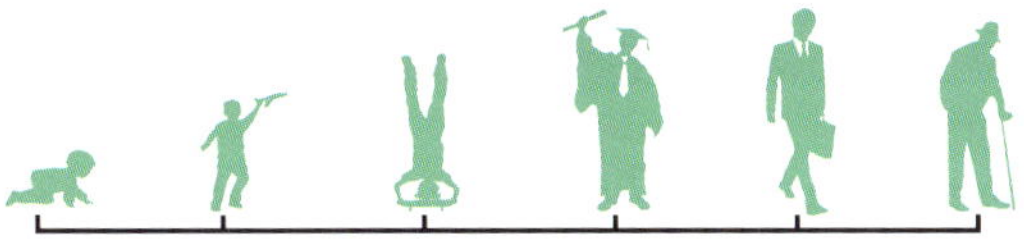

… we carry on polluting the planet, because we're sure that we'll find a way to clean it up some day …

THE OPTIMISM BIAS
This certainty that our future is bound to be better than our past and present is known as the 'Optimism Bias' and researchers have found that it is common to people all over the world and of all ages. Of course, the Optimism Bias can lead us to make some very bad decisions. Often, people don't take out travel insurance because they're sure everything will be all right, they don't worry about saving up for old age because the future looks fine, or they smoke cigarettes in spite of the health warnings on the packet because they believe 'it won't happen to me'. Or on a global scale, we carry on polluting the planet, because we're sure that we'll find a way to clean it up some day in the future.

OPTIMISM IS GOOD FOR YOU
But researchers believe that the Optimism Bias is actually good for us. People who expect the best are generally likely to be ambitious and adventurous, whereas people who expect the worst are likely to be more cautious, so optimism actually helps to make us successful. Optimists are also healthier because they feel less stress – they can relax because they think that everything is going to be just fine. Not only that, but the Optimism Bias may also have played an important part in our evolution as human beings. Because we hoped for the best, we were prepared to take risks such as hunting down dangerous animals and travelling across the sea to find new places to live and this is why we became so successful as a species. Even if our optimism is unrealistic and leads us to take risks, without it we might all still be living in caves, too afraid to go outside and explore the world in case we get eaten by wild animals.

Many people who fail exams are quite sure they were just unlucky with the questions …

UNIT 5

e Read the article again. Tick (✓) the five points made in the article.
  1 Pessimists usually have fewer friends than optimists.
  2 Humans are naturally positive about their future.
  3 Reality is often worse than we imagine it to be.
  4 People who live in warmer countries are usually more optimistic.
  5 We often act (or don't act) because we're confident everything will work out.
  6 If we imagine a better future, we will take more risks.
  7 Optimists spend a lot of time daydreaming.
  8 Optimism about the future makes us feel better in the present.

f Discuss the questions.
  • Look again at your results in the quiz. Do you think you have the 'Optimism Bias'?
  • Do you agree that it's better to be optimistic than realistic? Why / Why not?
  • How do you see yourself in 20 years' time?

2 VOCABULARY
Adjectives describing attitude

a Find adjectives in *Why we think we're going to have a long and happy life* which mean:
  1 expecting the future to be good
  2 seeing things as they are
  3 not seeing things as they are
  4 prepared to take risks
  5 not prepared to take risks
  6 wanting to be successful

b Which of these adjectives best describe you?

c ▶ Now go to Vocabulary Focus 5A on p.158

UNIT 5

3 LISTENING

a Read the statistics and guess which numbers complete the sentences.

> 8,000   6   18 million   1 million   4

WHAT ARE YOUR CHANCES?

Chance of living to be 100 (man):
1 in _____

Chance of living to be 100 (woman):
1 in _____

Chance of having a road accident:
1 in _____

Chance of winning the lottery:
1 in _____

Chance of being in a plane crash:
1 in _____

b ▶2.23 Listen and check your answers. Do you think any of the statistics would be different for your country?

c ▶2.23 According to the speaker, how can you increase your chances of doing these things? Listen again and check.

1 surviving a plane crash
2 getting to the airport safely
3 living to be 100

4 GRAMMAR Future probability

a ▶2.24 Complete the sentences with the words in the box. Then listen and check.

> likely   unlikely   could   may   probably (x2)
> certainly (x2)   chance

1 It's very _____ that your plane will crash.
2 Even if it does you'll _____ be fine, because 95% of people in plane crashes survive.
3 So, if you're worried about getting on that plane, don't be, because you'll almost _____ survive the journey.
4 You're more _____ to have an accident in the car going to the airport.
5 You have quite a good _____ of living to be 100.
6 Modern medicine _____ well make the chances higher still during your lifetime.
7 You _____ won't die in a plane crash and you _____ live to be 100.
8 But the bad news is, you almost _____ won't win the lottery.

b Find phrases in 4a which mean … ?

1 it's certain / nearly certain
2 it's probable
3 it's possible
4 it's not probable

c Which words in the box in 4a are used in these patterns?

1 will _____ (+ verb)
2 _____ won't (+ verb)
3 is/are _____ to (+ verb)
4 It's _____ that …
5 There's a _____ that …

d 💬 Change these predictions, using words from 4a.

1 I'll meet someone famous in my life – 70%.
2 I'll have children – 50–60%.
3 I'll fall in love at least once in my life – 90%.
4 I'll become a millionaire – 0.05%.
5 Someone will steal from me – 80%.
6 I'll live in the same place all my life – 20%.

e ▶ Now go to Grammar Focus 5A on p.142

5 SPEAKING

a Do you think these things will happen in your lifetime? Decide if each event is certain, probable, possible, unlikely to happen, or if it will certainly not happen. Then add a question of your own.

1 Will we find a cure for cancer?
2 Will people go to live on Mars?
3 Will the level of the oceans rise?
4 Will there be another world war?
5 Will people stop using cars?
6 Will Chinese become the world language?

b 💬 Ask other students their opinion.

c 💬 Tell the class what you found out.

- How many people agreed with your opinion?
- What were the most interesting comments?
- Are people in your class generally optimistic, pessimistic or realistic?

5B I'll be settling into my accommodation

Learn to prepare for a job interview

G Future perfect and future continuous
V The natural world

1 READING

a Look at the pictures of Antarctica and answer the questions.
1 What can you see in the pictures?
2 What do you know about Antarctica?
3 Would you like to go there? Why / Why not?

b Do the quiz. Then compare your answers with a partner.

THE UNKNOWN CONTINENT

1 HOW BIG IS ANTARCTICA?
(a) the size of Russia
(b) the size of the USA and Mexico
(c) the size of Australia

2 HOW MUCH OF ANTARCTICA IS COVERED BY ICE?
(a) 98%   (b) 86%   (c) 77%

3 WHICH OF THE FOLLOWING CAN'T YOU FIND IN ANTARCTICA?
(a) rivers   (c) trees
(b) deserts

4 WHICH OF THESE ANIMALS CAN YOU FIND THERE?
(a) polar bears
(b) seals
(c) wolves

5 WHO WAS THE FIRST PERSON TO REACH THE SOUTH POLE IN 1911?
(a) Richard Byrd (American)
(b) Robert Scott (British)
(c) Roald Amundsen (Norwegian)

c ▶ Communication 5B Now go to p.130.

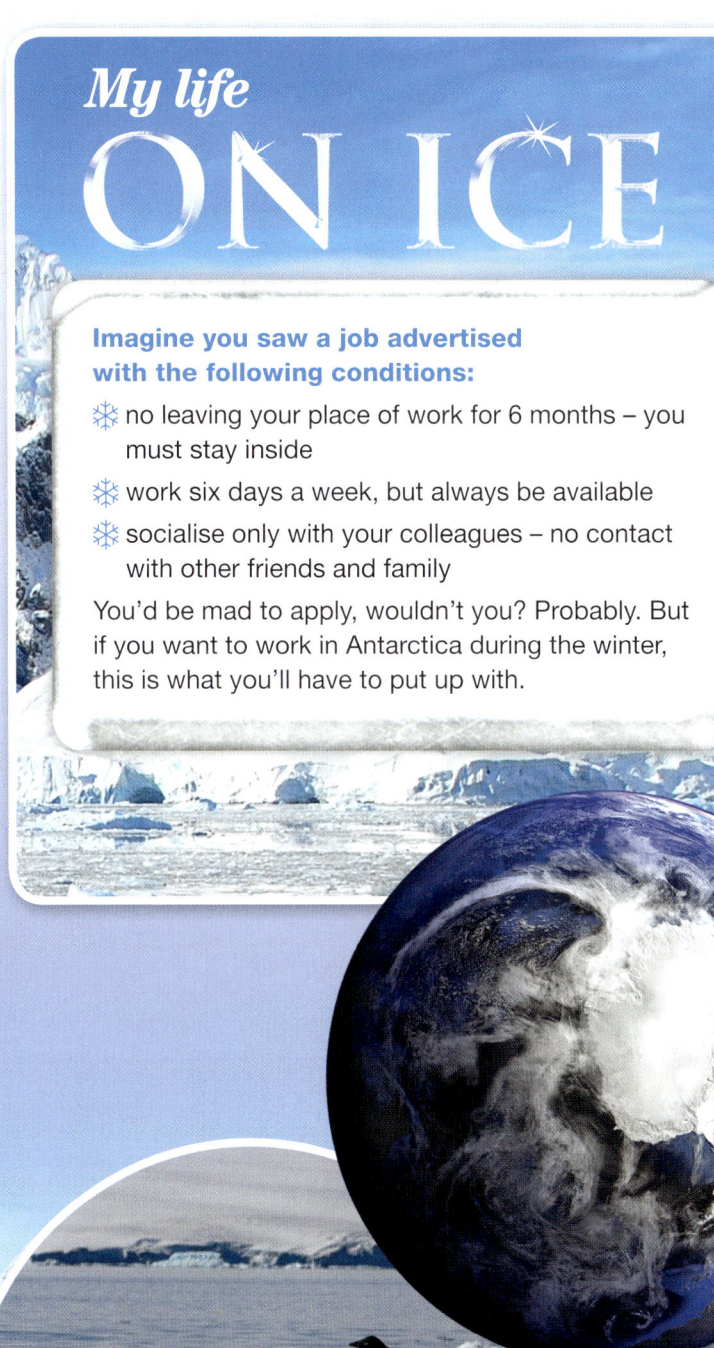

d Read the first part of an article about working in Antarctica. What would your reaction be to a job advert like this?

My life ON ICE

Imagine you saw a job advertised with the following conditions:

❄ no leaving your place of work for 6 months – you must stay inside
❄ work six days a week, but always be available
❄ socialise only with your colleagues – no contact with other friends and family

You'd be mad to apply, wouldn't you? Probably. But if you want to work in Antarctica during the winter, this is what you'll have to put up with.

UNIT 5

e 💬 Discuss the questions.
- Why do you think people want to work in Antarctica?
- What kinds of jobs can people do there?
- What kinds of leisure activities do they do during the winter months when it's difficult to go outside?

f Read *Cooking in Antarctica*. Does it include any of your ideas from 1e?

g Read the article again. Make notes about:
- Fleur's background
- her role at the base
- her free time
- her thoughts about Antarctica
- her colleagues at the base

h 💬 What do you think are … ?
- the advantages of a job like Fleur's
- possible frustrations in this kind of job

Would you ever consider doing a job like this?

2 VOCABULARY The natural world

a Cover the article *Cooking in Antarctica*. Match words from A with words from B to make collocations.

A	B
rough	environment
environmentally	energy
solar	atmosphere
fragile	footprint
ecological	weather
global	change
carbon	warming
climate	impact
the Earth's	friendly

b Check your answers in the article.

c Complete the sentences with the collocations in 2a.
1. We're going to change our energy supply to _____ _____ to reduce our _____ _____.
2. When the steam engine was invented, not many would have thought about the _____ _____ of burning so much coal.
3. Our boat trip was cancelled due to _____ _____.
4. The factories on the outskirts of town burn their waste and release toxic gases into _____ _____. I think they should be shut down.
5. If there is an oil spill from a ship, it will damage the _____ marine _____ in this bay.
6. Most scientists agree that irregular weather patterns are evidence of _____ _____ and _____ _____.
7. Travelling by train is slower but it's far more _____ _____ than going by plane.

Cooking in ANTARCTICA

When she saw an online advertisement for a Chef Manager at the British Antarctic Survey (BAS) base in Rothera, chef Fleur Wilson was certainly given food for thought. Fleur, in her mid-thirties, felt it was time for an adventure and a life experience that really was different.

Fleur is part of a group of key support staff at Rothera. The main focus of BAS is scientific research into the climate, the oceans and ecosystems of Antarctica. In order to carry out this research successfully, scientists need the help of people like Fleur to make their lives as comfortable as possible.

A key responsibility for Fleur is keeping everyone happy, and one of the best ways of doing this is by keeping them well fed. This doesn't mean preparing high-end restaurant food, but it does mean organising lots of social events to boost the mood. However, everyone has to play their part, and Fleur makes sure no one escapes doing the dishes.

One thing that all staff at BAS share is their love of the continent. 'I don't mind the rough weather,' Fleur says, 'and I've always found landscapes with ice and snow amazingly beautiful. Sure, I don't get to see much for six months of the year, but for the other six months there's plenty of light and the scenery is stunning.' But, quite apart from admiring the natural beauty of Antarctica, the staff all have a clear understanding of the fact that it's a fragile environment because, compared to the rest of the world, it is largely untouched. They're aware that the presence of human beings can have a significant ecological impact on the continent and, therefore, they treat it with care. BAS research stations use solar energy to heat air and hot water. 'We try to be as environmentally friendly as possible,' says Fleur; 'we don't want to leave a carbon footprint down here.'

As Fleur notes, 'Antarctica can tell us a lot about what's happening in the world. It can tell us a lot about global warming and climate change. In an extreme climate like this, you can really notice if things are changing.'

During the winter months, all Rothera staff try to keep themselves entertained either by making mid-winter gifts for each other or creating a murder mystery event. Fleur has also taught herself Spanish to intermediate level. However, during the summer months she does cross-country skiing and enjoys trips to do some penguin and whale watching.

Fleur realises that living and working in Antarctica isn't for everyone. 'If you're the kind of person that likes shopping, going out for dinner and clubbing, then forget it.' She's now in her fourth year here and still finds it a unique and rewarding experience.

'I was mad enough to apply for the job and I've been mad enough to stay. But it's a job that's given me so much – I've worked with some remarkable people and I'm living in a unique and fascinating part of the world.'

60

d Work on your own. Answer the questions and make notes.
- Are there any environments in your country that are considered fragile? What kind of environments are they?
- What different human inventions have a negative ecological impact?
- What kind of things could you do to reduce your carbon footprint?

e 💬 Discuss your answers.

3 LISTENING

a ▶2.27 Martha's going to Antarctica to do research on Adelie penguins. She talks to her friend Joe about her work. Listen and answer the questions.
1 How well does Joe understand Martha's research?
2 Are his questions serious or light-hearted?
3 What do we learn about the personality of the penguins?
4 Why is the research important?

b ▶2.27 Listen again. Number the actions in the correct order from 1 to 5.
☐ the eggs are laid
☐ tags are put on the penguins
☐ penguins get into pairs
☐ Martha arrives in Antarctica
☐ penguin chicks are born

4 GRAMMAR
Future perfect and future continuous

a Look at these future verb forms from the conversation in 3a and match them to the uses a–c below.
1 … this time next week **I'll be settling** into my accommodation.
2 … I think **I'll be doing** similar things every day.
3 … by the time I arrive **the penguins will already have got** into pairs.

a talk about an action that will be in progress at a specific time in the future
b talk about an action that will be completed before a specific time in the future
c talk about planned actions in the future

b ▶ Now go to Grammar Focus 5B on p.142

c Work on your own. Make notes about the questions.
- Where do you think you'll be living this time next year?
- What do you think you'll have achieved in five years' time?

d 💬 Tell each other your answers to 4c and ask follow-up questions.

5 SPEAKING

a Read the job advert. Would you like this job?

http://arctic_jobs_(UK)

Communications Officer in Antarctica

Responsibilities:
❋ interview researchers and collect information about their projects
❋ update our blog regularly
❋ assist all staff with IT

You need a friendly personality and excellent people skills.
This job is from October to March.

b Prepare a job interview role play for the job in 5a.
Student A: You want to apply for the job. Imagine you have the skills and experience that make you a suitable job applicant. Think of questions you can ask the interviewer.
Student B: You are the interviewer. Think of questions you can ask the applicant. Think of any useful information you can tell the applicant.

c 💬 Work in pairs. Do the role play.
Student A: Do you still want the job?
Student B: Do you think Student A is suitable for the job? Why / Why not?

5C Everyday English
We're not making enough money

Learn to discuss advantages and disadvantages
- **P** Tone groups
- **S** Responding to an idea

1 SPEAKING and LISTENING

a 💬 Discuss the questions below.
- What kind of cafés are there near where you live? e.g traditional, modern, part of a chain
- What kind of cafés do you like? Why?
- What do you usually do in a café?

b ▶ 2.30 Watch or listen to Part 1. Put four of these events in the correct order. One event doesn't appear in the scene. Which is it?
- ☐ Sam talks about money.
- ☐ Becky offers to help.
- ☐ Phil finishes his chapter.
- ☐ Phil asks about Tessa.
- ☐ Phil suggests staying open longer.

c ▶ 2.30 Answer the questions. Watch or listen again and check.
1. Why is Sam worried?
2. What are the problems with serving meals?
3. Why does Phil think serving meals is a good idea?
4. What does Phil want to know about Tessa?

2 LISTENING

a ▶ 2.31 Look at photo b of Sam and Emma. Which of these topics do you think they're talking about? Listen to Part 2 and check.

> money problems   staying open later   Sam's birthday
> hiring a cook   investing money in the café

b ▶ 2.31 Watch or listen again. Make notes about the ideas Sam and Emma discuss. What are the positive and negative points for each idea?

3 USEFUL LANGUAGE
Discussing advantages and disadvantages

a Sam and Emma discuss the advantages and disadvantages of making changes to the café. What do you think they say? Complete the sentences.
1. Of course, the _____ is we'd have to invest even more money.
2. Yes, but the _____ is, it might be a way to get more business.

b ▶ 2.32 Listen and check.

c Which of these words/phrases could you use in the sentences in 3a?

> problem   advantage   disadvantage
> best thing   drawback

d ▶ 2.33 Add prepositions from the box to the expressions. Then listen and check.

> of (x2)   with (x2)   about

one good thing _____
the advantage/disadvantage _____
the only drawback _____
another problem _____
the trouble _____

e Look at some people's ideas for the future. Use an expression from 3d in each second sentence.
1. 'I might sell my car and go everywhere by bike. I'd get fit.'
2. 'I'd love to live in London. It would be very expensive.'
3. 'I could work in China for a year. I don't speak the language.'

4 PRONUNCIATION Tone groups

a ▶2.34 Listen to these sentences. Answer the questions.

The good thing about it is it might be a good way to get more business.
The trouble is it means investing even more money.
1 Where do you hear a slight pause?
2 Which words are stressed in the **bold** phrase?
3 Does Sam's voice go up (↗) or down (↘) on the word *is*?

b ▶2.35 Listen to these sentences. Practise saying them, pausing after *is*.
1 The trouble is we don't have enough money.
2 The point is we still owe money to the bank.
3 The problem is we'd need to employ more staff.
4 The advantage is we'd attract more customers.

5 LISTENING

a ▶2.36 Watch or listen to Part 3. Who suggests doing these things (Sam or Emma) and what do they say about it?
1 have live music
2 get students to play music
3 have photo exhibitions
4 ask people to read poems and stories

b Which of these adjectives and phrases describe Emma? Which describe Sam?

full of ideas   cautious in making decisions
enthusiastic   worried about the future
careful with money   fair to other people

6 CONVERSATION SKILLS Responding to an idea

a Read what the speakers say. Complete the replies with the words in the box.

bad   possibility   lovely   worth

1 **A** I don't know, it's a big risk.
  B I think it's a _____ idea.
2 **B** Well, how about entertainment? We could have live music, get locals to play at the weekend.
  A That might be _____ a try.
3 **B** Or display paintings or photos.
  A That's not a _____ idea.
4 **B** Or readings. Have poetry readings.
  A Yeah, that's a _____.

b ▶2.37 Listen and check. Which of the replies is … ?
1 more enthusiastic   2 more cautious

c Look at these ways to respond to an idea. Order them from 1–6 (1 = very cautious, 6 = very enthusiastic).
☐ It's an idea, I suppose.
☐ Yes, that makes sense.
☐ That's a great idea.
☐ What a brilliant idea!
☐ 1 Mm, I don't know about that.
☐ Yes, good idea.

d You want to do something with the whole class at the end of the course. Write down three ideas.

We could go on a day trip

e 💬 Work in groups. Take turns to suggest your ideas. Respond to other students' ideas, using expressions in 6a and 6c. Which idea is the best?

7 SPEAKING

a ▶ **Communication 5C** Now go to p.129.

b Take a class vote. Whose café sounds the best?

Unit Progress Test

CHECK YOUR PROGRESS

You can now do the Unit Progress Test.

5D Skills for Writing
The weather is getting more extreme

Learn to write an argument for and against an idea

W Arguing for and against an idea

1 SPEAKING and LISTENING

a Discuss the questions.
1. What extreme weather events are shown in photos a–d?
2. What kinds of extreme weather might affect your country or region? What can people do to protect themselves against it?

b ▶2.38 Listen to the news reports and match them with photos a–d. What key words helped you decide?

c ▶2.38 What did the news reports say about these topics?
1. farmland – cattle – villages – rivers
2. around Boston – the Boston to New York highway – residents
3. the weather in March – emergency supplies – the rice harvest
4. winds – residents – food and shelter

Re-tell the reports. Listen again if necessary.

d Discuss the questions.
1. Have you ever heard a news report like those in 1b about your own country or a country you know? What happened?
2. Which of these statements do you agree with most and why?
   - 'The climate does seem to be changing, but it's probably just a natural process.'
   - 'The weather is getting more extreme all over the world. This is clearly a sign of man-made climate change.'
3. What action (if any) do you think governments and world leaders should take to manage climate change?

Are extreme weather events a sign of CLIMATE CHANGE?

Leon

[1] People have always complained about the weather, but the number of extreme weather events – such as droughts, hurricanes and heavy snow – seems to have increased in recent years. Naturally, people are worried about this. But are these events a sign that our climate is changing?

[2] Many people believe that extreme weather is part of a general pattern of climate change. Scientists predicted that global warming would lead to more unstable weather and this is exactly what seems to be happening. Furthermore, most scientists agree that these changes are happening faster than expected and that they are a direct result of human activity. Many scientists also warn that this is only the beginning and things will almost certainly get worse if we don't take action.

[3] However, not everyone agrees with this point of view. Some people point out that there have always been extreme weather events, but we are simply more aware of them now. They say it's not certain that climate change is a result of human activity, so we should try to find out the facts before we spend millions on fighting it.

[4] On balance, it seems that extreme weather is probably linked to climate change, but we can't be completely sure about this. My own view is that we can't take the risk of waiting until we are absolutely certain about climate change, as by then it will be too late to stop it. It's far cheaper to invest in cleaner forms of energy now than to fight climate change in the future, and rich countries should lead the way doing it.

UNIT 5

2 READING

a Leon wrote an essay discussing the topic of climate change. Read the essay and answer the questions.

1 Which of these sentences best summarises the essay?
   a He considers arguments for and against climate change and then draws a conclusion.
   b He sets out to prove that climate change is really happening.
2 What is his conclusion?
   a We don't know enough about it to act now.
   b We should act against climate change now or it will be too late.

b Read the essay again and make notes on the points Leon makes for and against extreme weather being a sign of climate change.

3 WRITING SKILLS Reporting opinions

a Match four of the descriptions below to paragraphs 1–4 in the essay.

- Introduction – stating the problem
- Introduction – giving Leon's point of view
- Arguments against the existence of climate change
- Arguments for the existence of climate change
- Conclusion – re-stating the problem
- Conclusion – summarising the main points and giving Leon's point of view

b Answer the questions.

1 Why does Leon ask a question in the first paragraph?
2 How does Leon make his arguments seem more objective (i.e. not just his own opinion)?

c Find linking expressions in the essay that mean:

1 considering the various arguments   3 also
2 I think   4 but

d Notice how Leon uses expressions like these to report people's opinions.

> Most scientists agree that …
> Many people believe that …

Find more expressions in the essay that:

1 report what scientists say or think (x2)
2 report what other people say or think (x4)
3 report how people feel (x1).

e Write sentences for and against these questions, using expressions from 3d. Compare your sentences with other students.

Should investment in cleaner forms of energy continue?
Is the climate changing faster now than ever before?
Is it already too late to stop climate change?

4 WRITING

a Work in pairs. Choose one of the essay topics below.

Should air fares be increased to discourage people from travelling by plane?
Does recycling household rubbish really make any difference to the planet?
Is building nuclear power stations the best way to provide 'clean' energy?

b 💬 Discuss the topic you chose and make notes on possible arguments for and against. Then decide on your conclusion.

c Work on your own. Plan your essay using the structure in 3a.

d 💬 Compare your notes with your partner and explain roughly what you plan to write.

e Write the essay in about 150–200 words, using expressions in 3b–3d.

f Swap essays with another student. Does the essay … ?

1 have a clear structure
2 set out the arguments in a clear way
3 use suitable expressions for reporting opinions

Do you agree with the conclusion?

UNIT 5
Review and extension

1 GRAMMAR

a Change these sentences using the words in brackets, so that the meaning stays the same.
1 Cities will probably become more dangerous over the next 50 years. (likely)
2 Scientists will probably find a way to delay the ageing process soon. (chance)
3 It's quite possible that the Democratic Party will win the election. (could well)
4 There are bears in this forest, but you probably won't see one. (unlikely)

b Complete the gaps with the verbs in brackets. Use either future continuous (*will be + -ing*) or future perfect (*will have* + past participle).

I'm in my 20s, but I sometimes imagine my life at 70. When I'm 70, I'll ¹_____ (retire), so I won't ²_____ (work) and I'll have plenty of free time. But I will ³_____ (have) a successful career and I will ⁴_____ (save) lots of money, so I'll be rich. I will ⁵_____ (get) married in my 30s and we will ⁶_____ (have) two or three children. By the time we're 70 we'll have a nice house by the sea, and our children will ⁷_____ (live) nearby.
Of course, my life could turn out quite differently, but it's always good to have positive dreams!

c 💬 Imagine yourself 30 years from now. What will you be doing? What will you have done?

2 VOCABULARY

a What adjective could describe these people? Use words from the box.

well-organised   critical   adventurous
reliable   sympathetic   realistic

1 Dana has started a rock group but she knows she probably won't ever become famous.
2 Ivana always keeps her desk tidy and she knows where to find everything.
3 Tom listens to people's problems and knows how to make them feel better.
4 Pierre gave up work for six months to travel through Central America on a motorbike.
5 Christine's very hard to please. If you get something wrong, she'll notice it and she'll tell you.
6 If you ask Hamid to do a job, he'll always do it well and on time.

b What is the opposite of these words?
1 reliable   3 responsible   5 well-organised
2 sensitive   4 thoughtful   6 realistic

c 💬 Work in pairs. Which words in 2b (or their opposites) are true of people you know? Tell your partner and give a few examples of things the people do or don't do.

3 WORDPOWER *side*

a Look at these examples and match the word *side* with the meanings in the box.

group or team   point of view   part of a person's character

1 She's friendly but she also has a rather unpleasant **side**.
2 He usually plays for Liverpool but today he's playing for the national **side**.
3 We need to look at both **sides** of the argument.

b Here are some common expressions with *side*. Use them instead of the underlined parts of the sentences.

on your side   look on the bright side
to one side   from side to side   on the side
side by side   see the funny side

1 They sat on the bench next to each other without talking.
2 We think he was wrong. We're all supporting you.
3 Well, let's see things positively – we're both still alive.
4 I didn't earn much as a taxi driver, but I made quite a bit of money doing other work.
5 I was very embarrassed at the time, but now I can laugh about what happened.
6 She took me away from the other people and said quietly, 'I'll phone you this evening.'
7 As the sea got rougher, the lamp in my cabin started swinging from left to right.

c Read these extracts from stories. Which sentences from 3b do you think go in the gaps?

① The first few days of the voyage were calm, but then the weather changed. _____
I lay in my bed watching it, feeling sick.

② She saw a man approaching. It was Tom. 'OK if I sit here?' he asked. She nodded. _____
Then he turned to her and said, 'Do you still have the letter?'

d Work in pairs. Choose another sentence from 3b. Imagine it's from a story, and write a sentence before and after it.

e 💬 Read out your sentences. Which were the most interesting?

🔄 REVIEW YOUR PROGRESS

How well did you do in this unit? Write 3, 2 or 1 for each objective.
3 = very well   2 = well   1 = not so well

I CAN ...

discuss possible future events	☐
prepare for a job interview	☐
discuss advantages and disadvantages	☐
write an argument for and against an idea	☐

Communication Plus

4C Student A

a Look at the photos of Cambridge, England. Imagine you visited this place. Prepare to present your photos to other students. Decide:
  - what the photos show
  - what you will say about them
  - which expressions in 2a on p. 50 you can use.

  Notes: The photos show a row of buildings in the city centre. Photos A and C also show bicycles (everyone uses them in Cambridge). Photo A: your favourite café.

b ▶ Now go back to p.50

4C Student B

a Prepare to give an opinion on one of the topics below. Plan what you will say about it.
  - a film or book
  - a café or restaurant
  - the town/city you're in now

b Listen to Student A's opinion about their topic. Express careful disagreement. Use language in 4c on p.51.

c Tell Student A your opinion about the topic you have chosen.

d ▶ Now go back to p.51

4A Student A

a Read about Sharon Tirabassi. Use these questions and keywords to help you focus on the main points.
  1 What was Sharon's life like before she won the lottery? (job, apartment)
  2 How much did she win?
  3 What did she do then? (trips, shopping, house, cars)
  4 Who did she give money to? (family, rent, friends)
  5 What's her life like now? (house, bike, work)
  6 Why is she happier now? (lifestyle, kids)

Sharon Tirabassi

Nine years after her huge lottery win, Sharon Tirabassi is catching the bus to her part-time job. Tirabassi, one of this city's biggest lottery winners, has gone from being very rich to living from pay day to pay day with just enough money.

Before her win, Tirabassi used to live in a small apartment with her three children and couldn't afford a car. But in April 2004, she won $10.5 million from a Lotto Super Seven ticket. She was unprepared for the change to her lifestyle. She would take friends on wild shopping trips and pay for everything herself. She and her husband bought a huge house in the wealthiest part of town and owned four cars. Besides the house and the cars, a lot of the cash went to family and friends – too much, as she admits now. She bought several houses in the city, renting them out at affordable rates to her family. A lot of friends suddenly appeared when news broke of her win – and a lot of them she never heard from again.

But all that has changed. Today, Tirabassi is living in a rented house on a quiet industrial street – not far from where she started. She no longer has the expensive cars. These days, she rides an electric bike when she's not taking the bus.

But she says she's happier now than she used to be and she lives life more fully than she did before. 'When I had lots of money, I used to spend all my time shopping, but now other things are more important to me.' Tirabassi's now concentrating on raising her children with good family values. 'I'm trying to get them to learn that they have to work for money,' she says.

b ▶ Now go back to p.45

5C

a You're opening a café in your town. You want it to be different from other cafés. Make notes about:
  - furniture
  - food and drinks
  - music and entertainment
  - special things you could offer.

b Explain your ideas and respond to other students' ideas. Use language from 6a and 6c on p. 63.

c ▶ Now go back to p.63

129

4A Student B

a Read about Ihsan Khan. Use these questions and keywords to help you focus on the main points.

1 What was Kahn's life like before his win? (job, money)
2 What was his dream? (diamonds, number)
3 How much did he win?
4 What did he do then? (taxi, car, houses, Pakistan, mayor)
5 Then what happened? (earthquake, medicine, school)
6 Why isn't he satisfied? (money, greedy)
7 What happened later? (parliament, votes)

Ihsan Khan

Before he won the lottery, Ihsan Khan used to work as a taxi driver and security guard in the USA – first in Chicago and then in Washington. He would usually send most of what he earned back to his family in Pakistan. 'It was the worst job in the world,' Khan says now. And then, one night, he had a dream in which he saw diamonds and also a number: 246 1725. He played those numbers on the lottery for 10 years. Then one day he struck lucky. Ihsan Khan won the jackpot and found he had $55 million. He immediately gave up his job as a taxi driver and bought an expensive car and two luxury houses.

But then he did something surprising. Instead of living in the USA and spending the money on luxuries, he went back to his hometown of Battagram and ran in the election to become mayor. He saw it as a way to pay back some of what he'd gained. Khan believes that it's wrong to save money for yourself and that we have a responsibility to help others who are not so well off as ourselves. Although he was competing against a candidate whose family had been in local politics for 35 years, Khan was elected mayor. Then, just after he was elected, the region was hit by a huge earthquake which killed 3,000 people in Battagram. Mayor Khan took the opportunity to use his lottery money to help people directly. He spent $300,000 on medicine and on repairs to homes, and he also gave money to build a new school.

But Khan isn't fully satisfied with what he's done and feels that simply giving people money is never enough. He used to think he could use his money to fix everything, but he no longer believes that. He has discovered that people are often greedy and they never seem satisfied with what they are given.

In 2008, he resigned as mayor and ran for election to the Pakistan parliament, but this time he wasn't a winner. The winning candidate received over 22,000 votes. Ihsan Khan only received 5,000. It seems his luck had run out.

b ▶ Now go back to p.45

4C Student A

a Prepare to give an opinion on one of the topics below. Plan what you will say about it.
- a recent sports event
- a famous person
- your classroom

b Tell Student B your opinion about the topic you have chosen.

c Listen to Student B's opinion about their topic. Express careful disagreement. Use language in 4c on p.51.

d ▶ Now go back to p.51

5B

a Read the text and check your answers to the quiz in 1b on p.59.

Antarctica is the fifth largest continent in the world and is completely surrounded by the Southern Ocean. It is approximately the size of the USA and Mexico. About 98% of Antarctica is covered by ice that averages 1.6 km in thickness. It is the coldest, driest and windiest continent in the world. Temperatures reach minimums of between –80 °C and –90 °C in the winter. The landscape is considered a kind of desert, because there is very little rainfall. There are mountains, glaciers and rivers, but no trees or bushes. There is a variety of animal life on the continent, but the two most well known are penguins and seals. The continent is positioned around the southern-most point of the planet, the South Pole. The first person to reach the South Pole was the Norwegian Roald Amundsen.

b ▶ Now go back to p.59

3C Student B

a You'd like to go somewhere fun with Student A after class. You're not very keen on shopping unless it means going to a shop or department store that sells video games. It might be fun to go to a new juice bar that opened last week. You could also go to the movies. Make careful suggestions and try to agree on what you can do after class.

b ▶ Now go back to p.39

4C Student B

a Look at the photos of Moscow, Russia. Imagine you visited this place. Prepare to present your photos to other students. Decide:
- what the photos show
- what you will say about them
- which expressions in 2a on p.50 you can use.

Notes: The photos show Moscow State University, built in 1953.

b ▶ Now go back to p.50

5A

a Are you an optimist or a pessimist? Read the descriptions below to find out.

Mostly a) answers:
You're an optimist. You expect things to turn out well for you, and when you encounter problems you believe you can overcome them. When things go well, you usually see it as the result of your own ability or hard work. When things go badly, you see it as just bad luck and expect it to be better next time.

Mostly b) answers:
You're a bit of a pessimist. You don't always expect things to turn out well for you, and when you encounter problems you believe you are generally unlucky. When things go well, you usually see it as the result of chance or what other people have done. When things go badly, you see it as a result of your own weaknesses.

b ▶ Now go back to p.56

3C Student A

a You need to buy a new jacket. You'd like Student B to come with you after class, because you need someone's advice on the best jacket to buy. You're not sure if Student B is keen on shopping. Perhaps suggest doing something nice as well, for example having a coffee together. Make careful suggestions and try to agree on what you can do after class.

b ▶ Now go back to p.39

2B

a Read the texts and check your answers to 1f on p.24.

Wolf
If you see a wolf before it sees you, walk away silently. If the wolf sees you, back away slowly and avoid eye contact. Wolves see eye contact as a challenge. If the wolf runs towards you, don't run away, as wolves are faster than you. Instead, turn to face the wolf. If the wolf attacks you, curl up in a ball, or defend yourself with a stick. A wolf's nose is very sensitive, so if you hit it on the nose it will probably run away. Wolves are also easy to distract with food, so if you have some food, throw it to the wolf, then move slowly away, still facing the wolf.

Shark
Don't lie on the surface of the water in areas where there are sharks, as this makes you look like a seal. Instead try to keep vertical in the water. Sharks normally won't attack unless they smell your blood or they think you're food. So if a shark comes towards you, keep still or swim slowly towards the shark. As long as you don't panic, it will probably swim away. If the shark bites you, hit it in the eye.

Bear
In bear country, always wear a bell or hit trees with a stick to make a noise. This will make any bears that are near go away. If a bear comes towards you, lie on the ground and 'play dead'. Provided you stay absolutely still, the bear will lose interest. If you are on a hill, run away downhill, going from side to side. Bears find it hard to run fast downhill because they are so heavy and they can't turn quickly.

b Imagine that you had to encounter one of these three animals. Which would you prefer? Why?

c ▶ Now go back to p.24

Grammar Focus

1A Review of tenses

▶ 1.2

Present simple
We use the **present simple**:
- for habits, repeated actions, facts and things which are generally true
  *I usually **do** my homework in the evening.*
  *She **writes** crime stories.*
- with state verbs for short-term states, verbs of preference and verbs of the senses.
  *I **want** to go home.*

Present perfect simple
We use the **present perfect simple**:
- for experiences in our life without saying when they happened
  *I**'ve seen** this film three times.*
- to focus on present states which started in the past and have continued up to the present
  *I**'ve lived** here since I was a child.*
- to focus on past completed actions which are recent (often with *just*) or which have a connection with the present.
  *I**'ve posted** your letter.*

Present continuous
We use the **present continuous**:
- for actions in progress now (at the moment of speaking) or around now
  *Sorry, I can't talk now – I**'m doing** my homework.*
  *She**'s writing** a book about her life.*
- for temporary situations.
  *I**'m studying** English in Cambridge this semester but normally I work in Milan.*

Past simple
We use the **past simple**:
- to talk about completed past actions and states. We often specify the time in the past with the past simple:
  *I **lost** my phone last week, but then I **found** it in my car.*

Past perfect simple
We use the **past perfect simple**:
- for actions and events that happened before a particular moment in time
- for reasons (after *because*).
  *I decided to walk home because I **had forgotten** my bus pass.*

Past continuous
We use the **past continuous**:
- to describe actions that were in progress at a particular moment in the past
- for actions or events in progress at the time of a shorter, past simple action.
  *He phoned while I **was doing** my homework.*

1B Question forms

▶ 1.13 **Positive and negative questions**
Most questions have an auxiliary verb (e.g. *be, do, have* or modal verbs) before the subject. The auxiliary verb can be positive or negative:
*How **do** you spell that?*   *Why **isn't** my computer working?*

Prepositions usually come at the end of questions.
*Where are you **from**?* NOT *~~From where are you?~~*

In very formal questions they can go at the beginning.

> 💡 **Tip** We can make short questions from *who / what / where* + preposition:
> **A:** *I'm going to a party tonight.*   **B: Who with**?
> **A:** *Can I borrow your phone?*   **B: What for**? *(Why?)*

We use negative questions to express surprise:
***Haven't** they **finished** yet?* (I'm surprised)

When we ask about the subject of a sentence the word order doesn't change and we don't use an auxiliary verb.
***Somebody** wrote this book.* → ***Who** wrote this book?*
NOT *~~Who did write this book?~~*

▶ 1.14 **Indirect questions**
We use indirect questions to sound polite. Start indirect questions with *Can you tell me… / Do you know…* We don't use an auxiliary verb and the word order doesn't change: Use *if* in indirect yes / no questions.
*Why **did she become** famous?* → ***Do you know why** she became famous?*
Do you like foreign films? → ***Can you tell me if** you like foreign films?*

We can also use indirect questions in sentences starting with:
I'm not sure… I know / don't know… I wonder… I can't remember… etc.
Is this answer correct? → ***I'm not sure** if this answer is correct.*
Where have they been? → *I **wonder** where they've been.*

> 💡 **Tip** We use **which** + **noun** when there is a limited number of options and **what** + **noun** when there are many possibilities:
> *We can have our meeting at 10.00, 12.15 or 14.30. **Which time** would you prefer?*
> *I'm free all day. **What time** do you want to meet?*

134

Grammar Focus

1A Review of tenses

a Correct the mistakes in the sentences. Think about spelling, tense and form.

1. I'm studing hard at the moment because I try to pass my final exams.   *I'm studying, I'm trying*
2. Internet shopping becomes more and more popular these days.   _____
3. We looking for new members of our group. Do you want to join?   _____
4. This food is tasting a bit strange. I think I prefer food from my own country.   _____
5. We think of buying a new car but they're costing a lot of money.   _____
6. I write to apply for the job of sales assistant. I send my C.V. with this letter.   _____

b Match the sentence halves.

1. ☐ When I arrived …   a … I was watching television.
2. ☐ While my brother was cooking …   b … twice in my life.
3. ☐ I was waiting for the plumber …   c … Sally had already left.
4. ☐ I have been to Istanbul …   d … when he phoned me to cancel.
5. ☐ Robert stayed in my flat …   e … in 2004 to work abroad for a year.
6. ☐ I moved to Singapore …   f … both this summer and last summer too.

c ▶ Now go back to p.9

1B Question forms

a Choose the best word or phrase to complete each question.

1. Where *we are / are we* going to eat?
2. What *you thought / did you think* of the film? Did you enjoy it?
3. We've got cheese sandwiches and egg sandwiches. *What / Which* flavour do you prefer?
4. Why *you didn't / didn't you* call me?
5. I hear you're a musician. *What / Which* kind of music do you play?
6. I got this watch for my birthday. *Who from? / What from?*
7. What *happened / was happened* to the window?

b Write questions about the underlined words and phrases.

1. *Who discovered pulsars?*   <u>Jocelyn Bell-Burnell</u> discovered pulsars.
2. _____   She's interested in <u>classical</u> music.
3. _____   <u>Over 2000</u> people watched the match.
4. _____   They haven't started yet <u>because they're waiting for you</u>.
5. _____   My <u>left</u> foot hurts.
6. _____   She heard the news from <u>Ralph</u>.

c Rewrite the sentences and questions using the prompts.

1. What do you want?
   I don't know …   *what you want.*
2. Why didn't they come back?
   I wonder …   _____
3. Where are they going?
   Where do you think …   _____
4. Have you ever met him?
   Can you tell me …   _____
5. Who wrote this story?
   Do you know …   _____
6. Does this pen work?
   I wonder …   _____
7. What's your sister's name?
   Can you tell me …   _____
8. When will it be ready?
   When do you think …   _____

d ▶ Now go back to p.13

2A Narrative tenses

We use narrative tenses to tell stories about what happened in the past. The most important narrative tenses are: past simple, past continuous, past perfect simple and past perfect continuous.

▶ 1.30

We use the past simple for completed past actions and states which happened at a specific time in the past:
We **spotted** them on the mountain so we **rescued** them and **took** them to hospital.

We use the past continuous for actions (not states) that were in progress at the time of the main events in the story:
When we spotted them, they **were standing** next to some stones. They **were waving** their arms but we couldn't hear what they **were shouting**.

We use the past perfect simple / continuous for events and activities that happened before the main events in the story and to give explanations or reasons. It often occurs after *because*.
We spotted them because they **had built** the word *help* out of stones.
We finally spotted them after we **had been searching** for over a week.

Past perfect simple or continuous?

We use the past perfect simple:
- To focus on the results of an earlier completed action:
  We **spotted** them (result) because they**'d built** a big sign (earlier action).
- To talk about 'time up to then' with a state verb (e.g. know, have, be):
  When we found them, they**'d been** on the mountain for a week.

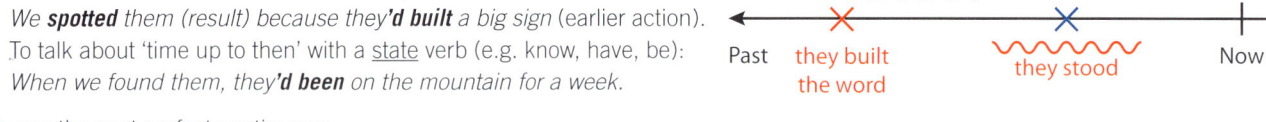

We use the past perfect continuous:
- before a result in the past to show the effect of an earlier activity:
  They **were tired** (result) because they**'d been building** a big sign (earlier activity).
- To emphasize the duration of time with an action verb (e.g. wait, search, drive):
  We found them after we**'d been searching** for a week.

2B Future time clauses and conditionals

We use future time clauses to talk about future possibilities, future plans or to give advice. We can normally use *will*, *be going to*, or the imperative in the main clause.

We normally use a present tense in the subordinate clause with words like *if*, *when*, *as soon as*, *unless*, *as long as*, *provided*, *in case*, etc. We can also use the same time clauses to talk about facts and things which are generally true. In these sentences we often use a present tense verb in the main clause.

▶ 1.31

When we **go** hiking next weekend, we'll try a new path.
If you **see** a bear, don't run.
It won't attack you **provided** you**'re standing** still.
Unless you know the way well, **bring** a map.
Always bring a snack **in case** you **get** hungry.
As soon as it **gets** too cold, we'll go home.

> 💡 **Tip**
>
> When *if* means *whether*, we normally need *will* or *going to* to refer to the future:
> I don't know **if / whether I'll** see any wild animals when I'm on holiday.
> NOT: … *if I see* …

▶ 1.32 *as soon as*
As soon as shows that something will happen immediately after another thing:
As soon as I get home, I'll email you.

> 💡 **Tip**
>
> We can use present perfect or present simple after words like *as soon as* or *when* to talk about completed processes in the future. There is little difference in meaning:
> We'll leave **when / as soon as I've finished** my work. (Or: … *I finish* …)

▶ 1.33 *if, unless, as long as, provided* and *in case*

Unless means *if not*. The verb after *unless* is usually positive:
You won't see any animals **unless** you **stay** quiet.
(You won't see any animals if you don't stay quiet)

As long as and *provided* are similar to *only if*:
We'll be safe **provided / as long as** we stay here.
(But only if we stay here).
You can go out tonight **as long as** you're back by 10. (But only if you're back by 10).

We use *in case* to talk about preparations for possible future situations:
Take your keys **in case** we're out when you get home.

Grammar Focus

2A Narrative tenses

a Complete the sentences with the past simple or past continuous form of the verbs in brackets.
1. While he __was walking__ (walk) in the forest, he __tripped__ (trip) and __cut__ (cut) his knee.
2. I _____ (not / notice) what the thief _____ (wear) because I _____ (hide) under the desk the whole time.
3. When I _____ (get) home, everyone _____ (watch) TV. Nobody _____ (even / say) 'hello'.
4. **A:** Where _____ (you / be) when you _____ (hear) the news?
   B: I _____ (be) on the bus – I _____ (travel) to work.
5. Fortunately, I _____ (not / hurt) myself when I _____ (fall) because I _____ (wear) a helmet.
6. **A:** What page number _____ (the teacher / just / say)?
   B: Sorry, I _____ (not / hear) anything. I _____ (not / listen).

b Choose the best verb form.
1. She was out of breath because *she'd run / she'd been running*.
2. It was sad to sell my old car – *I'd had / I'd been having* it since I was a student.
3. The party was great. *They'd planned / They'd been planning* it for months.
4. We were really pleased because *we'd finished / we'd been finishing* our project.
5. Everything was wet because it *had rained / had been raining*.
6. How long *had they known / had they been knowing* each other when they decided to get married?
7. They weren't very happy because *they'd waited / they'd been waiting* for six hours.
8. I didn't watch the film because *I'd already seen / I'd already been seeing* it four times.

c Choose the best verb forms.

It [1]*happened / had happened* on the last day of our holiday. We [2]*were getting / got* up and [3]*saw / were seeing* that, at last, the sun [4]*was shining / had shone*. We [5]*were leaving / left* the hotel and [6]*were starting / started* walking along the narrow cliff path. Then, after [7]*we'd been walking / we walked* for about two hours, the path [8]*was suddenly becoming / suddenly became* much narrower – it was no more than 10cm wide. There [9]*had been being / had been* a storm the previous night, and the sea [10]*had washed / was washing* part of the path away.

The cliff wasn't very high, so [11]*we'd decided / we decided* to keep going, along the narrow path. I [12]*went / was going* first, and [13]*had made / made* it safely to the other side. But then I [14]*was hearing / heard* a shout and a splash. Mike [15]*had fallen / fell* into the sea below. There were sharp rocks all around him, but luckily [16]*he'd landed / he'd been landing* safely in the water, and [17]*wasn't hurting / hadn't hurt* himself. So I [18]*climbed / was climbing* down the cliff to help him to safety.

Later, back at the hotel, he [19]*had been explaining / explained* what had gone wrong: [20]*he'd been trying / he tried* to take a photograph at the time of his fall.

d ▶ Now go back to p.22

2B Future time clauses and conditionals

a Tick (✓) the correct sentences. Correct the mistakes.
1. I'll send you a postcard when we'll be on holiday.
2. We'll come out as soon as we've eaten dinner.
3. My parents don't mind if I go out as long as I'll tell them where I'm going.
4. You won't pass the exam unless you don't study harder.
5. If it's still raining when you'll finish work, I'll pick you up.
6. I'm going to leave my laptop at home in case it'll get damaged.
7. I lend you my car provided you won't drive too fast.

☐ incorrect   when we're on holiday
✓ _____
☐ _____
☐ _____
☐ _____
☐ _____
☐ _____

b Join the sentences using the words in brackets.
1. Maybe I'll see Joseph. I'll tell him to call you. (if)
2. She'll finish university. She wants to be a teacher. (when)
3. They'll be late if they don't hurry up. (unless)
4. I'll check your work. Then I'll send it back to you immediately. (as soon as)
5. You can take photographs but you mustn't use a flash. (provided)
6. You should take some money because you might need to take a taxi. (in case)
7. He won't bite you but you must be careful. (as long as)
8. You'll only understand if you listen very carefully. (unless)

I'll __tell Joseph to call you if I see him.__
She _____.
They'll _____.
I'll _____.
You _____.
You _____.
As _____.
You _____.

c ▶ Now go back to p.24

3A Multi-word verbs

▶ 1.45 Multi-word verbs consist of a verb and one or two particles:
*We **came up with** some good ideas, and decided to **try** them **out**.*

Sometimes the meaning of the multi-word verb is clear from the meaning of the verb and the particle (e.g. *sit down*), but often you have to learn the meaning of each multi-word verb.

Transitive and Intransitive multi-word verbs
- Transitive multi-word verbs need an object. The object can come before the particle (e.g. *throw **sth** away*) or after the particle (e.g. *look after **sb***), depending on the type of multi-word verb.
- Intransitive multi-word verbs don't have an object, e.g. *go away* NOT *go somebody away*

Type 1 has no direct object (intransitive): verb + particle	wake up; go away; fall over; stay up; break up; sit down; take off; calm down
Type 2 has an object (transitive): verb + noun / pronoun + particle OR verb + particle + noun / pronoun	wake up; fall over; take off; calm down; try sth out; figure sth out; make sth up; throw sth away; pick sth up; let sb down
Type 3 has an object (transitive): verb + particle + noun / pronoun	look into sth; focus on sth; believe in sth; live for sth; be into sth; look after sb
Type 4 has two particles and always has an object: verb + particle 1 + particle 2 + noun / pronoun	come up with sth; look down on sb; look up to sb; run out of sth; fall out with sb; go on about sth; get away with sth

💡 **Tip** Many multi-word verbs are both transitive and intransitive (e.g. *wake up; fall over; take off; calm down*):
*When you **wake up** (intransitive), try not to **wake** the dog **up** (transitive) too!*
*After the plane **took off** (intransitive) I **took** my shoes **off** (transitive).* Use a dictionary to find out if a multi-word verb is transitive or intransitive.

Type 2 multi-word verbs
When the object is a long noun phrase, it normally comes after the particle:
*Please **throw away** those old shoes that are nearly falling apart!*
When the object is a pronoun (e.g. it, me, sb), it almost always comes before the particle:
*Those shoes are really old. Please **throw** them **away**!* NOT: *Please throw away them!*
When the object is a short noun phrase (e.g. up to three words), it can come before or after the particle:
*Please **throw** those old shoes **away** / Please **throw away** those old shoes.*

3B Present perfect simple and continuous

▶ 1.50 We use the **present perfect simple**:
- to talk about experiences without saying when they happened
  *He**'s tried** to run a marathon four times in his life.*
- for experiences during any present period of time
  *What **have** you **learnt** so far **this year**?*
- with superlatives
  *She**'s the nicest** person I**'ve ever met**.*
- for recent completed actions which have a result in the present.
  *Oh no! I**'ve broken** my key.*
- with *already, just* and *yet*
  *I**'ve already done** the shopping, I**'ve just put** the food in the oven, but I **haven't laid** the table **yet**.*
- to talk about *how long* with state verbs (with *for / since*)
  *I**'ve known** them **for** years but I **haven't seen** them **since** January.*
- with *how many, how much* and *how often* to talk about experiences
  *How many essays **have** you **written**?*

We use the **present perfect continuous**:
- when a recently completed action has a result now
  *She's tired because she**'s been training** hard.*
- to describe repeated activities which started recently
  *I**'ve been going** to the gym a lot recently.*
- to talk about unfinished activities using *how long* and *for / since*
  *We**'ve been walking since** the sun came up.*

138

Grammar Focus

3A Multi-word verbs

a Tick the correct sentences. Sometimes more than one sentence is correct.

1. a I don't **believe in** these new language learning techniques.
   b I don't **believe** these new language learning techniques **in**.
   c I don't **believe in** them.
   d I don't **believe** them **in**.

2. a Do you want **to try** the new guitar I got for my birthday **out**?
   b Do you want to **try out** the new guitar I got for my birthday?
   c Do you want to **try out** it?
   d Do you want to **try** it **out**?

3. a We've **fallen out** with our neighbours.
   b We've **fallen with** our neighbours **out**.
   c We've **fallen** them **out with**.
   d We've **fallen out with** them.

4. a Did you **make up** that story?
   b Did you **make** that story **up**?
   c Did you **make up** it?
   d Did you **make** it **up**?

b Rewrite these sentences replacing the verbs in bold with multi-word verbs. Use a verb from A and one or two particles from B.

A

| come | be | go | take | look | let | figure | run |

B

| up | into | out | off | about | of | with | into | out | down | on |

1. How did you **invent** a name for your shop? — *How did you come up with a name for your shop?*
2. Have you **investigated** the cause of the accident? ___
3. I've **liked** jazz since I was at university. ___
4. We've almost **used all** our food. ___
5. I hate to **disappoint** you. ___
6. I can't **understand** it. ___
7. I know I was wrong. Stop **repeating** it! ___
8. Do you think this product will **be successful**? ___

c ▶ Now go back to p.34

3B Present perfect simple and continuous

a What are the most likely combinations? Match the sentence halves.

1. a ☐ I'm really proud of myself because …
2. b ☐ I'm exhausted because …

   1 … I've been building a wall in my garden.
   2 … I've built a wall in my garden.

3. a ☐ They've been on holiday …
4. b ☐ They've been going on holiday …

   1 … three times this year.
   2 … to the same place for 20 years.

5. a ☐ I've written ….
6. b ☐ I've been writing …

   1 … six emails already.
   2 … emails all morning.

7. a ☐ She's been playing …
8. b ☐ She's played …

   1 … tennis twice this week.
   2 … a lot of tennis recently.

b Tick (✓) the correct sentences. Correct the mistakes.

1. How long have you worked here? ✓
2. Please don't come in – we haven't been finishing yet. *incorrect   haven't finished*
3. Have you ever been sailing? ___
4. We've been giving three presentations this week. ___
5. This room has been empty since our son left home. ___
6. I've been watching a lot of films lately … maybe too many. ___
7. I haven't been hearing that old song since I was a child. ___
8. Those people have been calling me five times today. ___

c Complete the sentences with the correct form of the verbs in brackets. Use the present perfect simple or the present perfect continuous.

1. I *'ve just spent* (just / spend) over £100 on football classes for you, and now you're saying you don't like football!
2. Can you hurry up? We _____ (wait) for ages!
3. How long _____ (you / study) to become a doctor?
4. She _____ (not / say) a word all day – I think she's angry with me.
5. _____ (you / clean) the car yet, or is it still dirty?
6. **A:** Your eyes are red. _____ ? (you / cry) **B:** No, I _____ (chop) onions!

d ▶ Now go back to p.37

139

4A *used to* and *would*

▶ 2.2 *used to* and *would*

We often use *used to* to describe past situations. In general, these situations continued for a long time and are not true now. They can be states (e.g. *like*, *live*, *have*) or habits (= repeated actions):
When I was a child, I **didn't use to** like vegetables, but now I love them.
When we were students, we **used to** go dancing every week.

We can also use *would* to describe past habits. Don't use *would* for past states:
When we were students, we**'d go** dancing every week.

We often use a mixture of *used to*, *would* and the past simple when talking about our past:
When I was young, we never **used to** go on holiday. Instead, we'd **spend** the whole summer playing in the fields near our house. We **loved** it.

💡 **Tip** Don't use *used to* or *would* for things that happened only once, or when we say how many times something happened in the past:
I read that book **once / a few times** when I was a teenager. NOT I used to read …

▶ 2.3 *no longer* and *any more*

We use *no longer* before a positive verb or after *be*:
We **no longer** go to the old forest. It's **no longer** there.
We use *any more* at the end of a sentence with a negative verb:
We **don't** go to the old forest **any more**. It's **not** there **any more**.

▶ 2.4 *be / get used to*

Don't confuse *used to* with *be / get used to*. They have very different meanings. After *be / get used to*, we use a gerund or a noun phrase:
I **used to** study for many years. (This was my habit in the past.)
I**'m getting used to** working in an office. (It's becoming normal for me now.)
I**'m used to** the job now. (It's normal for me. It's not difficult.)

💡 **Tip** We can also use *usually* + the present simple to talk about habits in the present tense:
I **usually get up** at 6.30 am.

4B Obligation and permission

▶ 2.11

	The speaker is making a rule	The speaker is describing somebody else's rule	
		Present	Past
Strong positive obligation	You **must** wear a helmet. I won't let you ride without it.	We **have to / need to** wear a helmet. It's the law.	We **had to / needed to** wear a helmet to go on the motorbike.
Strong negative obligation	You **must not / mustn't** remove your helmet. It's far too dangerous.	We**'re not allowed to / can't** remove our helmets. The instructor will get very cross with us.	We **weren't allowed to** remove our helmets.
Positive obligation	I think you **should** give / **ought to** give the money back.	I**'m supposed to** give the money back, but I don't want to.	I **was supposed to** give the money back, but I forgot.
No obligation	You **don't have to / don't need to / needn't** buy a ticket.		You **didn't have to / didn't need to** buy a ticket.
Permission	Yes, it's OK, you **can** go home.	I **can** / I**'m allowed to** go home now.	I **could / was allowed to** go home before 5pm.
No permission	No, I'm sorry. You **cannot / can't** go home yet.	I **can't** / I**'m not allowed to** go home yet.	I **couldn't / I wasn't allowed to** go home early.

- *must* and *mustn't* are very strong. In most situations, it's more natural to use *have to*, *need to*, *needn't*, *can't*, *be not allowed to*, etc. Questions with *must* are very rare.
- *should* is much more common than *ought to*. Questions and negatives with *ought to* are very rare.
- *Need to* is like *have to* whereas *need* (usually found in the negative) is a modal.

▶ 2.12 *make* and *let*; *be forced to* and *be allowed to*

make and *let* are special because they are followed by an object + infinitive without *to*:
They **made** me **pay** extra. NOT They made me to pay extra.
They **let** me **come** in for free. NOT They let me to come in for free.
We often use the verbs *force* and *allow* in passive constructions. Both are followed by *to* + -infinitive:
I **was forced to** pay extra. (Less common: I was made to pay extra)
I **was allowed to** come in for free. NOT I was let come in for free.

140

Grammar Focus

4A *used to* and *would*

a Tick (✓) the possible forms in each sentence.
1. She _____ good at maths when she was little.
   a used to be ✓   b would be ☐
2. Laura was my best friend – we _____ for hours every day.
   a used to talk ☐   b would talk ☐
3. I _____ five swimming competitions when I was at school.
   a won ☐   b would win ☐
4. Our teacher, Mr Williams, was very strict. He _____ allow us to speak at all during lessons.
   a didn't use to ☐   b wouldn't ☐
5. I'll never forget the time I _____ my leg. I couldn't walk for weeks!
   a used to break ☐   b broke ☐
6. We _____ a dog but he died about five years ago.
   a used to have ☐   b would have ☐

b Choose the correct form.
1. I *used to / would be* really good at football when I was young, but now I'm terrible at it.
2. I *didn't use to / didn't used to* like jazz, but now it's my favourite type of music.
3. I*'m used to / used to* living on my own. It was strange at first, but now it's fine.
4. I don't think I'll ever *get used to / get use to* writing on a tablet computer – it's much easier on a laptop.
5. Where did you *use to go / used to go* on holiday when you were a child?
6. How long did it take you to *get used to / used to* working from home?

c ▶ Now go back to p.45

4B Obligation and permission

a Rewrite the sentences using the words in brackets.
1. You can wear whatever you want. [need to]   _You don't need to wear_ a uniform.
2. I think you should write to them. [ought]   I think _____.
3. They made me give them my phone. [forced]   They _____.
4. They won't let you park there. [allowed]   You won't _____.
5. You don't have to stay here. [can]   _____ if you like.
6. They advised us to bring strong shoes. [supposed]   We _____.
7. I wasn't allowed to use a dictionary. [let]   They _____.
8. It was raining so we were forced to stop. [made]   The rain _____.

b Look at the rules for a computer training course. Andy explains the rules to his friend Dan. Complete the conversation with one word or a contraction (e.g. mustn't) in each space.

- All users must change their passwords after first logging in.
- You are not allowed to access the computer system without a new password.
- You can choose your own password.
- Your new password must be at least 20 characters long.
- Your password should be easy to remember but it shouldn't be easy to guess.
- You must not tell anyone else your password.

Dan: So how was the course?
Andy: It was OK, but the security was really tight. We _had / needed_ to change our password straight away.
Dan: Why?
Andy: They said we ²_____ access the system without a new one. We were ³_____ to choose our own passwords, but it ⁴_____ to contain at least 20 characters?
Dan: Wow … that's long!
Andy: Yes, but it was ⁵_____ to be something that's easy to remember.
Dan: OK, so the name of your football team then?
Andy: No, it was ⁶_____ to be something that's not easy to guess.
Dan: So what was it?
Andy: I ⁷_____ tell you! We're not ⁸_____ to tell anyone else!

c ▶ Now go back to p.49

141

5A Future probability

We use a wide range of modals verbs, adverbs, adjectives, etc. to describe what we think is the probability of future events:

Degree of probability	Modal verbs	Other expressions	Adjectives
100% high	We **will** go. We **will certainly** go. We **will probably** go	I'm **sure** we'll go.	It's **certain** that we'll go.
	We **could well** go. We **may well** go. We **might well** go.		It's (very) **likely** that we'll go.
50% medium	We **could** go. We **may** go. We **might** go.	There's a (good) **chance** that we'll go.	It's **possible** that we'll go.
	We **probably won't** go.	I **don't suppose** we'll go. I **doubt if** we'll go. I **shouldn't think** we'll go.	It's (very) **unlikely** that we'll go.
0% low	We **won't** go. We **certainly won't** go.	There's **no chance** that we'll go. I **can't imagine** that we'll go.	

▶ 2.25 Positive and negative forms
We can make negative statements of probability with *might not* or *may not*. Don't use *couldn't* in this way – it refers to the past ability, not future probability:
We **could** go out on Friday. (= it's possible that we'll go out next Friday).
We **couldn't** go out on Friday. (= we weren't able to go out last Friday).

Adverbs like *certainly* and *probably* increase or decrease the level of certainty and come after *will*, but they come before *won't*:
It**'ll probably** be a nice day today but it **probably won't** be nice tomorrow.

▶ 2.26 Adjective + *to* + infinitive
With the adjectives *sure / likely / unlikely / certain / bound* we can use the pattern: *be* + adjective + *to* + infinitive:

They**'re sure to be** late. (= I'm sure that they'll be late.)
He**'s certain / likely / unlikely to see** you.
There**'s bound to be** someone who knows the answer.
(= I'm sure someone knows the answer)

5B Future perfect and future continuous

▶ 2.28 Future perfect

Positive	Negative	Question	Short answer
We'll have left.	She won't have left.	Will they have left?	Yes, they will / No, they won't.

We use future perfect to describe what we expect to happen before a specific time in the future:
I don't know exactly when somebody will buy my car. I hope **I'll have sold** it by the end of the month.

> **Tip** We often use future perfect with *by*.
> We'll have finished **by Friday / by the time** they get here.

▶ 2.29 Future continuous

Positive	Negative	Question	Short answer
He'll be driving.	We won't be driving.	Will you be driving?	Yes, I will / No, I won't.

We use future continuous for activities that will be in progress around a particular time in the future:
Don't phone me at 5pm. I'll still **be driving** home from work at that time.

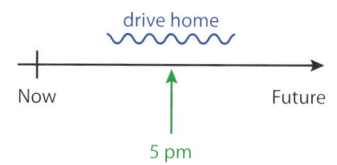

We can also use future continuous for things that are already planned:
It'll be tough in my new job – **I'll be getting** up at 4am every day.

Grammar Focus

5A Future probability

a Complete the sentences with one word from the box. Use each word once.

can't chance if likely might no probably shouldn't suppose sure

1. I'll _probably_ get up at about 8 tomorrow.
2. I don't _____ I'll ever see them again.
3. It's very _____ that you'll get a better job soon.
4. I _____ imagine that they'll move to another country.
5. There's _____ chance that we'll win, but we can try.
6. That _____ well be the best idea.
7. I'm _____ you'll have a brilliant time.
8. I _____ think too many people will be interested.
9. There's a good _____ that I'll be back before 10.
10. I doubt _____ they'll be able to fix my printer.

b Rewrite the sentences using the words in brackets. Keep the meaning the same as the original.

1. It's certain that he'll pay you. (to)
   He's _____ _certain to pay you._
2. It's very unlikely that we'll leave. (probably)
   We _____.
3. He'll certainly win a medal. (bound)
   He's _____.
4. These new phones are unlikely to sell well. (unlikely)
   It's _____.
5. It's possible that she won't notice. (might)
   She _____.
6. I'm sure there'll be another chance. (to be)
   There's _____.

c ▶ Now go back to p.58

5B Future perfect and future continuous

a Tick (✓) the sentences which are correct. Correct the mistakes.

1. I'd prefer to visit you in August because I'll be finishing my exams then. □ _incorrect_   _I'll have finished_
2. I don't want to be late – they'll have eaten all the food before we get there! ✓ _correct_
3. I can't take you to the airport at 10 because I'll have attended a very important meeting at that time. □ _____
4. The presentation is scheduled for the 15th, so I'm sure I'll be writing it then. □ _____
5. Thursday is the best day to call me at home because I'll have worked from home then. □ _____
6. I can pass the message on to Arthur – I'll be seeing him tomorrow at college. □ _____
7. A: How will I recognize you at the airport? B: I'll have carried a sign with your name on it. □ _____
8. I can't access the internet right now. Can you try again in 10 minutes – hopefully it'll be working again then. □ _____

b Look at Christina's calendar for tomorrow. Complete her conversation with Zofia with the future continuous or future perfect form of the verb in brackets.

Zofia: So, what time can I come and visit you tomorrow? What about 8.30?
Christina: No, sorry, ¹_I'll still be taking_ (I / still / take) the kids to school at that time.
Zofia: OK, so maybe when you're back home. ²_____ (you / get) back by 9.30?
Christina: Yes, probably. But ³_____ (I / still / deal) with my emails then. I've got some urgent emails that I need to reply to. But you could come at about 11. I'm sure ⁴_____ (I / finish) before. Does that suit you?
Zofia: Er … not really. Could we make it a bit later? What about 14.00?
Christina: Yes, that's fine, but it'll only give us an hour. ⁵_____ (I / leave) about 15.00 to pick the kids up from school.
Zofia: OK, yes, an hour should be perfect. Oh, one thing. Can you lend me that DVD you were telling me about?
Christina: Well, Hannah's got it at the moment. She wants to watch it tonight. But ⁶_____ (I / see) her tomorrow, so I can ask her to bring it. ⁷_____ (she / watch) it by then.

Monday

8.00 – 9.00
Take children to school

9.00 – 10.45(?)
Deal with emails

12.30 – 14.00
Meet Hannah

15.00 – 16.00
Pick up children from school

c ▶ Now go back to p.61

143

Vocabulary Focus

1A Character adjectives

a Read the descriptions of people's characters. Which is personal and which is more formal?

Fred currently works as a researcher here at Bio-Tech. He's been a very **loyal** member of our staff, and has worked here for over ten years now. He's **passionate** about alternative energies and this can be seen in the energy and enthusiasm he puts into his work. He's also **self-confident**, so he is never afraid to work independently or to work on difficult tasks. Finally, he's always **optimistic**, even when he comes across problems in his work.

We've got this new colleague at work, Sheila. She's only been here for two weeks and already I don't like her very much. She's one of those **ambitious** people who's got lots of plans, but she's so **arrogant** about it all. She thinks she's better than everyone else. But if you try and suggest a different idea, she gets really upset. So she's a strange mix of being very sure of herself, but incredibly **sensitive** at the same time. She told me that she wants to be our team leader. If she thinks that's going to happen overnight, she's really **naive**!

b Match the bold character adjectives in **a** with the definitions.

1 when you don't have much experience of the world and believe things too easily
2 when you easily get upset by what people say about you
3 when you believe or behave as if you know more or are more important than other people
4 when you feel sure about yourself and your abilities
5 when you like something and have strong feelings about it
6 when you have a strong wish to be successful, powerful or rich
7 when you always support something or someone, even when other people don't
8 when you always think good things will happen

c ▶1.7 Complete the sentences with the adjectives from the texts in **a**. Listen and check.

1 He's very _____. If I give him any negative feedback, he gets angry and shouts at me.
2 I'm sure he won't be nervous when he gives the speech. He always seems very _____.
3 I feel quite _____ that this project will be successful – everything is going according to plan.
4 They both think they're fantastic and everyone else is stupid. I've never met a couple who are so _____.
5 She's helped and supported me since we were at school. She's a very _____ friend – I know I can always rely on her.
6 Phil is really _____ about being a doctor. He loves the job and looks forward to going to work every day.
7 She works really hard because she's _____ and wants to do well in her career.
8 Martin is a little _____ – he honestly thought his boss would listen to his suggestions but of course in the end he didn't. He really is very young.

d 💬 Think of three family members or friends. Make notes on their character. Tell your partner.

My father's very passionate, particularly about his work.

I really like my aunt. She's a very successful lawyer. Some people think she's arrogant, but I don't.

PRONUNCIATION Word stress

a ▶1.8 Listen to these adjectives and underline the stressed syllable. Which syllable is stressed: the first, second, third or fourth?

optimistic   unsympathetic   arrogant   ambitious

b ▶1.9 Write these words in the table. Then listen and check your answers. Practise saying the words.

passionate   self-confident   sensitive   determined
determination   pessimistic   environment
environmental   influential   television

1st syllable stressed	2nd syllable stressed
3rd syllable stressed	4th syllable stressed

c 💬 Test each other. Student A: Choose a word from **b** and say a sentence.
Student B: Did Student A say the adjective correctly?

I'm determined to become a millionaire.

d ▶ Now go back to p.10

154

Vocabulary Focus

2A Expressions with *get*

a Read what Emma and Martin say. Who did they have a problem with?

> **Emma:**
> Last year I decided to join the social club at work. I always thought the social club was a bit boring and I wanted to improve it. I talked to some other people in the club and we tried to work out a way to **get rid of** the man running the club – the secretary – because we really thought he was the problem. Everyone liked this idea and we all **got a bit carried away** and decided a direct approach would be the best one. At the next meeting, we were about to say something when all of a sudden he said, 'Look, I'll **get straight to the point**. I think the social club's getting a bit boring and we need some fresh ideas.' We couldn't believe his sudden change. Now the club is much more interesting and lots of new people have **got involved**.

> **Martin:**
> My son's really **getting on my nerves** at the moment. He won't study at all. I can't **get across** to him the importance of doing well at school. He just won't listen and it's **getting me down**. The problem is he **got through** his exams very easily last year without studying. He thinks he can do the same thing this year, but I'm not so sure.

b Match the *get* expressions in bold in a with definitions 1–8.
1. to say something important immediately and in a direct way
2. to make someone understand something
3. to take part in an activity or organisation
4. to be successful in an examination or competition
5. when something annoys you
6. to become excited about something so that you are no longer careful
7. when something makes you feel sad or depressed
8. to send or throw someone or something away

c ▶1.26 **Pronunciation** Notice the linking between **get** and the word after in this example.

Lots of new people have got‿involved

Listen to these examples. In which sentences is there linking between *get* and the word after? What does that tell you about linking?
1. We tried to work out a way to get rid of the man running the club.
2. We all got a bit carried away.
3. I'll get straight to the point.
4. I can't get across to him the importance of doing well.

d Think of examples of these things.
1. a time that you got rid of something you didn't want
2. something that gets on your nerves
3. a time when you got through an exam, test or interview
4. a situation where you got a bit carried away
5. a club or organisation you got involved in

e Tell each other about your examples in d.

PRONUNCIATION Sounds and spelling: *g*

a ▶1.27 Listen to the words. In which words does *g* have … ?
1. a hard sound /g/
2. a soft sound /dʒ/

get   negative   manage

b ▶1.28 Decide which sound the *g* has in these words – /g/ or /dʒ/. Then listen and practise saying them.

guard   gymnastics   guide   generous
biology   together   religion   agree
dangerous   forget   bridge   gardener

c Look at your answers to b.
1. If *g* is followed by a consonant or *a*, *o* or *u* is it hard or soft?
2. If *g* is followed by *e*, *I* or *y*, is it hard or soft? Are there exceptions to this rule?

d ▶ Now turn to p.21

155

3B Words connected with sport

Jack Taylor will once again **represent** Australia at next year's Olympics. He already holds the **world record** for the 400m after his brilliant performance in 2011. During that race, he **led** from the start.

Referee Eno Koskinen gave Rodriguez a red card and **awarded** a penalty kick to Chelsea. But the **spectators** weren't at all happy with the decision and **cheered** Rodriguez as he left the **pitch**.

a Find words in the sports reports which mean:
1 play for your country or city
2 the people watching a match
3 be ahead during a game or competition
4 give (a prize or a point) for something you have done
5 shout to show you think someone is good
6 the best or fastest that has ever been achieved
7 the person who makes decisions during a sports game
8 the area where a football match is played

b Underline the correct words.
1 Even though she holds the *world record / spectator* in the 1500m, Kirabo Sanaa probably won't *represent / award* her country at next year's Olympic Games.
2 The spectators *cheered / represented* as the players walked onto the *pitch / referee*.
3 Sasha Spyridon *cheered / led* the race from the beginning and was *awarded / cheered* a gold medal.

c Write two short sports reports, using two of the sentence starters. Use the words in bold in the texts and your own ideas.
1 Ten minutes into the match …
2 18-year-old Martina Bereskova from Belarus …
3 Kenyan runner Pamela Abasi …

d 💬 Read out your reports. Who has the most interesting sports report?

PRONUNCIATION Word stress

a Add the words in the box to the table.

training competition victor competitor performance championship trainer athletic competitive athletics victorious performer professional

Verb	Noun (event or activity)	Noun (person)	Adjective
compete	*competition*		
		athlete	
	victory		
		champion	
train			
perform			
	profession		professional

b ▶1.46 Which syllable is stressed in each word in the table? Does the stress stay the same in all the word forms or does it change? Listen and check.

c ▶1.47 How does the vowel sound in **bold** change in each pair of words? Listen and check.

athl**e**te   athl**e**tics
vict**o**ry   vict**o**rious
comp**e**te   comp**e**titor

d 💬 Work in pairs. Cover the table and test each other.

Student A: say a sentence with one of the words.
Student B: make a follow-up sentence with a similar meaning, using a different word.

> He entered the championship.

> He wanted to be the champion.

e ▶ Now go back to p.36

Vocabulary Focus

4B Talking about difficulty

a Underline a word or phrase in each sentence that means (to be) difficult.
1 Working as a waiter in a busy restaurant is one of the most demanding jobs I've ever had.
2 I find it quite awkward when I have to speak to my staff about mistakes they've made.
3 Teaching a class on my own for the first time was a very testing experience.
4 Doing the outdoor survival training course really challenged me.
5 I have to talk to my teacher because I'm not happy with her lessons; it's a very delicate subject and I'm not sure what to say exactly.
6 Unfortunately, it's often not very straightforward for students here to find part-time work.
7 When I lived in Budapest, it was a struggle to learn Hungarian well.
8 I think I understand how computers work, but learning a programming language really stretched me.

b Which two words in **a** do we use to describe situations that are embarrassing or need to be dealt with very carefully?

c Complete the sentences with words from **a**. There may be more than one answer.
1 My final exams at university were really _____ / _____ – I needed a long holiday after I finished!
2 I can't come to my best friend's wedding because I'm going on holiday. It's a really _____ / _____ situation and I'm not sure how to tell her.
3 I'm really busy at work at the moment and I'm finding it a _____ to get my work done by the end of the day.
4 I thought connecting my new printer to my computer would be easy but actually it's not _____ at all.
5 I'm not very confident, so giving a presentation at university last week in front of 50 people really _____ / _____ me.

d Think of an experience you've had for three of the things below:
1 an outdoor experience that stretched you
2 the most demanding thing about learning a language
3 a book you once read that wasn't straightforward
4 an awkward meeting you once had
5 a sport that it was a struggle for you to learn
6 a delicate question that you had to ask someone
7 something you studied that really challenged you
8 a testing experience you had in a new place or country

e Now tell each other about the things you chose in **d**.

PRONUNCIATION Sounds and spelling: u

a ▶2.8 Listen to the words.

include   struggle   cushion   busy

b Match the vowel sounds in the words in **a** with the sounds in words 1–4.
1 cup
2 put
3 true
4 thin

c ▶2.9 What sound does u have in these words? Listen to check and add them to the table.

subject	focus	punish
pullover	amusing	assume
unfortunately	super	pudding
business	supper	helpful

sound 1 /ʌ/	sound 2 /ʊ/	sound 3 /uː/ or /juː/	sound 4 /ɪ/

d Write a sentence with two of the words in **a** or **b**. Read out your sentence to other students and check if you pronounced u correctly.

e ▶ Now go back to p.49

5A Adjectives describing attitude

a Read about Tamara's family and add adjectives in the gaps.

> thoughtful   critical   disorganised   unreliable
> well-organised   irresponsible   sympathetic   competitive

My brother Nick is very [1]_____ – his desk is a mess and he can never find anything. But my sister Vera is a very [2]_____ person. She plans her day carefully and she always knows exactly where everything is. She's also so [3]_____. She wants to be the best – it's all she thinks about. I would say my grandmother is a very [4]_____ person – you can go to her if you're in trouble and she'll always listen and make you feel better. My cousin, Maude, is very [5]_____. She's always thinking about how she can help other people. She remembers everyone's birthday and always sends presents. I like my other cousin, Becky, but she can be quite [6]_____. She never tells anyone where she's going when she goes out, and she sometimes leaves the front door open or doesn't lock her car. She's also terribly [7]_____. If you arrange to meet her somewhere she'll probably be late or she won't even show up. And what about me? Everyone in the family complains that I'm always commenting on what people are like. Some of them say I'm too [8]_____ and I only see the bad things in them. I can't imagine why they should think that.

b Complete the table with the opposite of the adjectives in **a**.

thoughtful	
well-organised	disorganised
	unreliable
	irresponsible
sympathetic	
competitive	
critical	

c Make a list of the prefixes and suffixes we can add to adjectives to make them negative.

d ▶2.20 Look at the sentences. Decide if the word in bold is correct or not. Then listen and check.

1 He often arrives late to meetings and doesn't bring everything he needs.
   He's very **disorganised**.
2 She always makes sensible decisions and she never does anything silly.
   She's very **irresponsible**.
3 She often expresses negative opinions about things and other people. She's very **critical**.
4 If he says he's going to do something, he always does it.
   He's very **reliable**.
5 He doesn't think about how the things he says might affect other people.
   He's totally **thoughtful**.
6 When you tell her your problems, she listens and tries to understand how
   you feel. She's **unsympathetic**.
7 He always wants to do better than everyone else. He's quite **competitive**.

e Look through the adjectives and their opposites and note down your own personality 'profile'.

f 💬 Tell your partner and mention a few examples of things you do.

> I think I'm fairly thoughtful and caring. For example, I always phone my grandmother once a week to ask how she is …

PRONUNCIATION Sounds and spelling: *th*

a ▶2.21 Listen to *th* in these words. What two different sounds do you hear?

> thoughtful   clothes
> weather   seventh
> sympathetic

b ▶2.22 Which sound does *th* have in these words? Listen to check, then add them to the table.

> leather   north
> thumb   northern
> month   Netherlands
> together   healthy
> something   enthusiastic
> therefore   worth

/θ/ (think)	/ð/ (the)

c ▶ Now turn to p.58

Audioscripts

Unit 1

1.4

CHLOE What's that book you're reading?
AMELIA It's about astronomy – black holes, planets, the big bang …
C Hmm, not exactly a light read, but I suppose you like that sort of thing. Me, I like to relax when I read.
A It's just I read this article online the other day.
C Uh-huh?
A It was about this physicist. She discovered these things called pulsars which are like … well, they're an incredible kind of star.
C Uh-huh … She?
A Yeah, yeah, her name's Jocelyn Bell-Burnell. She's a respected physicist. Well, that's the thing, that's what got me interested. There aren't many women working in that area.
C But hang on, she discovered these stars?
A Yeah, she was a postgraduate student at the time, but the guy who was her supervisor got all the credit.
C You're kidding?
A No, he won the Nobel Prize.
C So who did you say this woman was?
A Jocelyn Bell-Burnell.
C But I've never even heard of her.
A Well, no. That's the point. On this website it talks about … well, it's got a whole lot of information on people like her … you know, people who work behind the scenes and don't get the credit or don't become famous. It was really interesting.
C Yeah, I bet there are a lot of people like that.
A I mean, she really is an inspiring woman. Even when she was at high school, they weren't going to let her join the science class …
C When was this?
A Back in the fifties.
C Really? Even in the fifties?
A Yeah. And then at the end of the year, she came top of her class! And when she was doing her PhD and made her amazing discovery, she had a young child and was having to manage a whole lot of things in her private life, too. I mean, she was really determined, but in a quiet way. And then, when the newspapers wanted to interview her, they didn't want to know about her research, they just asked a lot of stupid questions about her height, her clothes, that sort of thing.
C That's terrible, isn't it? So is that a biography of her that you're reading?
A Well, no, it's just a book about astrophysics.
C Astrophysics? Just? So you're going to become … what? A rocket scientist or something?
A Well, no … I don't know. The thing is … after I read the article, I found an interview with Jocelyn Bell-Burnell online. And she was talking about how even today there still aren't many women who go into science and become scientists.
C So now you want to go back to university and do a physics degree?
A Maybe. But, you know, why not? I've always been good at science and I used to really enjoy physics.
C But are you really prepared to study and put in all that effort?
A Yeah, I think I am.
C Well, you've always been motivated, that's for sure. And stubborn …
A But I'm still thinking about it … doing some reading, that kind of thing.
C Well, actually … good on you. Why not make a change – take a risk? I admire that.
A Yeah. Actually that's what she says in the interview: 'Be prepared to take a risk – you'll probably surprise yourself.' And she said something else very simple about women wanting to be scientists: 'Go for it!' And I thought, yeah, why shouldn't I?

1.10

INTERVIEWER So Alison, you went to find out about the 30-day challenge. What is it and how does it work?
ALISON Yes, I went to a one-day seminar about it. The basic idea is that, according to psychologists, 30 days is about the time it takes to really develop a new habit because that's how long it takes for our brains to shift to a new direction. So often if we try something new, we give up after about a week or two because our brain hasn't adapted. So the idea of the 30-day challenge is, you choose something you want to do, like drink less coffee, for example, and you keep going for exactly 30 days.
I So, if you manage to do it for 30 days and you feel good about it, you'll probably keep to it, is that the idea?
A That's right, yes. But the other thing about it is that 30 days isn't a very long time. 30 days goes past quite quickly anyway. So if you decide to do something completely new – let's say you decide to get up at dawn every day and see the sun rise – maybe you wouldn't want to keep it up for your whole life, but it might be fun to do it for just 30 days. So it's also a chance to try something different, and if you're successful it's great, but if it doesn't work out it doesn't matter too much.
I I see, so it's not just about giving up bad habits. The idea is really that you try out something new.
A Yes, very much so. There were people at the seminar, for example, who'd written a short poem every day for 30 days, and someone else had tried to eat something new every day for 30 days. So it's a chance to do something you've always wanted to do or maybe something new that you'd never thought of doing.
I It sounds a lot of fun, if you've got time for it.
A Yes, well you can either do something that doesn't really get in the way of your life, like writing a poem – you can do that in your lunch break, it's easy. Or you can take time out and have a go at something you've always wanted to do, like paint a picture or climb mountains or something. Obviously to do something like that you need to make an effort and, of course, you have to give yourself a time limit of 30 days.
I So, it sounds like you think it's a good idea.
A I think it's a great idea, yes. I came away convinced!
I So, are you planning to try the 30-day challenge yourself?
A Yes, in fact I already am. I decided to put my car keys in a drawer and I'm going to cycle everywhere for 30 days, even if it rains.
I And how's it going so far?
A Really well. I'm finding it much easier than I expected.
I And when did you start?
A Erm … this morning.
I Well, good luck with that, Alison. Now, Alison's only just started, but next up on the Life and Style podcast we're going to talk to a few more people who've been doing the 30-day challenge. They're all about half-way through, and they've done it successfully so far …

1.12

INTERVIEWER What made you decide to become vegetarian, Farah?
FARAH Well, for quite a long time now I've been trying to eat less meat, partly for health reasons. I think vegetables are better for you.
I But didn't you ever think of being vegetarian before?
F Yes, but I always thought I'd miss meat too much. But the idea of being a vegetarian for 30 days was really good, because I could give it a try and then see how I feel.
I And how do you feel? Are you finding it difficult?
F No, I feel really good. Actually, I don't miss meat at all, so I think I'll easily manage the 30 days and I might try carrying on longer. I certainly think I'm a bit healthier than I used to be.
I Mona, why did you decide to draw something every day?
MONA Well, I've never been very good at drawing, but I've always thought I'd like to start drawing things around me. It's one of those things that you think about doing, but you never get round to.
I What have you drawn pictures of so far?
M All kinds of things. At the start I drew objects around me at home. Then I went out in my lunch break and started drawing things outdoors, like yesterday I drew a duck in the park – that was really difficult!
I So do you feel it has been worthwhile?
M Oh yes, definitely. I'm still not very good at drawing, but it's been lots of fun and it's very relaxing.
I Steve, what language did you decide to learn?
STEVE Well, I thought I'd choose a language that isn't too different from English, so I decided to try Italian.
I Isn't it difficult to keep going with it?
S Yes, it is. I've had to be very strict with myself. I'm using a book with a CD, so I usually try to cover one lesson a night.
I And who do you practise with? Or are you just working alone?
S Well, there's an Italian restaurant just round the corner and I'm friends with the owner, so I go there and I chat to him. That's one reason I chose Italian.
I And do you think you'll carry on after the 30 days?
S Maybe, or I might try a different language every month. I'm thinking of trying Japanese next.

1.15 PART 1

BECKY That was a really interesting lecture. There's so much to learn, though. I'm going to try and get all my homework done tonight.
TESSA Oh, I'm going out tonight. Can't be bothered with homework. I'll do mine later. You always study too much! Do you want a coffee?
B Sorry, I can't. I've got to go to work. It's my first day!
T Oh, of course, at your cousin's café. Well, good luck! Oh, by the way, when is that assignment due?
B Friday. Really must go now, I'll be late. See you tomorrow.
T Bye!

1.16 PART 2

BECKY Hi, Tom. I'm just on my way to the café.
TOM Oh OK …
B I'm late.
T Look, this evening … do you want to come over? I wanted to talk over a few things … about the wedding …
B I'd love to but I've got to study tonight.
T OK. Never mind. Well, good luck with your first day at work.
B Thanks. I'm sure it'll be fine.
T Don't spill coffee over anyone!
B I'll try not to. Oh, must run. Here comes my bus. No time to talk now. See you tomorrow. Bye.

1.19 PART 3

SAM OK, so what was I showing you? The food. The sandwiches are all here. The most important thing is, don't touch the food. Remember to always use these tongs to pick food up. And what else? Oh, the espresso machine. Uh, the coffee goes in here, the cup there, and you press this button. Is that clear?
BECKY OK, I'll remember that.
S Another thing to remember is the tables – they're all numbered. So it starts with one over there and goes round to fifteen. OK, have you got that?
B Yes, sure. I think I can count to 15!
S Hah – I still get them mixed up myself. Oh, say hello to Phil. He's our most regular customer. This is my cousin Becky. She's just started here.

Audioscripts

PHIL Hi, nice to meet you.
B Hi.
S Phil's writing a novel.
B A novel! Amazing.
P Well, it's just a science fiction story. Haven't got very far yet.
S He comes to the café to write. We call him JK. You know – like JK Rowling. She wrote the first Harry Potter book in a café.
B Oh, right!
EMMA Oh, there you are. Lovely to see you, Becky. We're really pleased you're working here.
B Me too. I'm going to enjoy it, I'm sure.
E Is my husband looking after you and explaining everything?
B Oh yes, I'm getting the hang of it – slowly.
P She's doing really well.
E And I see you've met Phil. He's going to make the café famous one day, you'll see.

▶ 1.20 PART 4

TOM Large cappuccino please, with extra milk.
BECKY With extra m – oh Tom! Sorry. Wasn't expecting you.
T I was just passing by. How's it going?
B There's a lot to learn, but I think I'll be OK. Is it OK if I take my break now?
SAM Yeah.
B I'll make a coffee for both of us.
T Sure that's OK?
B Yeah, it's fine. You came at a quiet time. So, what was it you wanted to talk to me about tonight?
T Er, the wedding?
B The wedding?
T Yes, our wedding!
B Of course. We need to start thinking about it.

▶ 1.23

GITTA Most people at work think my boss, Michaela, is an inspiring woman who's had an amazing career – we work for a public relations company. She always looks very busy and people find that impressive, but I find her a bit arrogant, to tell you the truth. The other day, we were having a performance review meeting – she was reviewing me – and in the middle of the meeting her mobile phone rang. She answered the call and just ignored me! When she finished the call, she then spent a long time writing an email on her phone whilst I was just sitting there – waiting. When she'd finished, she didn't apologise or anything and just said, 'OK, what were we talking about?' Maybe I'm being too sensitive, but she didn't seem to care about our meeting – or me – and was far more interested in her phone call and email. I really think people should switch off their phones during meetings. I was really upset, to be honest.

DEREK For years, I resisted getting a mobile phone. Don't get me wrong – I'm not a techno-phobe. I've been using a computer for years; in fact, I have two: a desktop and a laptop. It's just that mobile phones annoyed me. I didn't want to be available all the time and I thought the language people used in text messages was a bit silly. However, my niece, Emma, was determined that I should get a mobile phone. I run a small firm of accountants and she felt someone in my position needed to be 'more connected', as she put it. Emma has a smartphone and she explained to me how they were just like mini computers that you carry around in your pocket. And, of course, she was right. She let me borrow hers for a weekend. I didn't actually phone anyone, but she had a lot of clever apps on her phone and I found out that I could go online and check email really easily. Of course, I went out and bought a smartphone the following week. Emma was delighted – she had finally managed to convince me. I haven't told her that I still don't ring anyone or send text messages, but now she thinks I'm more connected. For me, it's a great new toy – lots of fun.

Unit 2

▶ 1.25

ABBY So, when are you off to South Africa?
ROB End of next week. I can't wait to get away.
A I absolutely loved it when I went there last year. So, what have you got planned?
R You know – the usual things – Cape Town first. I'll definitely go to Robben Island.
A Great.
R And one thing I want to try while I'm there is surfing. Apparently, there are some really great schools you can go to.
A Yeah, there are loads.
R I've always wanted to learn how to surf and I'll finally get to do it – you know, with proper waves! Cool!
A That's a great thing to do – I went to one of those schools.
R And was it good? Did you learn a lot?
A Yeah – yeah I did. But … but you've got to be a bit careful in the water there. Actually, I got into a bit of trouble once.
R What, in the water?
A Yeah, when I was first learning to surf I went out one time by myself. I was trying to catch this wave, but I came off my board, and stupidly, I'd forgotten to attach a leg rope from my ankle to the board.
R So you lost the board?
A Yeah, I tried to get hold of it, but it got swept away by the wave.
R So what did you do – just swim to the shore?
A Well, sort of. I started swimming and I soon realised that I wasn't getting anywhere. Then very gradually I got the feeling I was being pulled out to sea.
R You were caught in a current?
A Yeah, and when I realised this, I began to panic a bit. So I waved to get someone's attention. Luckily a life-guard had already seen that I was in trouble. And he came to rescue me in his lifeboat.
R Bet you were pleased to see him!
A Yeah! But the idea of being carried right out to sea is really frightening. I don't think you could survive very long. I'm quite a strong swimmer, but even so …
R Yeah, I think you'd start to really feel the cold in the water.
A Well, I was wearing a wet suit. But they say if you get caught in a current you shouldn't try and swim against it. The thing is, the water there is ocean, not sea. The waves are really powerful.
R Hmm, maybe I'll have another think about it.
A About surfing you mean?
R Yeah.
A No, honestly you'll love it. It really is the most amazing feeling. I just had a bad experience. I got myself a new surfboard, and as soon as I'd had some lessons and knew what I was doing, it was fantastic. It's just you and the board, and you have this incredible sense of freedom. And when you catch the wave at the right time …
R Yeah, you're right, it sounds amazing.
A Yeah, it's fantastic. Oh, but, just watch out for sharks.
R Yeah, I'll … watch out for what?!

▶ 1.34

INTERVIEWER Miles, tell us about the story. What happened?
MILES Well, one day in the winter of 1997, in eastern Siberia, one of the wildest and most natural habitats on Earth, a hunter came across a Siberian tiger. He shot the tiger and wounded it and then took part of the dead animal that the tiger was about to eat. Of course, the tiger wasn't happy. It attacked and killed Markov but it didn't do this immediately. It waited 48 hours before attacking. In other words, it remembered what had happened and carefully planned the attack. So while Markov was away hunting, the tiger found its way to his hut in the forest and broke in through the door. The tiger then took Markov's mattress outside and laid on it, waiting for him to return. When Markov finally appeared, the tiger dragged him into the forest and ate him, leaving only his boots. They found the boots later and figured out what had happened.
I So these are very dangerous animals, obviously.
M Yes, very dangerous if you make them angry, certainly. They're also not just any tiger, they're the largest species of cat walking on earth. The Siberian Tiger is a very impressive animal. They can be up to four metres long and they weigh more than 250 kilos. They can jump about ten metres if they need to. So imagine a creature that's as active as a cat and has the weight of an industrial refrigerator – that's what a Siberian tiger's like! …

▶ 1.35

INTERVIEWER … So what happened then?
MILES Well of course, a group of men hunted the tiger down and killed it.
I I suppose they had to, really.
M But did they?
I What do you mean?
M Well, when you read the story, you're not sure whose side you're on, the tiger's or the humans'. As Vaillant says, the tiger's response is quite 'logical' and the tiger is 'just trying to be a tiger', and it's a human who interferes with that.
I So in a sense, it's the humans who are dangerous, rather than the tiger?
M In a way, yes. What's interesting is that humans and tigers hunt the same animals and share the same environment, and they've done this in Siberia for years but they don't normally disturb each other. But if you make the mistake of attacking a tiger, you're in trouble. People who live in the area say this has never happened before. There is no record ever of a tiger hunting a human being.
I So is that the message of the story – leave tigers alone?
M Well, yes, don't make a tiger angry, certainly, or it will take revenge. But also it makes you ask the question, 'Which is the dangerous animal, tigers or humans?' We think of tigers as dangerous, but of course we're not at risk because of tigers, they're at risk because of us. There are 40 million humans but only 500 tigers, so they really are an endangered species, and that's mainly because of us hunting them and living in their habitat and taking away their natural food.
I Miles, thank you. You heard Miles Holman talking about the book *The Tiger* by John Vaillant …

▶ 1.37 PART 1

BECKY Could you give me a hand with this please, Tessa?
TESSA Sure.
B I just, I just can't get the right height.
T OK.
B Great, thank you.
T No problem.
T Good shot?
B Not really. I think I need to be closer. It's quite difficult.
T Yeah, it's hard, isn't it? … Do you need all this equipment?
B I find it helps.
T Do you?
B Usually. Ah, this is fun.
T Yeah, much better than sitting in a lecture at college. All that theory!
B Well, that can be interesting …
T I'd really like to take a photo of something a bit more exciting – maybe a squirrel.
B A squirrel? That'll be good … if we can find one …

▶ 1.39 PART 2

TESSA Nice daffodils.
BECKY Gorgeous, aren't they?
B Can I have a look? Wow, what a great shot!
T It's all right.
B You know just how to get a really good shot. The light is amazing.
T Thanks. Guess it's not bad. Can I have a look at yours?
B It's pretty boring.
T Don't you want me to?

165

B No – I mean it's not a problem. I just feel it's a pretty ordinary shot. You know, just … nothing special. Compared to yours.
Have you ever worked as a photographer?
T Me? No. It was just something I kind of got into. Kind of a hobby. How about you?
B No, never. I used to have this job working in HR, but I've just given that up.
T Too stressful?
B Sort of.
T Or too boring?
B Well … both! My café job's enough to pay the bills – just. You?
T I'm just studying at the moment; I haven't got a job …
B Oh right …
T Shhh!
B What?
T Squirrel. Over there.
B Oh right. Great.
T We'll need to get a bit closer. But quietly.
B You go first.
T No, no. You go.
B No, really – you should go.
T It's fine. This is your shot.
B Sure?
T Yeah.
B OK. Oh no! It's run away. Ah, this is a really bad shot. The light's all wrong. I need a reflector.
T Can I have a look?
B I don't like it.
T This is great.
B Really?
T Yeah, it's your best shot.
B But I didn't have a chance to set it up.
T Maybe sometimes you don't need to.
B Hm. OK. Maybe not. You know, one thing I don't like about this assignment.
T What's that?
B It's so cold!
T Yeah, it's freezing, isn't it?
B My flat's not far away. Do you fancy a nice warm cup of coffee?
T OK. Yeah. Why not?
B Great. Let's go.

▶ 1.41

LUIZA I spent a year in Vancouver in Canada. I loved the National Parks there – they're very special environments full of rare and protected plants and animals. This one particular day I'd been exploring in the Pacific Rim National Park when I got in trouble in the forest. I'd been to see this waterfall. It was a very easy walk from the main track – less than an hour. On the way back I saw what I thought was a short cut that would get me back to the main track more quickly – a big mistake. After a couple of hours I realised that I was going round in circles and I wasn't getting anywhere. I'd got completely lost. I was beginning to get worried – that's for sure. All I had to eat was an energy bar and I had nothing to drink. Well, I waited until later in the afternoon because then I knew the sun would go down in the west and I knew roughly I should be going in an easterly direction. And I had a bit of luck – I came across a stream with fresh water. I followed the stream for a bit and I came to an open area – a kind of a clearing. I knew that eventually people would start looking for me – I'd told the forest ranger when I would be back and I was more than four hours late. And I knew it's better to sit in one place where you can be seen. So I was sitting quietly and thinking about how I could spend the night in the forest and I suddenly had this strange feeling I was not alone.

▶ 1.42

LUIZA I looked around the clearing and on the edge of it I saw a bear looking at me. I knew that you shouldn't run away or show fear. I stood up and said in a clear voice "I have a right to be here" and moved slowly backwards without looking at the bear in the eyes. I could sense the bear watching me. I tried to keep calm but inside I was really panicking. I was terrified. Suddenly, it started moving – thankfully it was away from me. It just disappeared back into the forest. I didn't know if I should stay where I was or keep moving. But then I could hear a helicopter in the distance coming towards me. I thought it might be looking for me. I jumped up and tried to see it, but it flew away before I could get its attention. It was so frustrating. But about fifteen minutes later it flew back and I was ready. I took off my jacket and turned it inside out – the lining was red and easy to see. This time they saw me and waved back. About a half an hour later rescuers arrived and guided me out. What I couldn't get over is the fact that I was only 10 minutes away from the main track.

Unit 3

▶ 1.43

NARRATOR My teacher will get angry if I make mistakes.
TEACHER I don't really think that's the case. Teachers really do prefer students who try hard, you know, make an effort. It doesn't matter if they make mistakes. In fact, it's better if they do because if we know what their mistakes are, we can help fix them.
N Children learn faster than adults.
T I guess you could say that children aren't as busy as adults – they probably have a bit less going on in their lives. And that helps. They're less distracted and, you could say, a bit more open to learning. But adults – well, they often have really good motivation. They're often quite focused and they're really keen to learn. So this motivation can make them faster learners than children.
N I must practise every day in order to make progress.
T Well, in my experience you can practise too much! It's actually better to take two or three days off each week. The thing is our brains need a bit of a rest. It's like muscles when you're doing physical exercise – you need to rest them. So we need to rest our brains when we're learning and practising something new.
N If something seems very easy, I must be doing it wrong.
T Yeah, a lot of people believe this, but I think the opposite is true. In reality, if it's easy, it probably means you're doing it right. But if something's difficult or it's a physical activity that's causing you pain, then you're probably doing something wrong. Learning doesn't always need to be hard!
N Long practice sessions are best.
T It's much, much better to have shorter practice sessions. You've got to remember that most people get tired after about fifteen minutes and they need a short break. The thing is, though, during the fifteen minutes of practice, you really want people to concentrate on what they're doing – really focus. They'll get more benefit that way.

▶ 1.44

SEAMUS Ever since I was first able to read I've loved comic books. I just think it's a brilliant way of telling a story. I've read literally thousands of them. But, at the same time, I discovered I was quite good at drawing. When I was about eight years old I started copying some of the pictures in comics and even my parents were surprised by how good my copies were. It wasn't long before I started making up my own stories. All of my friends were also really into comics, but none of them tried coming up with their own stories. But they quite liked reading mine, so I'd share the comics I wrote with them. This was helpful because it gave me a good idea of what worked and what didn't. I studied design at university and then got a job as a graphic designer. But all the time I was writing and drawing my own comics – comics for adults and children. I've just signed a contract with a major comics publisher in the USA and I can now give up my job as a graphic designer. I think my career in comics is beginning to take off … well, I hope to do really well. Ten thousand hours? You bet. I've probably spent more time than that, but I loved every minute of it.
FIONA I'm a chemist and I've been lucky enough to get a research position at a university. I love chemistry because it's all about the things that make up the world we live in. I find it fascinating. It's funny, whenever I say that I'm a chemist, one of the first things people mention is the table of elements – you know, all the symbols for all the different metals and gases. They can never figure out all those symbols. Well, I have this system where the letter or letters remind me of the name of a person, and that reminds me of a face and something about the way he or she looks reminds me of the element. One colleague pointed out that this wasn't a very scientific way of remembering these elements. In fact, some scientists look down on this kind of thing, but it works for me. I find all these ways of making your memory stronger really interesting and I think making associations to help you remember is really useful. I have to remember so much information in my research work, so I want to look into these techniques in more depth.
HENRY I'm a musician – I play saxophone in a band. We're just about to go on a tour so we're practising full-time to get ready. We've got so much to do before the tour – so much that it's getting us all down a bit. Apart from needing to practise playing together, we've got to write some new songs and learn some others. I read about this idea of learning different things at different times of the day, so we decided to try it out and see if it'd help. So now we focus on writing new material in the morning, and we also use that time to learn the words and music of some classic songs we want to play – actually studying the notes and remembering the words of songs. After lunch we play together – you know, do the physical learning. And I have to say it's working pretty well. We're putting in a lot of work and we feel we're using the time well. The songs are getting easier to remember and I think our playing in the afternoon is tighter – we're producing a better sound. The only problem is that some days we get a bit carried away in the afternoon and keep playing into the evening, which means we stay up late and aren't so good in the morning!

▶ 1.48

PETER This week on The Book Show we're talking about David Epstein's *The Sports Gene*, in which he claims that many sports professionals are so good simply because they're lucky enough to have the right genes. According to him, top athletes and other sportsmen are simply different from the rest of us. With us is athlete Barbara MacCallum, who is a professional runner and trainer. Barbara, you've read the book. Do you think Epstein is right – is it all about having the right genes?
BARBARA Well, I think he's right that genes are important. And, of course, we all know that many Kenyans are tall and thin and so on, and also as the book says they live at a high altitude – 1,000 metres – so they have more red blood cells. So these things are important. But I think there's much more worried to it than that.
P You've lived in Kenya yourself.
B Yes, I've lived in Kenya myself and I've trained with Kenyan runners, I've also worked with Kenyan children. And there really are lots of very good runners in Kenya. But it's not just about having long legs. They also have a culture of running, everyone runs, even small children, so they have this background, they all see themselves as runners, as good runners. And if you're poor in Kenya, becoming an athlete is a way to change your life, so everyone wants to be a runner.
P And they run in bare feet. Does that help?
B Yes, it does. It gives you a much better running technique, so that's important, too. So yes, I think it is partly genetic, but it's also to do with lots of other factors, like having lots of practice, lots of encouragement to run, believing in yourself, and also learning to run in the right way.
P So could I run as fast as a Kenyan?
B Well, yes, you could, but you'd have to start early in life and you'd have to get very fit.
P Well, I haven't run anywhere for years, so maybe it's a bit too late to start.
B Absolutely not, it's never too late. Start training now and you'll be amazed at what you can achieve.

Audioscripts

1.49

PETER Thank you, Barbara. Well, also with us now is Marta Fedorova. Marta, you've been playing tennis since you were a child and you've been a professional player for ten years.
MARTA Yes.
P You've also read the book. Do you think he's right? Are some sports people naturally better? Or is it a question of technique and practice, as Barbara says?
M Well, yes, I've been thinking a lot about this recently. I used to think that it was mainly practice and technique that were important. You know, if you practise a lot, if you get fit, if you improve your technique, then you'll win. But after reading this book I'm not so sure. For example, I've played maybe 50 serious matches this year. And I've won about half of them. If I think about the people who beat me, they all have certain things in common physically. Short bodies but longer arms, for example.
P Like you.
M Well, yes, I suppose so! And very good eyesight, obviously. And mostly aged 18 to 25. And these are things that you can't really change. So yes, there is something in it.
P So sport isn't as fair as we like to think?
M That's right, and that's really what he's saying in this book. When we watch the Olympics, for example, we think it's a fair competition between equals, but it isn't. We're watching a competition between very different types of people who have different natural advantages. So there will be people who need to train very hard to get where they are and others who don't need to train so much, and there will be some people who can naturally finish 40 seconds ahead of all the others, and so on. So fairness in sport doesn't really exist.

1.51 PART 1

BECKY So when are you going to tell your parents about your promotion?
TOM This weekend, I think. We're seeing them on Saturday, remember?
B Oh yes. Anyway, as I was saying – about Tessa …
T Tessa, yes, your classmate …
B She's just got this amazing natural ability.
T So have you.
B But I've been taking photos for years …
T Very good ones too …
B … and I've gradually got better, but Tessa …
T Maybe she's been practising for years, too. In secret! … So what's for dinner then?
B Well, I got some cheese, some chicken and some salad.
T Cheese? You mean the one on offer?
B Yeah. Two for one – bargain.
T Yes, it was a bargain. That's why I got some.
B Well, I guess I know what we are having for dinner.
T Cheese on toast?
B Cheese on toast.

1.52 PART 2

TOM Anyway, as I was saying … about the wedding. I was thinking we should start making some decisions if we want to get married in June.
BECKY Yes, you're right.
T So what do we need to think about?
B Well, the usual things … guests, a venue for the reception, the cake.
T So maybe the first thing to decide is …
B … who should we invite?
T I mean, do we want a large wedding with lots of guests or just a small one?
B How about … how about we invite no one?
T What?
B We can just have a secret wedding. You know, go to Las Vegas in America – or something like that.
T Seriously?
B It's an idea …
T Seriously Becky – don't you think it's a good idea to set a limit? Say, no more than 80 guests?
B Yes, I suppose it is.
T OK.
B And … Tessa!
T Sure – we can invite her.
B … well, yes … but I was thinking … we'll need a photographer.
T Well, yes.
B But don't you agree that Tessa would be perfect as the photographer?
T Um … Becky … that's kind of an unnecessary detail right now.
B Yes. Of course.
T To go back to the guests …
B OK, so how many relatives, how many friends?

1.55 PART 3

TOM So, if we just invite close family and friends …
BECKY We'll have to invite Aunt Clare.
T Your mad Aunt Clare?
B We have to invite her.
T Of course, we could sit her next to my Uncle Fred.
B But he never says anything.
T Exactly – the perfect pair.
B Who else? What about the people you work with?
T Hmm – I don't know about that.
B We could always invite them to the evening reception.
T Don't you agree that it'd be easier not to invite them?
B But I would like to invite Tessa.
T As I said – that's fine. Anyway, I think we need to limit it to close friends and family members. Even the scary ones.
B I sort of get both excited and nervous when I think about it.
T It'll be fine. So the next question is where?
B Well, there's that lovely old hotel … you know, near where my cousin lives.
T Oh … 'Regent's Lodge'.
B Actually … thinking about where … after we're married. Where are we going to live?
T Hm. Good question.
B What you might call a necessary detail?

1.57

REPORTER This is Marco Forlan reporting from the multi-million-pound Market Street Sports Complex. It's huge – it's got so many different courts for different sports – tracks for athletics and cycling. It's even got its own indoor snow slope. It's been up and running for a year now, so I've come down to see just how much use it's getting. So, Lizzie, you haven't been doing this long, have you?
LIZZIE No, just over six months.
R And before that?
L Well, nothing. I was one of those people who was pretty hopeless at sport at school. In basketball I could never catch the ball very well and I couldn't throw it far enough. And I've never been a fast runner.
R So you were always last to be picked for a team?
L Yeah, that was me! Everyone else was so much more talented and they looked down on me. But I wanted to do some kind of exercise, and, to be honest, I almost don't consider this a sport – it's just something I used to do to get to school. I train four days a week now and I do a mix of track and open road. It's my favourite part of the day.
R And in the future?
L Next month I'm going to compete in a race. It's just a small local one, but it gives me a goal to aim for. I've been training quite hard for the past six months now. I train here on the track, but also on the open road.
R Good luck with your race.
R Hey, Barry – that was quite an impressive jump.
BARRY Thanks.
R So how long have you been doing this?
B Just over a year. I took it up after I recovered from a foot injury. You see, I used to run marathons, but now I find it really uncomfortable to run long distances.
R And did you get started here at the centre?
B Yeah, that's right. In the beginning I was just having fun – you know … And then I realised I was quite good at it. What I enjoy is … it's mostly about skill and the way you use your whole body – so it's not just about strength.
R And have you ever tried it out in the open?
B Yeah, last winter I went to France and had my first go on real snow. I met a lot of amazing people there including a few professionals. They told me that I've got a naturally good style.
R Any plans for the future?
B I'm going to compete in some championships this winter and I've just bought myself this new board. I just wish we had real mountains in England.
R That's a great-looking board. Have fun! That was a pretty energetic game, Patricia.
PATRICIA Yeah, it was fun.
R So you're new to the game?
P Yeah, I started about nine months ago.
R How did you get into it?
P I took it up because I wanted a sport for myself. You see, I've spent the past six or seven years taking my two children to different sports events. They're older now and can get to sports practice on their own. So I had to figure out what I'd like to do.
R How did you decide?
P Well, I was always quite good at basketball, but I wanted to try something new. And I wanted a sport that would get me fit, and this certainly does. Once I'd looked into a range of options – the choice was easy.
R This is a fairly new sport in the UK …
P Yeah.
R So how is it different from basketball?
P Well, you can actually take three steps with the ball – so long as you do it in three seconds.
R That's not long. And how often do you practise?
P Once a week and then we have a friendly game. I enjoy the social side of things as much as the competing. Next year my team's thinking about entering some championships.
R Well, I hope you continue to enjoy it.

1.58

1
A Oh no. There's glass all over the floor.
B Well, you dropped it so I think you should clear it up.
A I can't, I've got to go. Couldn't you do it? Please?
2
A What does 'potential' mean?
B Um, I don't know. I'll have to look it up. I'll tell you in a minute.
3
A Did you manage to learn Spanish?
B Yeah, it was easy. I picked it up in about six months. But I never really learned the grammar.
4
A I think we should talk about having longer lunch breaks. Thirty minutes is much too short.
B Yes, I agree. Why don't you bring it up at the meeting?

Unit 4

2.5

PRESENTER Monica, we often hear stories about lottery winners who were unhappy or who spent their money unwisely.
MONICA Yes, that's true, you often read about lottery winners whose lives turned bad. For example, the Griffiths family recently – that was a big story. They won £1.8 million on the lottery and they spent it all on houses and cars and I don't know what else. And they ended up losing all their money, and soon after that their marriage broke up – it was a very sad story. And you do certainly hear stories like that.
P So does suddenly having a lot of money really influence people's behaviour? Or are these just isolated or unusual cases which make a good story?
M They're just isolated cases; in fact winning doesn't usually have a negative influence on people. Of course, people like to believe that winning money leads to disaster because that makes them feel better about not winning. But the idea that winning a lot of money causes misery is actually a myth, it's simply not true.
P There have been studies done on this, haven't there?

167

M Yes, that's right. According to most studies, suddenly having a lot of money is just as likely to have a positive effect on you as a negative effect. And most people don't in fact spend all their money.

P Can you give us some examples?

M Yes. For example, a recent study in Britain looked at how much of their money people spent if they won the lottery. And it found that people spent a lot in the first five years, but very few people spent all the money in their lifetime, only about 2–3%. So most people do spend a lot, but they save a lot as well. And then there was an interesting study in California, and they measured how happy people are as a result of winning the lottery. And they found that people get very happy when they win, which isn't surprising, but as they adjust to the idea of being rich and go back to normal again after a few months – they end up feeling just the same as before. So over the long term, getting richer doesn't actually affect how happy you are, you just stay the same … but with more money, of course.

P So, if you're happy anyway, you'll stay happy even if you get rich, is that the message?

M Yes, that's right. Money won't make you happy, but it won't stop you being happy either. And studies have also shown that it depends on how you spend the money. So people who buy lots of things, like clothes or houses or cars, are often not very happy. As soon as you've got a car you want a better car and so on, so that doesn't make you happy for long. But spending money on experiences usually results in longer-term happiness.

P Experiences?

M Yes, for example, going on the holiday of a lifetime or doing something you've always wanted to do. That'll make you happy while you're doing it, and it'll make you happy later because you also have good memories of it. So it's a better way to be happy.

P OK, so there we have it. When you win that £5 million, forget the cars and the new house, and go for a long holiday instead.

▶ 2.7

ALPHONSO For me, the thing that's changed my life most is having a baby. Things are just completely different now. We used to go out a lot, we used to travel as well, we'd go somewhere different every year, and we didn't use to care much about money, we both had good jobs and we had a small flat in town so we didn't need to care about money very much. But now of course the baby's the most important thing, so I'd say I've become a bit more cautious than I used to be. I used to be quite an adventurous person, I used to take all kinds of risks without thinking much about it. Whereas now I think more about having a family, having a home, having a steady job, things like that. Sounds terribly boring, doesn't it, but it doesn't feel boring!

DRAGANA A very big change in my life was going abroad to study. I grew up in Croatia in a fairly small town and I went to university there. But then I had the chance to go to Berlin for a year to study. And of course I had a good time there and I made new friends, but I think it also changed the way I look at life. Before I went I was quite shy and not very self-confident and I had quite a protected life, I suppose, and then in Berlin I had to look after myself and also adapt to a new culture, of course. And as a result of being there, I think I no longer see everything from a Croatian point of view but more internationally, so I'm much more open to different ideas than I used to be – I hope so, anyway.

▶ 2.10

MIRANDA I think the hardest part of drama school was actually getting into it. The audition process took for ever. First of all we had to perform two scenes from plays – one modern, one Shakespeare. Then we got called back to do the scenes again. I was supposed to prepare a song as well, but they forgot to let me know. So I just sang the first song that came into my head – can't even remember what it was. After that, there was a workshop for a day where they made us work on new scenes from plays and do movement and voice classes. After all of that I felt really lucky to get selected. There's no doubt the training was very thorough, I mean, we did everything – the usual voice and movement classes, but also specialised things like learning how to pretend to fight on stage. I really enjoyed those classes. The tutors were all very different – some were really strict and tough. For example, we had a movement teacher and in her class we weren't allowed to talk or use our voices in any way. That was really difficult. But our voice teacher was really relaxed – she was cool. During my second year I went through a bit of a difficult time because I wasn't sure if acting was what I really wanted to do. I mean, drama school is a huge sacrifice. The training sort of swallowed my life – like, I lived it every single moment of the day. I kind of felt like I wasn't having what you'd call 'a normal life' for a 20 year-old. The school was really flexible about this and they let me take a couple of weeks off to make up my mind. I decided to keep going and I'm glad that I did. I graduated last year and I've got an agent and I've just got a small part in a production at the Royal Shakespeare Company. So I guess you could say I'm on my way …

FRED I got into a football academy when I was eleven years old. I was playing at my local club and a scout from a professional club saw me and invited me to play in a trial match. I was really excited about this. My parents had their doubts – they were worried about me not having a normal childhood – but they could see this was a pretty unique opportunity, so they let me do it. Dad was really pleased about one thing – we were allowed to see all the club games for free. But I don't think any of us really understood just how difficult a commitment it would be. Mum and Dad were more or less forced to act as my chauffeurs and they had to drive me to practice three times a week and then to a match every Sunday. I had to do this and keep up with my school homework at the same time. And that meant I often wasn't allowed to go out and play with my friends when I wanted to. Still, in the academy we had the best coaches and there's no doubt that my playing got so much better. We also used to watch videos of matches all the time and analyse the strategy of the different players. I enjoyed this a whole lot more than I thought I would. In fact, one of the coaches once told me that this is one of the reasons why I stood out from some of the other boys in the academy. It's a really competitive environment and at the end of every year, there were some boys who were forced to give it all up because they didn't get invited back for the following year. I had one mate, Jack. We started at the same time, but when we turned 16, and it became possible for some of us to earn a salary, Jack wasn't selected. And it was like the previous five years were all for nothing. And he was like my best mate and I really missed him. I did get selected though, and now I've got a full professional contract, so things are pretty good. Did I have a normal childhood? No, probably not. I kind of regret that, but then I've been given an opportunity, haven't I? I guess you can't have it both ways.

▶ 2.13 PART 1

BECKY Now let's have a look at some of the most successful ones. Tessa took this one.

TESSA We really like the way the light is hitting the tree.

B And here's a similar shot, but from a different angle with a plane crossing the sky. We got some close-ups of flowers. We managed to get some good shots of daffodils.

T The light was really good for this one.

B And we were lucky and managed to get a couple of wildlife shots. Here's a shot of a swan that Tessa took. And finally … my shot of a squirrel.

B Thank you for listening.

TUTOR OK, thank you, Becky … and Tessa. Some very good work. There were some interesting close-up shots there, very sharp details and clear colours. Yes, a very good first assignment. Well done both of you. OK. Now for your next assignment - Bridges. Pick a bridge that you like. Photograph it and then write an essay to go with it. OK? We'll see how you get on. You've got one month.

▶ 2.14 PART 2

BECKY That went quite well.

TESSA Yeah.

B It was fun. So, bridges for the next assignment.

T Yes, bridges. So boring.

B Oh, I don't know, it's not that boring. All that fantastic architecture. That could be quite interesting.

T Yeah, maybe you're right, I'm not sure. But there's all that theory for the essay. I didn't take any notes in yesterday's lecture.

B Don't worry, I took loads of notes. You can borrow mine.

T Can I?

B Sure. Come round to the café later and I'll give them to you.

B Must go now. Bye!

▶ 2.16

1
A I thought the goalkeeper was useless. He was the weakest player in the team.
B Really, did you think so? I thought he played quite well.

2
A €60 for fish and a salad! That's far too much.
B I'm not sure about that. It doesn't seem that expensive.

3
A Did you see that bank managers earn an average of £100,000 a year? It's crazy!
B I know what you mean, but on the other hand it's a very responsible job.

4
A She's having a fancy dress party on her birthday. How boring!
B Oh I don't know. I think it could be quite good fun.

5
A It was a very boring film. I thought it was far too long.
B Maybe you're right, but I enjoyed some bits of it.

▶ 2.17

1
A I thought that was a really interesting lecture.
B Oh, I don't know. It wasn't that interesting.

2
A I find photography a very difficult subject.
B Oh, I don't know. It's not that difficult.

3
A Look at that bridge. It's so unusual.
B Oh, I don't know. It's not that unusual.

4
A I thought the questions in the exam were incredibly easy.
B Oh, I don't know. It wasn't that easy.

▶ 2.18 PART 3

BECKY Here you are. My lecture notes.

TESSA Ah great, thanks.

B And these…

T Thank you.

B And here are some other notes I made earlier.

T Ah, OK, thank you. Plenty to read here.

B It's not too much, is it?

T Um, well … no, thank you. You've saved my life.

B Don't worry, that's OK. I'm more into the theory than you are.

T You can say that again. I hate it.

B By the way, Tom and I were sorting out details of the wedding last night.

T Oh yeah?

B And well we thought – if you're interested – we'd love you to take the photos.

T Me? Are you serious?

B Yeah, why not?

T Well, I'm not … I don't think I'm good enough.

Audioscripts

B Oh don't be silly. Of course you are. Oh, will you? Please?
T Well, yes, if you want me to. I mean … I'd love to.
B Great. Better get back to work.
PHIL Oh no. No!
B What is it, Phil?
P I've just deleted the whole chapter. I only meant to delete the paragraph.
B Oh no.
T Who's that?
B That's Phil. He's always here. He's writing a book. Well, trying to, anyway. When he isn't accidentally deleting his work!
T A writer … that's interesting.
B See you later.
T Hi.
P Hi.
T Becky tells me you're writing a book.
P Sort of.
T That's great. I like books.
P Mm.
T I'd like to see what you've written, anyway. I'm sure it's really good.
P Thanks. I haven't written much yet.
T Ah well, I'd better let you get on, bye. …
P Bye …

2.19

EVA I got a chance to go to Toronto in Canada for a year to work for my company – I didn't have to go there, but I chose to go because I thought it would be interesting. And it was a great experience. And, of course, at the start it was all new and exciting, and there was so much to see, so many places to go out. I'm from quite a small town in Colombia, so it was a huge difference. The most difficult thing, I think, was getting to know people. I think in a big city everyone's busy with their own life, you know, everyone's in a hurry. It was really hard to meet people and make friends. Also, because it's really cold in winter, nothing goes on outside in the street, everyone does things indoors in their own homes and that's quite a big difference. Sometimes you walk down a street and you think, where is everyone? And it was so cold, that really affects your mood, it makes you just want to stay indoors and as a result I felt quite lonely sometimes. So yes, it was a good experience, I'm very glad I went there, but I was quite glad to come back home again and see all my friends.

NICK I got a job teaching English in a town called Katowice in Poland. When I first went there I was very lucky, because I stayed with a family who didn't speak English, so I was really forced to speak Polish. It was very difficult at first, I couldn't understand a word. But because I learned Polish, I very quickly got to know lots of people. I think a key to understanding a country is to learn the language – without that you only ever meet the people who speak English and you can't ever get to know the culture. Another thing is that people often go to places that are beautiful to look at, and that's fine if you're a tourist. But to live in a place, I think what it looks like is the least important thing. People are much more important. For example, I come from a very beautiful old town in England – it looks great in photographs, but there's not much going on there. Where I was in Katowice, it's just a big industrial town, nothing special about it, but the people were very friendly and welcoming, so I very quickly felt at home there and I had a really good time. I was supposed to stay there for three months but I ended up staying for a year!

JEAN I work for a large engineering company and I went to work in Oman, in the Gulf, for a year. And I had a very good time there. I had a good salary so I ate out a lot and, at weekends, I went diving and swimming and went on trips into the mountains or the desert. It's a very beautiful country. So, as I say, I had a good time there, but I don't feel I ever really got to know the culture. I never got under the surface of it, so as a result I remained an outsider. People were very friendly, very hospitable, and I spent some time with the local employees who worked with us – we often went out together. But I suppose because the culture is very different and you're working hard every day, it's easier to spend your time with other foreigners, so my friends were mostly Europeans. I know it's not a good excuse, but it's what most foreign visitors do – they end up in a group of expatriates and have their own lifestyle, and that results in them being like a separate community. Maybe I should have tried harder to learn Arabic, I did try to learn a bit, but I never learned to speak it well enough to have a real conversation with people.

Unit 5

2.23

Lots of people get scared when they fly and they're sure the plane's going to crash, but in fact it's one of the safest ways to travel. The odds of a plane crashing are only about one in a million and obviously they're much less if you use an airline with a good safety record. It's very unlikely that your plane will crash, but even if it does you'll probably be fine, because 95% of people in plane crashes survive. If you sit at the back of the plane or over the wing, near the exit, your chances get even better. So, if you're worried about getting on that plane, don't be, because you'll almost certainly survive the journey. You're more likely to have an accident in the car going to the airport – your chances of having a road accident are 1 in 8,000. So the safest way to travel is to take a train to the airport and then fly.

More good news is that you have quite a good chance of living to be 100, especially if you don't worry too much. According to a recent report, in richer countries of the world, women who are 25 now have a 1 in 4 chance of reaching their 100th birthday – men of 25 only have a 1 in 6 chance, not quite so good. But the chances are getting better all the time, so a girl born now has a 1 in 3 chance of living to 100 and a boy has a 1 in 4 chance. Of course, this depends on what country you're in. In some countries like Japan the chances are even higher and modern medicine may well make the chances higher still during your lifetime.

So, that's the good news. You probably won't die in a plane crash and you, or at least your children, could live to be 100. But the bad news is, you almost certainly won't win the lottery. The chances of winning a big prize in the lottery are only about 1 in 18 million – so that's extremely unlikely.

2.27

JOE So, when are you off?
MARTHA Monday of next week.
J Exciting.
M Sure is – this time next week I'll be settling into my accommodation.
J So, I mean, what is it you'll be doing? From what I understand … well, you're going down there to keep your eye on some penguins. Is that it?
M Well, I suppose that's one way of looking at it!
J Yeah, but, you know, what will you be doing on a daily basis?
M Well, I'm not entirely sure, but I think I'll be doing similar things every day. It's more or less a question of observing the penguins – counting them, taking photos, checking tags on some of them – that kind of thing.
J OK – so, just kind of standing around in the cold?
M Yes, well, that's the downside of the job. That and the attacks.
J What? From polar bears?
M Erm … at the South Pole? No, from penguins.
J You mean those sweet little birds attack you?
M Oh yes, they're full of attitude – if you get too close.
J And will they be waiting for you when you get there?
M Well, of course – they know I'm coming.
J Very funny. So, there they are – Mr and Mrs Penguin about to play happy families and …?
M Yeah, so, by the time I arrive the penguins will already have got into pairs and then, by the middle of November, each pair of penguins will have laid two eggs.
J You just watch them sit on their eggs? That must be … 'really interesting'.
M I'm sure they'll do something to keep me entertained.
J And then?
M Well, by the end of December, most of the chicks will have arrived and then after about three weeks we put metal tags on them.
J Unless you get attacked by those nasty, aggressive parents.
M We have our methods of defence.
J Sounds scary. OK, this is all very interesting, but, I mean, why? Why's it useful to know what these penguins do? It sounds like they kind of do the same old thing year after year.
M Nothing wrong with predictable – we scientists like that – but sometimes there can be changes, like maybe there are fewer chicks or maybe the parents aren't able to feed the chicks and not as many survive. This can tell us a lot about what's happening in the Antarctic ecosystem.
J Like what exactly?
M Ah, I'm a scientist – I never jump to easy conclusions.
J That's no fun.
M But, in a general sense, if there are changes in the number of penguins or changes in their behaviour, this can tell us that there has been a change in the climate of some sort. It's part of the evidence – the bigger picture, if you like. The work I'll be doing is just a small part in a big project that's been going on for some time. But because Antarctica is such an unspoilt environment the changes that take place there can tell us a lot about what's happening on the rest of the planet.
J And you get to hang out with those cute little penguins.
M Yeah, well … it's just one big penguin party.
J Sounds pretty cool to me.

2.30 PART 1

BECKY Phil? We're closing.
PHIL Nearly done. I'm just finishing this chapter. That's it – done. See you tomorrow, then. What's wrong, Sam?
SAM The usual. Not enough money coming in. I need to do something to get more customers.
P Hmm. You could stay open longer? In the evenings? You could serve meals. I'd eat here.
B You practically live here anyway. But it's an idea, why not?
S It'd be a long day.
B You could do just Friday and Saturday to start with.
S Hmm, I'd need to hire a cook. Set up the kitchen properly. On the other hand, the extra money would be good … I don't know.
B Anyway, time to go. Are you ready, Phil?
P Yeah, coming. Bye Sam.
S See you.
P Umm … that friend of yours … curly hair …
B Tessa?
P Tessa. Is she at college with you?
B Yeah.
P OK.
B Bye Phil.

2.31 PART 2

EMMA Bad day?
SAM The café. We're not making enough money.
E Come on, you're doing fine. Mid-week, it's bound to be slow.
S I'm just worried. We've put all our money in this. I don't want to lose it.
E No, of course you don't. I can see that.
S Phil had an idea today.
E Yeah?
S Stay open Friday and Saturday evenings and serve food.
E Interesting.
S Of course, the trouble is we'd have to invest even more money – money that we haven't got.
E Yes, but the good thing about it is, it might be a way to get more business.

169

S Well, we'd need to put in a proper kitchen, and that'll probably cost a fortune. And we'll have to hire someone to cook. People do often ask if we're open in the evening, so there is a demand … I don't know, it's a big risk …
E I think it's a lovely idea. I know the perfect person to do the cooking.
S Who?
E Me.
S You? Seriously?
E Why not? Promise I won't charge much!

▶ 2.36 PART 3

EMMA And maybe we could do a few other things.
SAM Such as?
E Well, how about entertainment? We could have live music, get locals to play at the weekend.
S Hmm, that might be worth a try … if they didn't cost too much. In fact, we can probably get some students to do it for free.
E No!
S If we give them some food or something.
E Sam! You should pay them. That's not fair!
S Hmm, maybe you're right.
E Or display paintings or photos.
S That's not a bad idea. Becky could help with that … or Tessa.
E I know what you're thinking.
S What?
E Look, if you want to use Tessa's photos you should pay her for them. What I mean is, that she can display them and we can sell them.
S Hmm …
E Or readings. Have poetry readings.
S Hmm, that's a possibility … I know who you're thinking of ….
BOTH Phil!
S And he'd definitely do it for free.
E [sighs]
S What?

▶ 2.38

1
Large areas of farmland were under water and cattle had to be moved to higher ground. Several villages were completely cut off and fire services rescued 53 people from their homes. More rain is expected, so river levels may rise further over the next few days and there is a chance that larger towns will be affected …

2
Temperatures around Boston dropped to −25°. Drivers on the main Boston to New York highway had to abandon their vehicles and several small towns were entirely cut off. Residents were warned not to go out unless absolutely necessary. Temperatures are likely to remain below −20° at least until the weekend, with further heavy snow expected. …

3
March is normally one of the wettest months in the region, but this year's rainfall was the lowest ever recorded, with only three days of rain in some parts of the country. Emergency supplies of water were brought into areas most badly affected. According to a government statement, if the dry weather continues the rice harvest could be severely threatened.

4
Winds of over 150 kilometres an hour are expected to strike the coast on Tuesday evening, and residents in coastal areas have been advised to leave. Centres have been set up in towns further inland to provide food and shelter for families who were forced to abandon their homes.

This page is intentionally left blank

Phonemic Symbols

Vowel sounds

Short

/ə/	/æ/	/ʊ/	/ɒ/
teach**er**	m**a**n	p**u**t	g**o**t
/ɪ/	/i/	/e/	/ʌ/
ch**i**p	happ**y**	m**e**n	b**u**t

Long

/ɜː/	/ɑː/	/uː/	/ɔː/	/iː/
sh**i**rt	p**a**rt	wh**o**	w**a**lk	ch**ea**p

Diphthongs (two vowel sounds)

/eə/	/ɪə/	/ʊə/	/ɔɪ/	/aɪ/	/eɪ/	/əʊ/	/aʊ/
h**air**	n**ear**	t**our**	b**oy**	f**i**ne	l**a**te	c**oa**t	n**ow**

Consonants

/p/	/b/	/f/	/v/	/t/	/d/	/k/	/g/	/θ/	/ð/	/tʃ/	/dʒ/
pill	**b**ook	**f**ace	**v**an	**t**ime	**d**og	**c**old	**g**o	**th**irty	**th**ey	**ch**oose	**j**eans
/s/	/z/	/ʃ/	/ʒ/	/m/	/n/	/ŋ/	/h/	/l/	/r/	/w/	/j/
say	**z**ero	**sh**op	u**s**ually	**m**e	**n**ow	si**ng**	**h**ot	**l**ate	**r**ed	**w**ent	**y**es

Irregular verbs

Infinitive	Past simple	Past participle
be	was /wɒz/ / were /wɜː/	been
become	became	become
blow	blew /bluː/	blown /bləʊn/
break /breɪk/	broke /brəʊk/	broken /ˈbrəʊkən/
bring /brɪŋ/	brought /brɔːt/	brought /brɔːt/
build /bɪld/	built /bɪlt/	built /bɪlt/
buy /baɪ/	bought /bɔːt/	bought /bɔːt/
catch /kætʃ/	caught /kɔːt/	caught /kɔːt/
choose /tʃuːz/	chose /tʃəʊz/	chosen /ˈtʃəʊzən/
come	came	come
cost	cost	cost
cut	cut	cut
deal /diːl/	dealt /delt/	dealt /delt/
do	did	done /dʌn/
draw /drɔː/	drew /druː/	drawn /drɔːn/
drink	drank	drunk
drive /draɪv/	drove /drəʊv/	driven /ˈdrɪvən/
eat /iːt/	ate /et/	eaten /ˈiːtən/
fall	fell	fallen
feel	felt	felt
find /faɪnd/	found /faʊnd/	found /faʊnd/
fly /flaɪ/	flew /fluː/	flown /fləʊn/
forget	forgot	forgotten
get	got	got
give /gɪv/	gave /geɪv/	given /ˈgɪvən/
go	went	gone /gɒn/
grow /grəʊ/	grew /gruː/	grown /grəʊn/
have /hæv/	had /hæd/	had /hæd/
hear /hɪə/	heard /hɜːd/	heard /hɜːd/
hide /haɪd/	hid /hɪd/	hidden /ˈhɪdn/
hit	hit	hit
hold /həʊld/	held	held
keep	kept	kept
know /nəʊ/	knew /njuː/	known /nəʊn/
lead /liːd/	led /led/	led /led/

Infinitive	Past simple	Past participle
learn /lɜːn/	learnt /lɜːnt/	learnt /lɜːnt/
leave /liːv/	left	left
lend	lent	lent
let	let	let
lose /luːz/	lost	lost
make	made	made
meet	met	met
pay /peɪ/	paid /peɪd/	paid /peɪd/
put	put	put
read /riːd/	read /red/	read /red/
ride /raɪd/	rode /rəʊd/	ridden /ˈrɪdən/
ring	rang	rung
run	ran	run
sink /sɪŋk/	sank /sæŋk/	sunk /sʌŋk/
say /seɪ/	said /sed/	said /sed/
see	saw /sɔː/	seen
sell	sold /səʊld/	sold /səʊld/
set	set	set
sing	sang	sung
sleep	slept	slept
speak /spiːk/	spoke /spəʊk/	spoken /ˈspəʊkən/
spend	spent	spent
stand	stood /stʊd/	stood /stʊd/
steal /stiːl/	stole /stəʊl/	stolen /ˈstəʊlən/
swim /swɪm/	swam /swæm/	swum /swʌm/
take /teɪk/	took /tʊk/	taken /ˈteɪkən/
teach /tiːtʃ/	taught /tɔːt/	taught /tɔːt/
tell	told /təʊld/	told /təʊld/
think	thought /θɔːt/	thought /θɔːt/
throw /θrəʊ/	threw /θruː/	thrown /θrəʊn/
understand	understood /ʌndəˈstʊd/	understood /ʌndəˈstʊd/
wake /weɪk/	woke /wəʊk/	woken /ˈwəʊkən/
wear /weə/	wore /wɔː/	worn /wɔːn/
win	won	won
write /raɪt/	wrote /rəʊt/	written /ˈrɪtən/

Acknowledgements

The publishers would like to thank the following teachers and ELT professionals for the invaluable feedback they have provided during the development of the B2 Student's book:

Andre Alipio, Brazil; Peggy Altpekin, Turkey and the Gulf; Natalia Bayrak, Russia; Kate Chomacki, UK; Leonor Corradi, Argentina; Sandra Aliotti, Argentina; Ludmila Gorodetskaya, Russia; Ludmila Kozhevnikova, Russia; Ralph Grayson, Peru; Steve Laslett, UK; Rabab Marouf, Syria; Christina Maurer Smolder, Australia; Mariusz Mirecki, Poland; Catherine Morley, Spain; Antonio Mota Cosano, Spain; Julian Oakley, UK; Litany Pires Ribeiro, Brazil; Elena Pro, Spain; Wayne Rimmer, Russia; Ruth Sánchez, Spain; Hilda Zubiria, Peru; Michael Ward, UK.

The publishers are grateful to the following contributors:

Gareth Boden: commissioned photography

Leon Chambers: audio recordings

Hilary Luckcock: picture research, commissioned photography

Rob Maidment and Sharp Focus Productions: video recordings, video stills

The authors and publishers acknowledge the following sources of copyright material and are grateful for the permissions granted. While every effort has been made, it has not always been possible to identify the sources of all the material used, or to trace all copyright holders. If any omissions are brought to our notice, we will be happy to include the appropriate acknowledgements on reprinting. The publisher has used its best endeavours to ensure that the URLs for external websites referred to in this book are correct and active at the time of going to press. However, the publisher has no responsibility for the websites and can make no guarantee that a site will remain live or that the content is or will remain appropriate.

The publishers are grateful to the following for permission to reproduce copyright photographs and material: The New Zealand Herald for the extract on p. 21 'Robert Hewitt's story of survival', *The New Zealand Herald* 19/03/2006; Encomium for the headline 'How I spent my prize money - Nigerian Idol Seasson III winner, Moses Obi' *Encomium* 01/11/2013; The extract on p. 44 '19 Lottery Winners who Blew it All', by Mandi Woodruff with permission from Business Insider; The Telegraph for the extract on p. 44 (Zsolt Pelardi) 'Brothers living in cave to inherit billions from lost grandmother', by Henry Samuel *The Telegraph* 02/12/2009; Hamilton Spectator for the extract on p. 44 (Sharon Tirabassi:)'Hamilton's penniless millionaire', by Molly Hayes *Hamilton Spectator* 21/03/2013.

Key: L = left, C = centre, R = right, T = top, B = bottom, b/g = background
p7: David Cooper via Getty Images; p8(BL): Corbis/Lance Iversen/San Francisco Chronicle; p8(BC): Alamy/Helen Sessions; p9(BL): Corbis/Louis Psihoyos; p9(BR): Getty Images; p10(L): SSPL via Getty Images; p10(b/g): Shutterstock/Clearviewstock; p11(T): Corbis/Rainer Holz; p11(C):Corbis/John Lund/Marc Romanelli/Blend Images; p11(B): Corbis/Heide Benser; p12(T): Getty/Julie Toy; p12(B): Shutterstock/Cameron Whitman; pp12/13(b/g): Getty/Jordan Siemens; p13: Shutterstock/Nadino; p16: Alamy/Cultura Creative; p17: Shutterstock/Yeko Photo Studio; p19: Getty/Justin Tallis/Stringer; p20(B): Getty/Georgette Douwma; p21(TC): Shutterstock/Joze Maucec; p21(BC): Shutterstock/Olgysha; p21(BR): Fairfax Media, New Zealand; p23: Getty/Betty Wiley; p25(T): Random House; p25(B): Thinkstock/Andrea Poole; p27(B): Alamy/Nigel Cattlin; p28(mountain): Shutterstock/Mogens Trolle; p28(forest): Shutterstock/Aleksander Bolbot; p28(beach): Alamy/Chris Pancewicz; p28(desert): Shutterstock/Keith Wheatley; p29: Shutterstock/Mogens Trolle; p31: Getty/Ben Stansall/Staff; p32(B): Shutterstock/Akos Nagy; p33(T): Corbis/Mika; p33(B): Shutterstock/Image Point Fr; p34(L): Corbis/Hero Images; p34(C): Alamy/UpperCut Images; p34(R): Shutterstock/Chad McDermott; p35(TL): Corbis/KCS Presse/Splash News; p35(TC): Boston Globe via Getty Images; p35(TR): Corbis/BPI/Marc Atkins; p35(CL): Getty Images; p35(CR): Corbis/Diego Azubel/epa; p35(BL): Corbis/Tim Clayton; p35(BR): Alamy/PCN Photography; p36(T): Penguin Group; pp36/37(B): Corbis/per-Anders Pettersson; p37(TR): Alamy/Richard Ellis; p37(BR): MLB Photos via Getty Images; p40: Shutterstock/Vito Zgonc; p41(R): Corbis/Sho Tamura/AFLO/Nippon News; p41(L): Corbis/Sean Burgess/Icon SMI; p43: Getty/Jean-Luc Luyssen; p44: Corbis/Michael A Keller; p46(T): Corbis/Sherrie Nickol; p46(B): Alamy/Blend Images; p47(TL): Getty/Digital Vision; p47(B): Corbis/John Carnemolla; p47(R): Corbis/Sebastian Kahnert/dpa; p47(BL): Alamy/Alaska Stock; p48: Shutterstock/Jack Q; p49(T): Shutterstock/Rostislav Glinsky; p49(C): Corbis/Alessandra Bianchi/Reuters; p49(B): Alamy/Nico Smit; p50(CL): Alamy/Derek Meijer; p50(CR): Shutterstock/Yuttasak Jannarong; p52(Toronto): Shutterstock/Lissandra Melo; p52(Katowice): Alamy/brimo; p52(Muscat): Alamy/image BROKER; p52(Eva): Getty/Image Source; p52(Nick): Shutterstock/Monkey Business Images; p52(Jean): Alamy/Radius Images; p52(BL): Alamy/Bill Cheyrou; p55: Getty/Louisa Gouliamaki/Stringer; p56(TR): istockphoto/Mlenny Photography; p56(TR)(bg): Alamy/Lourens Smak; p56(BR): Shutterstock/selfnouveau; p57(TL): Alamy/Lourens Smak; p57(B): Corbis/Will & Deni McIntyre; p59(CL): Alamy/Alaska Stock; p59(CR): istockphoto/Marcel C; 59(TR)(b/g): Shutterstock/fivepointsix; p59(B): Shutterstock/fivepointsix; p60(BL): Shutterstock/Aleksey Stemmer; p60(BR): Alamy/chefs; p61(TL): Alamy/Anna; p61(CL): Alamy/Huntstock Inc; p61(BL): Alamy/RGB Ventures/Superstock; p61(R): Alamy/Robert Harding Picture Library Ltd; p64(a): Alamy/Ellen McKnight; p64(b): Alamy/blickwinkel; p64(c): Thinkstock/tortoon; pp64/65(d): Alamy/epa European Pressphoto Agency creative account; p64(TR): Shutterstock/arek_malang; p131(A): Corbis/Konstantin Kokoshkin/Global Look; p131(B): Corbis/Sandro Di Carlo Darsa/es Photography; p131(C): Alamy/RIA Novosti; p156(T): Shutterstock/William Perugini; p156(B): Getty/Chris Ryan; p157: Alamy/Jeff Greenberg 5 of 6.

Commissioned photography by Sophie Clarke: p129(A,B,C).

We are grateful to Hertfordshire County Council for their help with the commissioned photography.

The following stills were taken on commission by Rob Maidment and Sharp Focus Productions for Cambridge University Press: pp14, 15, 26, 27(TC), 38, 39, 50(TR), 51, 62, 63.

Front cover photograph by Superstock/Cultura Ltd.

The publishers would like to thank the following illustrators: David Semple; Dusan Lakicevic; Gavin Reece; Jerome Mireault; Jo Goodberry; John (KJA Artists); Marie-Eve Tremblay; Mark Bird; Mark Duffin; Martin Sanders; Paul Williams; Roger Penwill; Sean (KJA Artists); Sean Sims.

Corpus Development of this publication has made use of the Cambridge English Corpus (CEC). The CEC is a computer database of contemporary spoken and written English, which currently stands at over one billion words. It includes British English, American English and other varieties of English. It also includes the Cambridge Learner Corpus, developed in collaboration with the University of Cambridge ESOL Examinations. Cambridge University Press has built up the CEC to provide evidence about language use that helps to produce better language teaching materials.

English Profile This product is informed by the English Vocabulary Profile, built as part of English Profile, a collaborative programme designed to enhance the learning, teaching and assessment of English worldwide. Its main funding partners are Cambridge University Press and Cambridge ESOL and its aim is to create a 'profile' for English linked to the Common European Framework of Reference for Languages (CEFR). English Profile outcomes, such as the English Vocabulary Profile, will provide detailed information about the language that learners can be expected to demonstrate at each CEFR level, offering a clear benchmark for learners' proficiency. For more information, please visit www.englishprofile.org

CALD The Cambridge Advanced Learner's Dictionary is the world's most widely used dictionary for learners of English. Including all the words and phrases that learners are likely to come across, it also has easy-to-understand definitions and example sentences to show how the word is used in context. The Cambridge Advanced Learner's Dictionary is available online at dictionary.cambridge.org. © Cambridge University Press, Third Edition, 2008 reproduced with permission.

This page is intentionally left blank

Cambridge English

EMPOWER

COMBO A
WORKBOOK
WITH ANSWERS

B2

Wayne Rimmer

Contents

				Page
Unit 1 Outstanding people				
1A	She is an inspiring woman	**Grammar** Review of tenses **Vocabulary** Character adjectives	**Pronunciation** Sound and spelling: *e*	4
1B	Are you finding it difficult?	**Grammar** Questions **Vocabulary** Trying and succeeding		5
1C	Don't touch the sandwiches!	**Everyday English** Explaining and checking understanding	**Pronunciation** Rapid speech	6
1D	I really missed my phone all day	**Reading** An article about technology and communication	**Writing skills** Organising an article **Writing** An article about means of transport	7
Reading and listening extension		**Reading** An article about an outstanding person	**Listening** The unluckiest man in the world	8
Review and extension		WORDPOWER *make*		9
Unit 2 Survival				
2A	It was getting late and I was lost	**Grammar** Narrative tenses **Vocabulary** Expressions with *get*	**Pronunciation** *had been*	10
2B	If it runs towards you, don't run away	**Grammar** Future time clauses and conditionals **Vocabulary** Animals and the environment		11
2C	What a great shot!	**Everyday English** Giving compliments and responding	**Pronunciation** Tone in question tags	12
2D	Make sure you know where you are going	**Reading** A leaflet on orienteering	**Writing skills** Organising guidelines in a leaflet **Writing** A leaflet about collecting mushrooms	13
Reading and listening extension		**Reading** An article about terrifying animals	**Listening** A news story about a missing person	14
Review and extension		WORDPOWER *face*		15
Unit 3 Talent				
3A	I'm not very good in the morning	**Grammar** Multi-word verbs **Vocabulary** Ability and achievement		16
3B	There are lots of good runners in Kenya	**Grammar** Present perfect simple and continuous **Vocabulary** Words connected with sport	**Pronunciation** Syllable stress	17
3C	Who should we invite?	**Everyday English** Making careful suggestions	**Pronunciation** Consonant sounds	18
3D	It doesn't really matter what sport people choose	**Reading** An article about a bar chart	**Writing skills** Describing data **Writing** An article about a bar chart	19
Reading and listening extension		**Reading** An article about Michael Johnson	**Listening** A conversation about school days	20
Review and extension		WORDPOWER *up*		21

	Unit 4 Life lessons			
4A	She's happier now than she used to be	**Grammar** used to and would **Vocabulary** Cause and result		22
4B	We weren't allowed to talk in class	**Grammar** Modality review 1; Obligation and permission **Vocabulary** Talking about difficulty	**Pronunciation** Sound and spelling: u	23
4C	Thank you, you've saved my life	**Everyday English** Expressing careful disagreement	**Pronunciation** Contrastive stress	24
4D	I'm good at communicating with people	**Reading** A job advertisement	**Writing skills** Giving a positive impression **Writing** An application email	25
	Reading and listening extension	**Reading** A blog post about unwritten rules	**Listening** Interviews with university graduates	26
	Review and extension	WORDPOWER as		27
	Unit 5 The natural world			
5A	You could live to be a hundred	**Grammar** Future probability **Vocabulary** Adjectives describing attitude	**Pronunciation** /θ/ and /ð/	28
5B	I'll be settling into my accommodation	**Grammar** Future perfect and future continuous **Vocabulary** The natural world		29
5C	We're not making enough money	**Everyday English** Discussing advantages and disadvantages	**Pronunciation** Tone groups	30
5D	The weather is getting more extreme	**Reading** An essay on population growth	**Writing skills** Reporting opinions **Writing** A for and against essay	31
	Reading and listening extension	**Reading** An article about optimistic people	**Listening** A conversation about an unusual supermarket	32
	Review and extension	WORDPOWER side		33
	Vox pop video			64
	Audioscripts			70
	Answer key			78

1A She is an inspiring woman

1 GRAMMAR Review of tenses

a Underline the correct words to complete the text.

The other day I was walking down the street when I ¹have seen / was seeing / saw Sam Carter, you know, the famous film director. I was really excited because he ²has been / is / was one of my favourite directors for ages and I watch his films all the time. 'What ³is he doing / does he do / has he done here?' I thought to myself. There was only one way to find out. Sam ⁴went / was going / has gone into a café, but I stopped him before he got inside and said, 'Hi, Sam!' He smiled at me and we started to talk outside. Me and Sam Carter! He always ⁵is looking / looks / has looked so serious in photos, but he's a really friendly guy. In the end, Sam ⁶invites / has invited / invited me for a coffee. Then he told me why he was in town. His film company ⁷made / have made / were making a new film and they ⁸have / have had / are having lots of new faces in it, just ordinary people, but they need some more. 'How about you?' Sam asked. ' ⁹Did you watch / Have you watched / Are you watching any of my films? Do you want to be in one?' I was so shocked I ¹⁰have dropped / was dropping / dropped my cup on the floor! The hot coffee went all over Sam; he screamed and ran outside. I lost my big chance!

b ▶1.1 Listen and check.

c Complete the sentences with the correct forms of the verbs in the box: present simple, present continuous, present perfect, past simple or past continuous.

| come | do | not finish | get | not have |
| meet | remember | think | ~~work~~ | write |

1 John _is working_ in a small marketing agency at the moment.
2 _____ you ever _____ anybody famous?
3 A What _____ you _____?
  B I'm a student.
4 Shakespeare _____ plays and poetry, and thousands of words in English come from them.
5 Our friends _____ for dinner, but had to cancel because they were ill.
6 Not many people _____ her well now.
7 He was rich and famous, but he _____ many friends.
8 The game _____ yet, there are five minutes to go.
9 Things _____ slowly _____ worse in the office now that Mrs Andrews has retired.
10 I _____ it's a great idea to go skiing while we've got some snow.

2 VOCABULARY Character adjectives

a Underline the correct words to complete the sentences.

1 Don't be so *motivated* / *stubborn* / *ambitious*! You know what I am saying makes sense.
2 I wanted him to help me, but he was very *unsympathetic* / *inspiring* / *passionate* and didn't want to do anything.
3 Margarita is a really *inspiring* / *sensitive* / *arrogant* woman and an example to everyone.
4 Susan is *motivated* / *optimistic* / *passionate* about basketball and trains every day.
5 He's rude and *sensitive* / *determined* / *arrogant* – he thinks he's better than everyone else.
6 If you are *motivated* / *self-confident* / *pessimistic*, you do things because you really want to do them.

b Complete the crossword puzzle.

(¹L O Y ²A L across; other cells blank)

→ Across
1 showing firm friendship or support
6 not listening to people's opinions or changing your mind
8 thinking about the future in a positive way

↓ Down
2 wanting to be successful
3 making a decision and not letting anyone stop you
4 easy to hurt or upset
5 people have a good opinion of you
7 having no experience and expecting things to be all right

3 PRONUNCIATION Sound and spelling: e

a How is the underlined letter *e* pronounced in each word in the box? Complete the table with the words.

conc<u>e</u>rned   d<u>e</u>sert   d<u>e</u>sire   d<u>e</u>ssert   h<u>e</u>lpful   id<u>e</u>ntity
pref<u>e</u>r   priz<u>e</u>s   r<u>e</u>vise   s<u>e</u>nsitive   s<u>e</u>rvice   sl<u>e</u>pt

Sound 1 /e/ (e.g. r*e*spected)	Sound 2 /ɪ/ (e.g. d*e*termined)	Sound 3 /ɜː/ (e.g. s*e*rve)
		concerned

b ▶1.2 Listen and check.

4

1B Are you finding it difficult?

1 GRAMMAR Questions

a Underline the correct words to complete the conversation.

FABIO Hi, there. [1]*You have / Have you got* five minutes?
GABRIELLA Sure, [2]*what / what did* you want to talk to me about?
FABIO Well, I'm doing a triathlon next month. [3]*Didn't / Weren't* you read my post?
GABRIELLA No, I haven't seen it. A triathlon, wow! [4]*What for? / For what?* It sounds really tough!
FABIO It's not easy, yeah, swimming, cycling, then running.
GABRIELLA [5]*What / Which* of those is the most difficult?
FABIO All of them! Er, [6]*weren't / didn't* you a good swimmer once?
GABRIELLA Yeah, once. What are you looking at me like [7]*that for / for that*?
FABIO Do you think [8]*could you / you could* coach me?
GABRIELLA I don't know [9]*whether / what* I've got enough time. [10]*Can / Shall* I think about it and phone you later?
FABIO No problem. That's great, I'll swim a lot faster with your help.
GABRIELLA Who [11]*knows / does know*? You might win!

b ▶1.3 Listen and check.

c Put the words in the correct order to make questions.
1 a / want / do / marathon / to / you / run ?
   Do you want to run a marathon?
2 to / this / going / is / do / why / she ?
   _____
3 the / register / who / competition / need to / for / doesn't ?
   _____
4 giving / why / our / aren't / tickets / they / us ?
   _____
5 of / which / to do / would you / the challenges / like ?
   _____
6 have / ever done / the most / you / difficult / what is / thing ?
   _____
7 for / did / hard training / what / this / we do / all ?
   _____
8 the / happened / of / what / at / end / the game ?
   _____
9 have / think we / of / a chance / you / do / winning ?
   _____
10 who / your / website / designed ?
   _____

2 VOCABULARY Trying and succeeding

a Complete the sentences with the phrases in the box. There is one extra phrase you do not need.

| succeed in | give up | keep to | keep it up |
| manage to | try out | ~~work out~~ |

1 Sandra likes to *work out* at the gym in her lunch break.
2 Simon wants to _____ a new recipe for lemon cake. 
3 We really need to _____ fast food. 
4 Charlie's kids told him to _____. 
5 The Smiths didn't _____ assemble their kitchen table. 
6 It won't be easy to _____ this diet. 

b Complete the sentences with the phrases in the box.

| give up | ~~have a go~~ | keep to | keep it up | make an effort |
| manage to | successfully complete | try out | work out |

1 I'd like to *have a go* at snowboarding, but I'm afraid of falling and breaking something.
2 To _____ the course, you need to pass all four modules.
3 If you _____ this training programme, you'll get back in shape very quickly.
4 I play tennis on Saturdays and I also _____ once or twice a week in a local gym.
5 My car is in the garage and I don't know if they will _____ repair it by Monday.
6 Fred went sailing with me twice and he's terrible at it, but he doesn't want to _____.
7 Your writing has improved a lot this semester so _____.
8 Would you like to _____ the new version of the software, sir?
9 I know Jade isn't interested in the project, but she could at least _____ to get involved.

5

1C Everyday English
Don't touch the sandwiches!

1 CONVERSATION SKILLS
Breaking off a conversation

a Tick (✓) the best way to break off the conversation.
1 Sorry, but _____ now.
   a ✓ I really must go
   b ☐ I have to finish
   c ☐ there's nothing else to say
2 _____ Speak to you soon.
   a ☐ I've nothing else to say.
   b ☐ Are we finished?
   c ☐ Got to go.
3 OK, _____.
   a ☐ I look forward to speaking to you
   b ☐ see you tomorrow
   c ☐ that's enough
4 _____, Irena.
   a ☐ Talk to you later
   b ☐ Tell me again
   c ☐ We'll speak about this
5 _____ Can you phone later?
   a ☐ This is not convenient.
   b ☐ Who's speaking?
   c ☐ Can't talk just now.
6 Well, I must _____.
   a ☐ leave
   b ☐ run
   c ☐ end
7 Bye, nice _____.
   a ☐ conversation
   b ☐ talking to you
   c ☐ day
8 Must be _____ now, but thanks for calling.
   a ☐ away
   b ☐ there
   c ☐ off

2 USEFUL LANGUAGE
Explaining and checking understanding

a Put the extracts in the correct order to explain how to take a good photograph.
   ☐ Always remember to keep still. If the camera moves about, you get a bad photo.
   ☐ Is that clear? Do you want me to explain any of this again?
   ☐ But whatever camera you buy, read the instructions carefully. Make sure you know what your camera can do. Have you got that?
   [1] You don't need to get a very expensive camera. These have a lot of functions you just don't need. Do you understand what I mean?
   ☐ Another thing to remember is to take your time. Only real professionals can take good photos in a hurry.
   ☐ When you take a photo, the most important thing is the light. Basically, the more light, the better, so choose the right time of the day and place. Do you get the idea?

b ▶ 1.4 Listen and check.

3 PRONUNCIATION Rapid speech

a ▶ 1.5 Listen. Tick (✓) the sentences where you hear the final /t/ of the underlined words.
1 ☐ I must go and see her soon.
2 ☐ The nurse said I must eat less bread.
3 ☐ We've got to have more help.
4 ☐ Sorry, you can't take one with you.
5 ☐ Haven't any of the people arrived?
6 ☐ Sarah said she didn't do the homework.
7 ☐ Claudia has been there, hasn't she?
8 ☐ The shop might open again.
9 ☐ We can't use our phones here.
10 ☐ Children mustn't play ball games.

6

1D Skills for Writing
I really missed my phone all day

1 READING

a Read the article. Are the sentences true or false?
1 The woman has the same opinion as most other people.
2 She has noticed an imbalance in communication.
3 The experiment involved the couple not communicating for a day.
4 It was a positive experience for them.
5 Technology has made us forget our priorities.
6 We don't need technology.

b Read the article again and tick (✓) the best ending for the sentences.
1 The purpose of the first paragraph is …
   a ✓ to explain the writer's motivation.
   b ☐ to compare different types of communication.
   c ☐ to introduce a theory about communication.
2 The main rule of the experiment was that they …
   a ☐ had to communicate as little as possible.
   b ☐ couldn't say anything to each other.
   c ☐ needed to explain things very simply.
3 The point about breakfast is that …
   a ☐ making meals involves technology.
   b ☐ it was an amusing situation.
   c ☐ everything was so simple.
4 The rest of the day showed that the experiment …
   a ☐ needed to continue for longer.
   b ☐ only worked until a friend got involved.
   c ☐ was not as easy as they thought.
5 She texted her husband to discuss …
   a ☐ plans for a party.
   b ☐ the effectiveness of the experiment.
   c ☐ her friend's communication problems.
6 The conclusion is that …
   a ☐ the experiment was mostly a failure.
   b ☐ technology has changed relationships between people.
   c ☐ speaking is still an effective kind of communication.

2 WRITING SKILLS
Organising an article

a Read the tips (1–8) for writing an article. Is the advice good or bad? Tick (✓) the correct box.

When you're writing an article …	Good	Bad
1 plan the structure of your article before you start writing it.	✓	
2 write the article in your own language first, then translate it.		
3 write short paragraphs with one or two sentences.		
4 include questions to engage the reader.		
5 use a dictionary to find interesting words and phrases.		
6 use linking words and expressions to join ideas.		
7 evaluate ideas – write what you think about them.		
8 check your writing when you have finished.		

Face-to-face texting

A lot of people think that technology brings people closer together, but I'm not so sure. People spend so much time texting and looking at computer screens that they hardly ever speak to one another. This made me think and I decided to do a little experiment.

One day my husband and I decided not to speak to each other at all. We could email, text, etc. but we couldn't actually communicate in words. So, at breakfast he sent me a text to ask if I wanted any more toast and I replied that I didn't but I wouldn't mind another cup of tea.

We both thought it was funny at first, but things got more complicated as the day went on. For example, a friend phoned me about a special party she was organising. I had to text my husband for about 20 minutes to discuss everything.

The whole thing made me appreciate that nothing can replace face-to-face communication – talking to each other. Communication may be easier because of technology, but people aren't machines. We sometimes forget that simple things are often the most important in life.

3 WRITING

a Imagine that for one week you had to walk or cycle to get around, rather than use a car or public transport. Write an article about your experience. Use the notes to help you, and your own ideas.

Introduction: how you usually get around, your feelings about walking / cycling vs. cars / public transport

Your experience: good things (exercise, see interesting things, cheaper)

Your experience: difficulties (takes longer, bad weather, dangerous?)

Evaluation: walking / cycling better in some situations, should use cars / public transport less

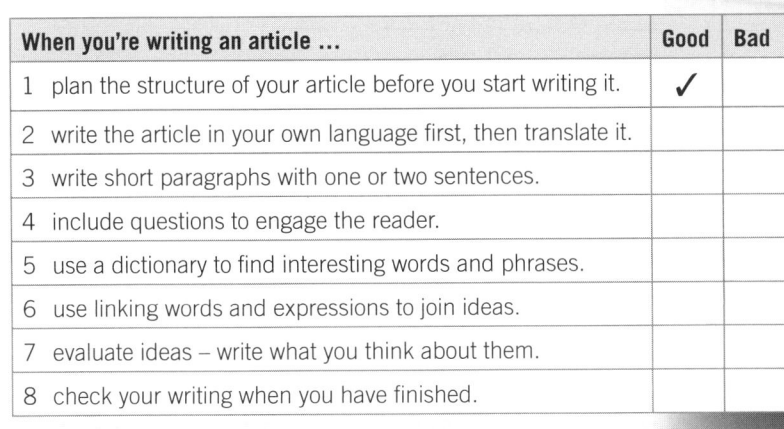

UNIT 1
Reading and listening extension

1 READING

a Read the article and tick (✓) the statement that matches Nick's attitude to his own body.
1. ☐ It's more difficult living without arms and legs now than when he was younger.
2. ☐ His physical condition means he is generally worried about trying new things.
3. ☐ He gets on with his life, even though he has no arms or legs.

b Read the article again and tick (✓) the correct answers.
1. Nick's parents knew he would be born without arms and legs.
   a ☐ true   b ✓ false   c ☐ doesn't say
2. Nick was sometimes unhappy when he was at school.
   a ☐ true   b ☐ false   c ☐ doesn't say
3. Nick could swim when he was just 18 months old.
   a ☐ true   b ☐ false   c ☐ doesn't say
4. Nick uses a mouse to operate a computer.
   a ☐ true   b ☐ false   c ☐ doesn't say
5. Nick uses the toe on his foot to do a sport.
   a ☐ true   b ☐ false   c ☐ doesn't say
6. The stadiums where Nick speaks are full.
   a ☐ true   b ☐ false   c ☐ doesn't say

c Write a paragraph about an outstanding person you know or have heard about, who has helped others. Remember to include:
- what the person does and why you are impressed by this
- any difficulties the person has had in their life
- how the person has helped other people.

Have you ever thought what it might be like to live just a single day without being able to use your hands or legs? This is everyday life for Nick Vujicic, who was born without any limbs. However, Nick doesn't let his condition stop him – he regularly takes part in sports, he has travelled all over the world and is also happily married with a young child. And unlike many able-bodied people, he can even swim and surf.

Before Nick Vujicic was born, his parents had no idea that he would go on to have any medical problems – none of the medical checks had ever shown a problem. However, when he was born, it was clear that his life would be different from that of other babies. Growing up would not be easy. His parents decided to send him to a normal school, where he would use a wheelchair, and where there were carers available to assist him. The experience was difficult, but Nick feels it was the best decision his parents could have made, because it would give him a sense of independence. Unsurprisingly, when he was at school, he sometimes felt depressed and lonely, and was sometimes bullied. But he always had the support of his loyal friends and family, and these people made him determined to overcome many problems. He even went on to study at university, where he was awarded a degree in Financial Planning and Real Estate.

What surprises many people is just how optimistic Nick can be, and how many different things he has managed to do. Much of this is down to his parents. His father put him in the water for the first time when he was 18 months, so that Nick would be self-confident enough to swim when he was older. He has one small foot which he can use to help him move around in the water. He is able to operate a computer by using the toe on this foot to type, something he learned to do when he was just six years old. And when he plays golf – yes, he even plays golf – he is able to hold the golf club under his chin.

A big part of Nick's life now is giving motivational talks. He travels around the world and has shared his inspiring story with millions of people, speaking to audiences in packed stadiums. Nick's message is that you should never give up, and that people should love themselves even when they fail.

2 LISTENING

a ▶1.6 Listen to Michael and Sarah talking about Frane Selak, who some people have called the unluckiest man in the world. Put the events in the order they happened.

- ☐ a plane crash
- ☐ a bus crash
- ☐ winning the lottery
- ☒1 a train crash
- ☐ a car accident
- ☐ being hit by a bus
- ☐ a car falling off a mountain

b Listen again and tick (✓) the correct answers.

1 What happened to Selak when he was in the train crash?
  a ☐ He was very seriously injured.
  b ☒ He had an injury.
  c ☐ He wasn't injured.

2 What is true about the plane crash that Selak survived?
  a ☐ Several other people also survived the crash.
  b ☐ He escaped through a door after it crashed.
  c ☐ He was helped by a problem with the plane.

3 What was the cause of the bus crash?
  a ☐ the weather
  b ☐ the speed of the bus
  c ☐ a technical problem with the bus

4 What is true about the first incident with a car that Selak had?
  a ☐ He was not driving the car when it developed a problem.
  b ☐ The car exploded just after he got out.
  c ☐ Flames came into the car from the engine while he was driving it.

5 Why did his car go off the side of the mountain in the later accident?
  a ☐ He was hit by a lorry.
  b ☐ He hit a tree and lost control.
  c ☐ He had to change direction to avoid a lorry.

6 Which of the following sentences is true about when Selak won the lottery?
  a ☐ He often played the lottery at that time.
  b ☐ He occasionally played the lottery at that time.
  c ☐ He had never played the lottery before.

7 What is Sarah's opinion of Selak's story?
  a ☐ She is sure it's true.
  b ☐ She is not sure if it's true.
  c ☐ She is sure it's untrue.

8 What does Michael say about Selak?
  a ☐ He thinks that Selak is probably telling the truth.
  b ☐ He thinks that Selak is wrong to invent stories.
  c ☐ He thinks it's strange that Selak gave away his lottery winnings.

c Write about a time when you were very lucky or unlucky. Use these questions to help you:
- What was the situation? What were you doing?
- Why were you lucky or unlucky?
- How did you feel?
- Was anybody else with you? How did he or she feel?
- Do you think this happens to a lot of people?

Review and extension

1 GRAMMAR

Tick (✓) the correct sentences. Correct the wrong sentences.

1 ☐ I write this letter to complain about the service.
   I am writing this letter to complain about the service.
2 ☐ Take any train, all of them go there.
3 ☐ I think I decided what to do.
4 ☐ Have you ever heard from her again afterwards?
5 ☐ I was having a shower when the water turned cold.
6 ☐ I don't know Tom. How is he?
7 ☐ Why you didn't tell me?
8 ☐ What is the currency in Thailand?

2 VOCABULARY

Tick (✓) the correct sentences. Correct the wrong sentences.

1 ☐ There are determined subjects everyone should study.
   There are certain subjects everyone should study.
2 ☐ Don't mention it to Laura. She's quite sensible about it.
3 ☐ The Mayor is very respective in this town.
4 ☐ The President gave a passionated speech about crime.
5 ☐ I'd love to have a go at diving.
6 ☐ I've got a plan and I'm going to keep to it.

3 WORDPOWER *make*

Match sentences 1–6 with responses a–f.

1 ☒a Shall we go by car or walk?
2 ☐ Why is it taking him such a long time to decide?
3 ☐ I'm really afraid of your dog.
4 ☐ Can't you just follow the instructions?
5 ☐ How can I stay in a place like this?
6 ☐ What are the flowers for?

a It makes no difference to me.
b He can never make up his mind.
c He's only trying to make friends with you.
d Just make the best of it.
e They don't make any sense.
f To make up for being late.

REVIEW YOUR PROGRESS

Look again at Review your progress on p.18 of the Student's Book. How well can you do these things now?

3 = very well   2 = well   1 = not so well

I CAN ...

talk about different forms of communication	☐
describe experiences in the present	☐
give and respond to opinions	☐
write a guide.	☐

9

2A It was getting late and I was lost

1 GRAMMAR Narrative tenses

a Underline the correct words to complete the sentences.
1. I *had* / *was having* / *had had* a quick shower and ran for the bus.
2. Sorry, when you called, I *spoke* / *was speaking* / *had spoken* to a customer.
3. By the time Jane arrived for dinner, everyone *left* / *had left* / *has left*.
4. He *set* / *had set* / *was setting* the watch to 00:00 and began to run the marathon.
5. The phone *had been* / *was* / *has been* ringing for about a minute when I answered it.
6. What *have you done* / *had you done* / *were you doing* in the garage all that time?
7. We *were buying* / *bought* / *had been buying* some fruit and went to the next shop.
8. Someone *had broken* / *was breaking* / *had been breaking* the window, but we didn't see who it was.
9. Hi, *had you waited* / *were you waiting* / *you waited* for me?
10. The manager stood up and *had made* / *was making* / *made* a speech.

b Complete the text with the correct forms of the words in brackets.

One evening some years ago, I ¹ _was thinking_ (think) about what to do when my friend Janice phoned. Janice was in a good mood because she ² _____ (finish) all her exams and she was free now. She ³ _____ (come) round and we decided to go for a walk. We ⁴ _____ (go) very far when we saw something very unusual inside the old building near the market. Years earlier the place ⁵ _____ (burn) down. No one knew how the fire ⁶ _____ (start), but ever since then the place had been empty. Anyway, in one of the windows we saw a face, the face of a young girl. She obviously ⁷ _____ (cry) because there were still tears on her face. It ⁸ _____ (get) dark by then, but we could still see her quite clearly. ⁹ _____ (you / see) that?' I whispered to Janice. We ¹⁰ _____ (never / be) in this building before and felt a bit scared, but we ¹¹ _____ (go) inside to find the girl. She ¹² _____ (wear) some really old clothes, they were dirty and smelt of smoke. 'I ¹³ _____ (get) out,' she said, crying again. 'I was too late!' We looked at each other and ¹⁴ _____ (run) all the way home. The place is now a restaurant and all our friends wonder why Janice and I will never go there with them!

c ▶ 2.1 Listen and check.

2 VOCABULARY Expressions with *get*

a Complete the sentences with the words in the box.

attention away ~~down~~ hold involved point rid swept

1. All this grey weather is really getting me _down_ and I feel quite depressed.
2. There isn't enough space. We need to get _____ of all this rubbish.
3. Simon is a very busy man. You can never get _____ of him when you need him.
4. The waves are really big, so be careful not to get _____ away.
5. Let's get straight to the _____ and not waste time.
6. To get the waiter's _____ in this restaurant you need to ring the bell.
7. It's been a very long term. I'd like to get _____ this summer – not sure where.
8. Don't get _____ in all Karen's problems. People will start blaming you.

b Complete the sentences under the pictures with the expressions in the box.

get through   ~~get to~~   get into trouble   get anywhere
get the feeling   get on my nerves

1. That looks fun. How do you _get to_ do this?
2. I'm not sure I'll _____ all this today. 
3. I _____ this will be over quickly. 
4. The company won't _____ with this new product. 
5. He might _____ walking into the house like that. 
6. All this crying is starting to _____. 

3 PRONUNCIATION *had been*

a ▶ 2.2 Listen to the sentences and tick (✓) the ones which include *had*.

Sentence 1 ✓   Sentence 6 ☐
Sentence 2 ☐   Sentence 7 ☐
Sentence 3 ☐   Sentence 8 ☐
Sentence 4 ☐   Sentence 9 ☐
Sentence 5 ☐   Sentence 10 ☐

2B If it runs towards you, don't run away

1 GRAMMAR
Future time clauses and conditionals

a Underline the correct words to complete the conversation.

MARIO Hi, Silvia. Are you coming camping with us?
SILVIA ¹*If / When* you still want me to, sure.
MARIO Great. It should be good fun ²*if / unless* the weather gets bad.
SILVIA ³*As long as / If* we get a couple of days of decent weather, I don't mind. What do I need to take?
MARIO The usual stuff. ⁴*When / If* I get home, I'll text you the list I've made just in case. You don't need to worry about food though. I've packed enough ⁵*in case / provided* you like pasta. That's the easiest thing to make.
SILVIA Fine. ⁶*If / In case* we run out of pasta, I'll take some tins and rice.
MARIO Good idea. ⁷*If / Provided* you want, bring some cards. We could play at night.
SILVIA I'll do that ⁸*when / provided* I don't forget. Text me tomorrow ⁹*as long as / as soon as* you get up.
MARIO OK. Remember to buy pepper spray because we might see bears.
SILVIA ¹⁰*If / Unless* I see a bear, I'll run all the way home!

b ▶2.3 Listen and check.

c Match 1–8 with a–h to make sentences.
1. [b] Phone your mum
2. [ ] It's perfectly safe
3. [ ] I like to go for a swim
4. [ ] It's ideal for a holiday
5. [ ] Take some sun cream
6. [ ] I'll go on the excursion
7. [ ] Don't go
8. [ ] You can go any time

a provided you like somewhere quiet.
b when you get there.
c unless you do something stupid.
d as long as you do.
e provided you tell me first.
f in case you need it.
g if you don't want to.
h if it's really warm.

2 VOCABULARY
Animals and the environment

a Find eight words about animals that match these clues.
1. a set of similar animals or plants
2. a living thing that is not a plant
3. the natural surroundings where we live
4. the place where an animal or plant naturally lives or grows
5. continue to live
6. animals or plants which could disappear without our help
7. uncommon and difficult to find
8. catch and kill animals for food or sport

A	E	N	V	I	R	O	N	M	E	N	T	E	U	L
K	N	C	R	H	B	E	X	U	D	D	O	X	K	E
X	D	T	S	G	T	I	C	U	L	E	T	C	E	L
S	A	D	S	N	P	C	L	N	Y	P	B	E	K	M
U	N	Q	E	T	B	S	R	I	A	R	N	P	Y	J
C	G	L	M	R	A	M	A	O	T	O	T	T	X	K
O	E	X	T	T	S	N	R	O	R	T	A	I	J	Z
C	R	E	A	T	U	R	E	Q	K	E	G	O	S	L
S	E	B	R	I	L	L	I	A	N	C	L	N	H	B
F	D	K	I	H	L	E	D	G	N	T	D	A	P	L
U	F	L	A	U	C	C	N	S	P	E	C	I	E	S
L	P	J	H	N	F	Y	Q	T	D	D	G	A	S	R
B	U	V	J	T	J	Z	Q	K	E	I	B	B	B	C
Y	Z	Z	I	I	R	M	P	H	A	B	I	T	A	T
S	K	T	S	X	A	Z	D	I	J	G	B	W	D	X

b Complete the text with the words in the box.

risk   creatures   environment   extinct
habitat   hunt   ~~shot~~   survive

Look at this ¹ _shot_ of a group of lions. This might be a very rare sight in the future. Lions are beautiful ² _____, but they are very much at ³ _____ in the modern world. The European lion has been ⁴ _____ for 2,000 years and now lions only ⁵ _____ in India and parts of Africa. People still ⁶ _____ lions and our damage to the ⁷ _____ is making it difficult for lions to find places to live and feed. We can help by protecting lions' natural ⁸ _____, which is the African savannah and the forests of Gujarat in India.

2C Everyday English
What a great shot!

1 CONVERSATION SKILLS Agreeing

a Complete the question tags in the conversations with the words in the box.

| aren't | could | did | don't | haven't | isn't | shall | wasn't |

MIKE It's a beautiful day!
LUCY It's lovely, ¹___isn't___ it? Why don't we go to the beach?
MIKE Yes, let's do that, ²_____ we?
LUCY We could drive but let's walk, we need the exercise.
MIKE We do, ³_____ we? I'll get my things.
LUCY Last time you forgot your towel.
MIKE I didn't have it with me, ⁴_____ I, so I borrowed yours. Anyway, let's go.

Later…
LUCY That was great, ⁵_____ it? I feel really hungry now.
MIKE Me too. This place looks good.
LUCY Yeah, we've been here before, ⁶_____ we? It does really good pizza.
MIKE That's right. Oh, I haven't got my wallet. You couldn't lend me some money, ⁷_____ you?
LUCY First a towel, then your wallet, you never remember anything.
MIKE Well, we're friends, ⁸_____ we? Let's go inside.

b ▶2.4 Listen and check.

2 USEFUL LANGUAGE
Giving compliments and responding

a Tick (✓) the best response for the sentences.
1 You're so good at singing.
   a ✓ Do you think so?
   b ☐ What do you think?
   c ☐ I'm glad you like it.
2 Your hair is amazing!
   a ☐ You're welcome.
   b ☐ I'm glad you like it.
   c ☐ I think so.
3 You really managed to get it just right.
   a ☐ Guess it's not bad.
   b ☐ Yes, I managed it.
   c ☐ Didn't I?
4 The colour is just perfect.
   a ☐ Yes, it is.
   b ☐ It's not bad, is it?
   c ☐ That's right, isn't it?
5 It's so tasty!
   a ☐ It's alright.
   b ☐ Not at all.
   c ☐ That's great.
6 That was a lovely present!
   a ☐ The same to you.
   b ☐ Yes, it was.
   c ☐ I'm glad you like it.

b ▶2.5 Listen and check.

3 PRONUNCIATION
Tone in question tags

a ▶2.6 Listen to the intonation in the questions. Is the speaker asking a real question or just checking information? Tick (✓) the correct box.

	Asking a question	Checking information
1 It was a great idea, wasn't it?		✓
2 You don't know where Oxford Street is, do you?		
3 That's obvious, isn't it?		
4 They just didn't understand, did they?		
5 He hasn't finished university yet, has he?		
6 I'm not on the team, am I?		
7 They will be able to do it, won't they?		
8 You've been there before, haven't you?		
9 She's forgotten all about it, hasn't she?		
10 She's not going to agree, is she?		

2D Skills for Writing
Make sure you know where you are going

1 READING

a Read the leaflet and <u>underline</u> the best heading for each section.

b Read the leaflet again. Are the sentences true or false?
1 It's easy to find an orienteering club.
2 Everyone should do the same training.
3 You should buy some running shoes.
4 You won't need to buy a map.
5 A fast start is important.
6 You should respect the environment you run through.
7 You only need a compass if you get lost.
8 The main thing is to have fun.

2 WRITING SKILLS
Organising guidelines in a leaflet

a Tick (✓) the best introduction to a leaflet about collecting mushrooms.
- a ☐ For centuries, people have collected mushrooms all over the world. The purpose of this leaflet is to discuss the reasons why mushroom picking is popular and to provide some practical suggestions to those who want to follow this tradition.
- b ☐ Collecting mushrooms might seem like a strange pastime, but it's very popular in many countries, especially in Eastern Europe. You need to be careful about which mushrooms you pick, but this is a fun way of spending time.
- c ☐ Why pick mushrooms? Many people think it is better to buy them from a supermarket, but there are advantages of getting them yourself provided that you don't pick the wrong ones!
- d ☐ One day I was at home when my friend phoned and suggested going out to the forest and picking some mushrooms. At first, I thought it was a crazy idea, but I went anyway and quite enjoyed it. Here is my advice for people who want to do the same.

3 WRITING

a Read the plan for the rest of the leaflet. Then complete the leaflet using these headings and notes.

Orienteering is a sport where you follow a route with a map and compass and try to get between the points as quickly as possible.

1 *Preparation / Getting into the sport / Advantages of orienteering*
- Orienteering is usually organised in forests. Just do a website search to find a club near you.

2 *Training / Dangers of forests / Running fast*
- You need to be fit to run around forests. If you're lucky, you might live near a forest, but most people will need to do some running in parks or on roads.
- Unless you are very fit already, start with fast walking and then build up to running.

3 *What you need / Expenses / Shopping for orienteering*
- You don't need to spend a lot of money on equipment, but a good pair of shoes is essential.
- You'll get a map at the course and you can borrow a compass as well.

4 *Win! / Be careful! / On the day*
- Set off slowly and save your energy.
- Don't damage any plants or trees. You are only there for the day, but the forest is there forever.
- You won't get lost provided you use your compass and go in a straight line.
- Enjoy yourself!

<u>Preparation</u>
1 When? (Autumn, mornings)
2 Where? (forests, near trees)
3 Need warm clothes, *good shoes/boots*
4 Check weather

<u>In the forest</u>
5 Be careful in forest – animals, accidents
6 Only pick mushrooms you know (*go with expert, use the Internet*)
7 Don't get lost!
8 Protect environment (litter)

<u>At home</u>
9 Eat or freeze mushrooms
10 Many recipes for mushrooms – *soup, pies, etc.*

UNIT 2
Reading and listening extension

1 READING

a Read an article about four animals and tick (✓) the things mentioned in the article.
1. ☐ an animal that lives in a different place from its ancestors
2. ☐ an animal that is becoming more and more widespread
3. ☐ an animal made famous in films
4. ☐ an animal that is now extinct
5. ☐ an animal that is important in many countries
6. ☐ an animal that lives close to a lot of humans

b Read the article again. Match the animals 1–4 with the descriptions a–d.
1. ☐ funnel-web spider
2. ☐ great white shark
3. ☐ Komodo dragon
4. ☐ tiger

a This animal has a special ability that allows it to follow other animals more easily.
b This animal may attack humans if they start living in the same environment.
c This animal has attacked humans by accident.
d This animal is often involved in attacks on younger people.

c Read the article again. Are the sentences true or false?
1. Great white sharks normally don't eat humans for food.
2. Attacks on humans from great white sharks are always fatal.
3. Tigers normally stay away from humans.
4. The total number of tigers is large and growing.
5. The Komodo dragon is larger than is typical for the group of animals it belongs to.
6. When hunting, the Komodo dragon generally kills the animal it attacks immediately.
7. Some aspects of the behaviour of the funnel-web spider are different from that of other spiders.
8. A bite from any type of funnel-web spider is equally serious.

d Write a paragraph about a special or unusual animal you know something about, or research one on the Internet. Remember to include:
- where it is found – its natural environment and habitat
- whether it is rare, at risk, protected, endangered or extinct
- how it gets its food
- any strategies it uses to find food, to survive or to get an advantage.

TERRIFYING ANIMALS

The animal kingdom is full of frightening creatures – animals you definitely wouldn't want to see close up, apart from perhaps in a zoo. Here are four very different – but equally terrifying – animals.

THE GREAT WHITE SHARK
Most people have heard of this animal – made famous in the *Jaws* films of the 1970s and 1980s. The great white shark has a reputation for being a killer, but perhaps unfairly, as these animals don't normally hunt humans – elephants kill more people than sharks do. But the problem for sports lovers is that a person swimming on top of a surfboard can, to a shark below the water, look very similar to a seal – its food of preference. If a great white shark does attack a human, the results are not always deadly – it's believed that sharks don't like the taste of humans.

THE KOMODO DRAGON
The Komodo dragon is a very large lizard – it can grow as long as three metres and weigh up to 70 kg. Experts think Komodo dragons are related to ancient lizards from Australia, but they're now found only in some islands in Indonesia. They are probably most famous for their unusual methods of killing. When hunting, they attack but don't kill the other animal right away. This is because they have a poisonous bite, so after attacking the animal, they follow it until it dies from the poison, a job made easier thanks to their excellent sense of smell. While attacks on humans are rare, they can and do happen.

THE FUNNEL-WEB SPIDER
Many people are afraid of spiders, although the vast majority are completely harmless to humans. But there are of course a number of species that can be dangerous, and the funnel-web spider is certainly among them. This spider's natural habitat is in the area around the Australian city of Sydney. It can be between one and five centimetres long, and is dark blue, brown or black. Unlike many other spiders, this species can be quite aggressive when it comes into contact with humans. When it attacks, it holds on tight and can bite several times. A bite from a Sydney funnel-web spider is extremely painful and can kill quickly, although bites from the females are less severe. Children are particularly at risk – 42% of attacks involve children rather than adults.

THE TIGER
The tiger is another animal that's probably familiar to most people, even though very few of us have ever seen one in the wild. Tigers have fascinated us since ancient times, and are very important to a number of cultures in Asia – they are the national animal of Bangladesh, India, Vietnam, Malaysia and South Korea. Tigers are the largest of all the cat species; they're fast runners, not to mention excellent swimmers. The good news is that they generally avoid contact with people, although they do attack, particularly when humans start to move into their natural habitats. It should also be added that tigers are now endangered and it's thought that humans play a very large role in this.

2 LISTENING

a ▶ 2.7 Listen to a news story and tick (✓) the correct answer.

1 ☐ A woman will probably recover after spending a week in her car.
2 ☐ A woman is currently in hospital after spending more than two weeks in her car.
3 ☐ A woman is very ill after spending over a month in her car.

b Listen again and tick (✓) the correct answers.

1 When Lone didn't come back by 9 pm, her family …
   a ☐ felt sure that something bad had happened.
   b ✓ were not immediately worried.
   c ☐ immediately called the police.
2 The police knew …
   a ☐ what time Lone had left work.
   b ☐ the route she had taken home.
   c ☐ where she had been planning to go after work.
3 The police think she turned from the main road …
   a ☐ because she had had a problem with her car.
   b ☐ because of the weather.
   c ☐ to have a break.
4 The police say Lone …
   a ☐ knew she would have to spend a long time in the car.
   b ☐ had turned the car round and driven back towards the main road.
   c ☐ wasn't able to move the car because the weather conditions had got worse.
5 The police …
   a ☐ have got all the details from Lone of what happened.
   b ☐ have only been able to speak to Lone for a short period of time.
   c ☐ haven't been able to visit the hospital yet.
6 The reason why nobody had found the car earlier was that …
   a ☐ few cars drive in that area at that time of year.
   b ☐ there was maintenance work, so no cars could reach the area.
   c ☐ the car was totally covered in snow.
7 The reason Lone survived might be that …
   a ☐ she had lots of food with her in the car.
   b ☐ she doesn't normally eat or drink much, so it was easier to adapt.
   c ☐ her body made a change to deal with the situation she was in.

c Write a conversation between two people discussing experiences of very bad weather conditions. Use these questions to help you:

- What kind of weather was it?
- Was the bad weather expected, or was it a surprise?
- What kinds of problems did it cause?
- How did they deal with the problems?

Review and extension

1 GRAMMAR

Tick (✓) the correct sentences. Correct the wrong sentences.

1 ☐ It's been a great week. On Tuesday, I have met an old friend.
   It's been a great week. On Tuesday, I met an old friend.
2 ☐ In those days, people spent more time outside.
3 ☐ I met Maria three years ago, when I had been a student.
4 ☐ She has been waiting for a chance and finally she got one.
5 ☐ Lucy had been seeing Michael for some time.
6 ☐ I'll watch it in case it's on TV.

2 VOCABULARY

Tick (✓) the correct sentences. Correct the wrong sentences.

1 ☐ The fish was too slippery for me to hold and it get away.
   The fish was too slippery for me to hold and it got away.
2 ☐ I can never get hold of an electrician when I need one.
3 ☐ I'm sorry, I got carried away and lost my temper.
4 ☐ People could do more to protect the enviroment.
5 ☐ Every year, hundreds of animal races just disappear.
6 ☐ The Siberian tiger could soon become extinguished.

3 WORDPOWER *face*

Complete the sentences with the expressions in the box.

can't face   face a difficult choice   ~~face fell~~
face the fact   face the music   say it to my face

1 Carmel really wanted the dress, but her ___face fell___ when she saw how expensive it was.
2 I have to _____ I'm not as young as I used to be.
3 John is so hypocritical. If he's unhappy with what I did, he should _____.
4 I _____ going to work today. I need a day off.
5 Is it better to get a job or go to university? Young people _____ nowadays.
6 My wife will be really angry, but I'm going to have to tell her the truth and _____.

REVIEW YOUR PROGRESS

Look again at Review your progress on p.30 of the Student's Book. How well can you do these things now?

3 = very well   2 = well   1 = not so well

I CAN …

discuss dangerous situations	☐
give advice on avoiding danger	☐
give and respond to compliments	☐
write guidelines in a leaflet.	☐

15

3A I'm not very good in the morning

1 GRAMMAR Multi-word verbs

a Underline the correct words to complete the text.

When I was at school, I didn't think I was good at anything. The other kids picked things ¹*out / in / up* really quickly but I didn't and everyone looked ²*down on / on down / down* me as some kind of loser. The only thing that interested me was cars and I spent ages in the garage with my mum's old car, checking ³*it out / out it / out*. My mum wasn't ⁴*at / by / into* cars at all though and she was tired of me going ⁵*in with / on about / with* them all the time. Anyway, one day there was a school trip. We set ⁶*by / off / on* by coach and were going down the road when the coach suddenly stopped. I thought we had run out ⁷*in / at / of* petrol, but the driver told us there was an engine problem and he would have to call the garage. I went to see for myself and quickly figured ⁸*out / by / through* what to do: I just needed to put back a cable. After ten minutes, the coach was on the road again. After that, everyone really looked ⁹*to me up / up to me / me up to* and I realised there was something I could do well. When I left school, I set ¹⁰*out / up / by* my own car repair business and now I'm doing really well.

b ▶3.1 Listen and check.

c Put the words in the correct order to make sentences and questions.
1 all / but / I / threw / sorry, / it / away .
  Sorry, but I threw it all away.
2 let / try / hardest and / your / us / down / don't .
  _____
3 fallen / not friends / out / I've / and we're / Tony / with .
  _____
4 away / you / like that / can't / get / mistakes / with .
  _____
5 yourself / for / it / and figure / go / out .
  _____
6 just / why / don't / it / you / out / try ?
  _____
7 made / Michelle / up / him / it / impress / to .
  _____
8 in / you / you're doing / what / to / believe / need .
  _____
9 up / anyone / a better / come / can / with / idea ?
  _____
10 picked / difficult, / I soon / it / but / is / French / up .
  _____

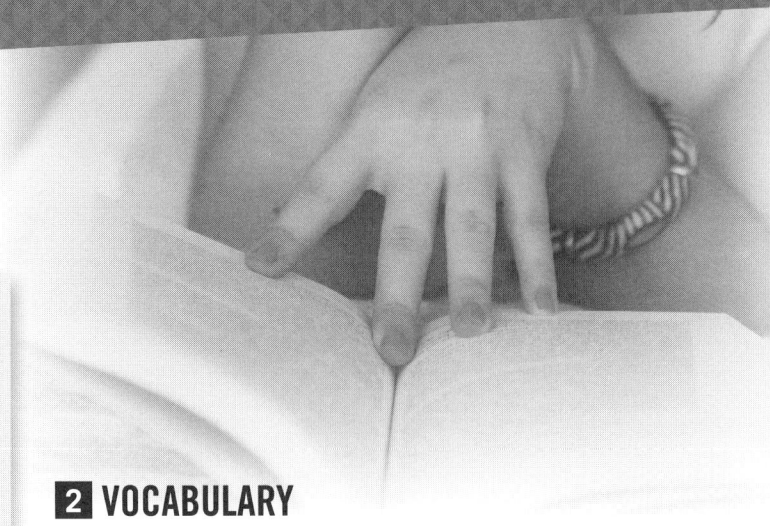

2 VOCABULARY Ability and achievement

a Underline the correct words to complete the conversation.
MARIANA Have you heard of this writer Daniel Kalder?
LOUIS Yes, I read *Strange Telescopes* some time ago. It's a ¹*talented / brilliant* book.
MARIANA I agree. Kalder has got this ²*ability / potential* to make a serious statement but make you laugh at the same time.
LOUIS It really is ³*able / outstanding*. I just wish I had some ⁴*ability / talent* for writing.
MARIANA Kalder is ⁵*successful / talented* because he's spent so many years improving his style. That kind of hard work is ⁶*successful / exceptional*.
LOUIS True. I don't think many people have heard of Kalder yet, but he has the ⁷*potential / brilliance* to be a really well-known writer.
MARIANA He is very ⁸*skilled / brilliant* at what he does, so good luck to him.

b ▶3.2 Listen and check.

c Correct the mistake in each sentence.
1 You need to have a talent to it.
  You need to have a talent for it.
2 Olympic athletes are all exceptional for their field.
  _____
3 She's quite successful by what she does.
  _____
4 I became quite skilled for the game.
  _____
5 The ability of running long distances is important.
  _____
6 Lesley is brilliant on most ball sports.
  _____
7 He has the potential of being world champion one day.
  _____
8 Carl Lewis was outstanding for the long jump.
  _____

3B There are lots of good runners in Kenya

1 GRAMMAR
Present perfect simple and continuous

a Underline the correct words to complete the sentences and questions.
1 *I've always loved* / *I always loved* baseball. It's my favourite sport.
2 *They've won* / *They won* the championship two years ago.
3 What *have you thought* / *did you think* of the match?
4 The players *have just arrived* / *just arrived* so the match can begin.
5 *I've been running* / *I was running* in the park when it happened.
6 Marina *has been doing* / *was doing* yoga since she was a teenager.
7 I have *completed* / *been completing* five marathons.
8 A Why is your shirt wet?
   B *I've run* / *I've been running*.
9 Joshua hasn't *played* / *been playing* tennis since he was at college.
10 Our judo trainer has *learned* / *been learning* Japanese for ten years.

b Complete the text with the correct forms of the verbs in brackets.

Samantha Hill ¹ *has just broken* (just / break) a new world record! Yesterday in Manchester she ² _____ (run) 100 metres backwards in 16.5 seconds. Samantha is only 17, but she ³ _____ (already / beat) all the best runners in the world. She ⁴ _____ (start) retro-running – running backwards – when she was 14 as a bit of fun, but soon she ⁵ _____ (win) lots of competitions and now she is the best in the world. We spoke to the new world-record holder.

'It's amazing! I ⁶ _____ (train) since January for this and I ⁷ _____ (try) three times to get this world record, but today was the day. I don't even have a trainer – I ⁸ _____ (look) for one for the past few years, but no one ⁹ _____ (contact) me yet. Sorry … I'm still very emotional. Excuse me …'

We could see she had been crying. Samantha then ran away – forwards – with tears running down her cheeks.

c ▶3.3 Listen and check.

2 VOCABULARY
Words connected with sport

a Read the definitions and write the words.
1 the act of winning a competition — *victory*
2 a person who is in charge of a sports game _____
3 shout approval or encouragement _____
4 people who watch a sports event _____
5 be in a competition for your country _____
6 an area for playing sports, especially football _____

b Complete the text with the correct forms of the words in brackets.

Everyone thinks that ¹ *professional* (profession) sportspeople get paid a lot of money to ² _____ (competitor), but this is not always true. The top ³ _____ (athletics) in smaller sports like handball, mountain running and women's cricket don't earn much money. Such sports are very ⁴ _____ (competition) and the athletes ⁵ _____ (training) hard, but even if they ⁶ _____ (representation) their country, they often can't make a living from their sport. Unfortunately, ⁷ _____ (victor) in ⁸ _____ (champion) and new world ⁹ _____ (recording) very often don't mean money, especially if the sport isn't popular on TV. But maybe this doesn't matter if the athletes enjoy what they do and spectators are happy to watch them perform and ¹⁰ _____ (cheerful) for them. Money isn't everything, after all.

c ▶3.4 Listen and check.

3 PRONUNCIATION Syllable stress

a ▶3.5 Listen to the conversation and underline the stressed syllables in the highlighted words.

ELENA I know you like ¹ath<u>le</u>tics, but do you ever take part in ²competitions?
DIMA Sometimes – in fact I'm going to ³compete in the national ⁴championships next weekend.
ELENA So you're almost a ⁵professional ⁶athlete then?
DIMA Not really, it's hardly a ⁷profession, but I do a lot of ⁸training and I'm hoping for a good ⁹performance. There'll be a lot of strong ¹⁰competitors and I'll have to ¹¹perform really well on the day.
ELENA So ¹²victory might be yours then and we'll welcome the ¹³victorious champion home?
DIMA Don't laugh, I might win!

3C Everyday English
Who should we invite?

1 USEFUL LANGUAGE Making careful suggestions; Keeping to the topic of the conversation

a Put the words in the correct order to make sentences and questions.
1 could / go / swimming / we / day / always / another .
   We could always go swimming another day.
2 thing / price / remember / another / to / is the .
   _____
3 stay / maybe / I / should / home / at / think / we .
   _____
4 idea / ask / think / to / a / don't you / it's / good ?
   _____
5 how / sound / we watch / does / on Sunday / a / film / if / it ?
   _____
6 to / that / but / easier / it'd / eat out / agree / be / don't you ?
   _____

b Correct the mistake in each sentence.
1 Don't you think it's a good idea take some food?
   Don't you think it's a good idea to take some food?
2 Anyway, as I was speaking, Tessa needs to decide.
   _____
3 Another idea might be for going the day before.
   _____
4 Just going to what I was saying before.
   _____
5 I thought maybe we could to invite Simon.
   _____
6 Of course, we could always checking on the Internet.
   _____
7 But don't you agree that it's be better to ask first?
   _____
8 So, to get back at Martin and his problems.
   _____

2 PRONUNCIATION Consonant sounds

a Decide which of the underlined letters has a voiced sound and which unvoiced. Write V (voiced) or U (unvoiced).
1 ga*m*e [V]   ca*m*e [U]   6 sa*v*e [ ]   sa*f*e [ ]
2 *b*each [ ]   *p*each [ ]   7 *p*ie [ ]   *b*uy [ ]
3 *f*erry [ ]   *v*ery [ ]   8 *p*ig [ ]   *p*ick [ ]
4 sim*p*le [ ] sym*b*ol [ ] 9 *p*ack [ ]   *b*ack [ ]
5 *g*irl [ ]   *c*url [ ]   10 ha*v*e a [ ] ha*v*e to [ ]

b ▶3.6 Listen and check.

18

3D Skills for Writing
It doesn't really matter what sport people choose

1 READING

a Look at the bar chart and read the article. Match paragraphs 1–5 with their functions a–e.
- a ☐ Adds extra information not shown in the data.
- b ☐ Interprets the data in more detail.
- c ☐ States the main conclusion you can draw from the data.
- d ☐ Outlines the issue that the data tries to answer.
- e ☐ Explains what the bar chart is about.

b Look at the bar chart and read the article again. Tick (✓) the correct answers.

1 The chart includes thirteen-year-olds from Scotland.
   a ✓ true   b ☐ false   c ☐ doesn't say
2 Each category is quite specific.
   a ☐ true   b ☐ false   c ☐ doesn't say
3 Older teenagers are doing more homework.
   a ☐ true   b ☐ false   c ☐ doesn't say
4 There is no great change between the figures for sport.
   a ☐ true   b ☐ false   c ☐ doesn't say
5 There are no major patterns in the data.
   a ☐ true   b ☐ false   c ☐ doesn't say
6 Face-to-face communication is better.
   a ☐ true   b ☐ false   c ☐ doesn't say
7 The article ends with a reference to the future.
   a ☐ true   b ☐ false   c ☐ doesn't say

2 WRITING SKILLS Describing data

a Look at the bar chart below and complete the sentences with the numbers and words in the box. There are two extra ones you do not need.

| 5 | ~~22~~ | 34 | 50 | decrease | increase | least | most |

1 About __22__ % of people today get their information from television.
2 In fact, nowadays _____ people follow sport on the Internet.
3 The _____ popular way of following sport is attending events.
4 There's an obvious _____ in reading newspapers.
5 There's about a _____ % drop in watching TV.
6 Only about _____ % of people now read about sport in newspapers.

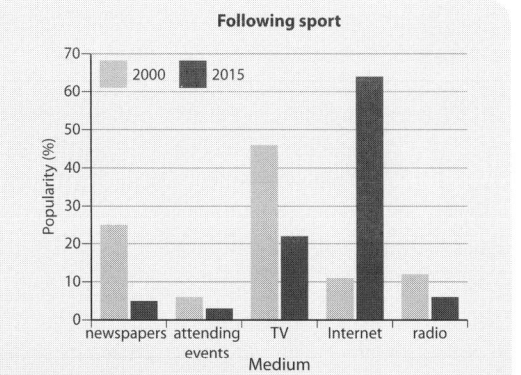

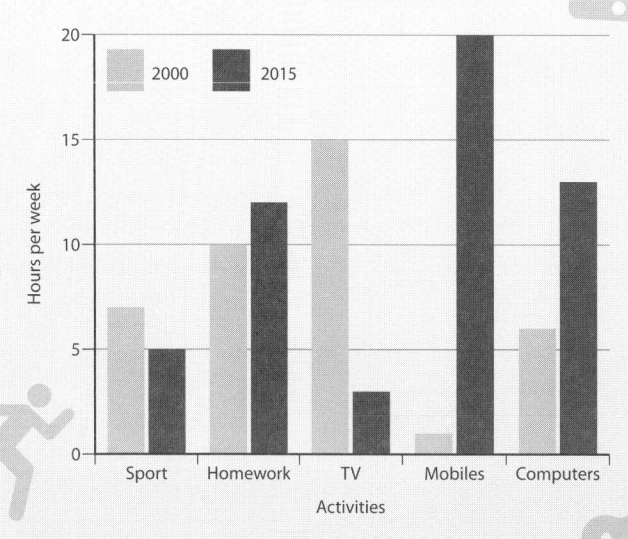

UK teenagers' out-of-school activities (2000, 2015)

1 School is a big part of teenagers' lives, but there are many ways of spending the rest of their time. Are teenagers basically the same these days, or are their needs and interests changing?

2 The bar chart looks at five different activities, quantified in hours per week, which teenagers do outside school. One point to note is that they are very broad categories: sport, for example, could include many activities.

3 As you can see, there are big differences in how teenagers spend their time. Sport and homework are comparable, but the other categories have changed considerably.

4 The most noticeable trend is from watching TV to using newer technologies, especially mobile phones. Mobiles were around in 2000, but they were much more primitive – you can watch films on your phone today.

5 It is important to remember that these are not the only ways teenagers spend their time, for example the chart doesn't mention meeting friends face to face. Things have changed a lot over the last 15 years, so it will be interesting to see what the future brings.

3 WRITING

a Look at the bar chart in 2a again. Then write an article about how people follow sport today. Use the notes to help you.

- newspapers – not free, 'old' news, people prefer to read online
- attending events – difficult, expensive
- TV – not so popular today, time may be inconvenient
- Internet – free instant news all the time
- radio – no pictures, best in car

Following sport (2000, 2015)

19

UNIT 3
Reading and listening extension

1 READING

a Read an article about one of the greatest runners of all time. Tick (✓) the statements that are true.

1. ☐ Johnson's running style was considered strange.
2. ☐ Johnson had the potential to win more than he did.
3. ☐ Johnson loved the attention he got from his success.
4. ☐ Johnson had a different style from Usain Bolt.

b Read the article again and tick (✓) the correct answers.

1. The fact that Michael Johnson's friends laughed at his running style made him want to run even faster.
   a ☐ true   b ☐ false
   c ✓ doesn't say

2. It was considered surprising that Johnson was able to win both the 200 and 400 metres.
   a ☐ true   b ☐ false
   c ☐ doesn't say

3. Johnson was the first person to win the 400 metres at one Olympic Games and then win it again in the following Olympic Games.
   a ☐ true   b ☐ false
   c ☐ doesn't say

4. Johnson was injured during the 1988 Olympic Games.
   a ☐ true   b ☐ false
   c ☐ doesn't say

5. Johnson didn't race in the 200 metres final at the Barcelona Olympics.
   a ☐ true   b ☐ false
   c ☐ doesn't say

6. Johnson often refused to speak to journalists when he was very famous.
   a ☐ true   b ☐ false
   c ☐ doesn't say

7. Johnson now says that he might have been more successful if he'd been as relaxed as Usain Bolt.
   a ☐ true   b ☐ false
   c ☐ doesn't say

8. Usain Bolt is currently trying to beat Johnson's 400 metres world record.
   a ☐ true   b ☐ false
   c ☐ doesn't say

c Write a paragraph about someone who has achieved a lot. Remember to include:
- some basic information about the person
- what he/she achieved and how he/she achieved it
- what other people think of him/her.

MICHAEL JOHNSON
THE MAN IN THE GOLDEN SHOES

Michael Johnson is one of the most successful professional athletes of all time. He won four Olympic gold medals and eight World Championship golds. People used to think that it was impossible for the same person to win the 200 metres as well as the 400 metres, but Johnson won both at the 1996 Atlanta Olympics, setting a new world record for both – 19.32 seconds and 43.49 seconds. He then went on to win the 400 metres again in Sydney in 2000 – the first time anyone had ever won the race in two Olympic Games in a row.

Anyone who saw Johnson perform in a race – even on TV – will remember him. He was an outstanding athlete, of course, but he also had a very unusual running style – short steps and a very straight back. When he was a child, his friends used to laugh at him because of how he ran. They said it was 'funny'. Johnson later said he'd found it funny too, but for another reason – the style was helping him to win all his races.

Many people think that with better luck, Johnson might have won even more medals – he was expected to be part of the team which went to the 1988 Olympics, but he had an injury and wasn't selected. Then in 1992, he got ill after eating in a restaurant two weeks before the start of the Barcelona Olympics. As a result, he didn't get as far as the final that he had been expected to win. In 1996, he avoided bad luck and the success story began.

Johnson's success made him rich and famous, and he was one of athletics' first 'superstars' – well known to the general public around the world, not just to athletics fans. But he didn't always seem to enjoy the fame – he sometimes sounded bad tempered in interviews and, with the golden shoes that he started to wear when racing, some called him arrogant. After retiring, he explained that he'd found the press attention annoying.

Johnson, of course, had a natural talent for running, but many people say that it was his ability to focus and his dedication to training that made him so exceptional. The big running star of today – Usain Bolt – is famously relaxed, almost the opposite of Johnson. Whether Johnson could have run faster if he'd taken Bolt's more relaxed approach is up for debate – Johnson has said he certainly doesn't think so.

Johnson has since lost his 200 metres world record to Bolt and has encouraged him to try the 400 metres as well, even though this might mean Johnson loses his world record. One thing is for sure – it would be fascinating to know who would win a race between Bolt and Johnson at his best.

Review and extension

1 GRAMMAR

Tick (✓) the correct sentences. Correct the wrong sentences.

1. ☐ The police are trying to check who stole the money.
   The police are trying to find out who stole the money.
2. ☐ He's too young. He's still growing up.
3. ☐ It's warm, put your jumper off.
4. ☐ We're finding a new secretary at the moment.
5. ☐ What ideas have you come up with then?
6. ☐ Sheila was just told about it and needs time to think.
7. ☐ Don't worry. I already sent the letter.
8. ☐ I'm waiting for you for ages!
9. ☐ I'm sure you've heard of the Loch Ness Monster.
10. ☐ I don't know. I didn't decide yet.

2 VOCABULARY

Tick (✓) the correct sentences. Correct the wrong sentences.

1. ☐ What are the secrets of success people?
   What are the secrets of successful people?
2. ☐ It's not able to get there by public transport.
3. ☐ No one doubts her capacity to get to the very top.
4. ☐ It was another fantastic performance by the Kenyan.
5. ☐ There is a training course for all new staff tomorrow.
6. ☐ Professional sport is very competitive.
7. ☐ What did the spectators think of the film?
8. ☐ And the footballers are just coming out on to the court.

3 WORDPOWER *up*

Read the sentences. Write *up* in the correct places.
1. We came early, but Greg turned late.
   We came early, but Greg turned up late.
2. If you don't know it, look it online.
3. She thought about it and decided not to bring the matter.
4. I used it all yesterday, so I went and bought some more.
5. We looked at the bill and added it again.
6. I went running with Sarah, but I couldn't keep with her.
7. I started to learn Spanish and picked it quite quickly.
8. He works so hard and I've always looked to him.

◉ REVIEW YOUR PROGRESS

Look again at Review your progress on p.42 of the Student's Book. How well can you do these things now?
3 = very well   2 = well   1 = not so well

I CAN ...

discuss ability and achievement	☐
discuss sports activities and issues	☐
make careful suggestions	☐
write a description of data.	☐

2 LISTENING

a ▶ 3.7 Listen to a conversation between two friends about their school days. Match names 1–5 with a–e to make sentences.

1. ☐ Julia   a argued with Mark.
2. ☐ Martina   b believed in Mark.
3. ☐ Mr Edwards   c was good at maths.
4. ☐ Sarah   d was good at sports.
5. ☐ Mrs Taylor   e was good at teaching grammar.

b Listen again. Look at the opinions. Who has these opinions – Tina, Mark, or both? Tick (✓) the correct box.

	Tina	Mark	Both Mark and Tina
1 Martina is likely to have a successful career now.			✓
2 Julia was very arrogant.			
3 Mr Edwards was a very good teacher.			
4 Sarah didn't have a good relationship with anybody at the school.			
5 Learning French at school wasn't very enjoyable.			
6 The school trips were not always educational.			

c Write a conversation between two people discussing their school days. Person A tells Person B about a subject they were good at. Person B tells Person A about a subject they were bad at. Use these questions to help you:
- Why was Person A good at their school subject?
- Was Person A naturally good at the school subject, or did he/she have to study hard?
- Why was Person B bad at their school subject?
- Is Person B good at this school subject now?

21

4A She's happier now than she used to be

1 GRAMMAR used to and would

a Underline the correct words to complete the sentences.
1. Yesterday my boss *used to come* / *came* to work late.
2. People *used to* / *would* believe the Sun went round the Earth.
3. One hundred years ago, it *couldn't* / *wouldn't* snow at all in winter.
4. We *lived* / *would live* in a small village before we moved to London.
5. I *would* / *used to* have a car, but I sold it.
6. That really *wasn't* / *didn't use to be* the best decision.
7. Julia *is used to working* / *used to work* in a shop before she started her own business.
8. Sam *got used to* / *used to* sharing a flat when he was a university student.
9. I *wasn't used to* / *got used to* getting up so early, so the first morning was a shock.
10. It took me a long time to *be* / *get* used to wearing a uniform at work.

b ▶ 4.1 Underline the correct words to complete the text. Then listen and check.

Richard Morgan lives on a boat on a canal in London. His life [1]*would* / *used to* / *was used to* be very different a few months ago. Richard [2]*left* / *used to leave* / *would leave* university in 2005 and got a great job in a law firm. It was interesting and well paid, but a very hard job. Richard [3]*was used to* / *got used to* / *used to* work 12–14 hours a day and sometimes he [4]*would sleep* / *was used to sleeping* / *got used to sleeping* at the office because it was so late. Richard [5]*used to realise* / *would realise* / *realised* that this kind of life was killing him. 'I [6]*was used to* / *used to* / *would* spending all my time at work. It was normal for me, that was the frightening thing,' Richard says.

On Sundays, Richard [7]*used to going* / *got used to go* / *would go* for a walk down the canal and he always enjoyed this. So one day, when he had had enough, he [8]*decided* / *used to decide* / *was used to deciding* to change his life completely. He gave up his job, bought a boat and said goodbye to his stressful life as a lawyer. 'It was a big contrast, I still haven't [9]*used to* / *got used to* / *been used to* the ducks waking me up, but it's a great life,' he says. 'My family and friends were shocked at first, but now they [10]*get used to visiting* / *are used to visiting* / *used to visiting* me on my boat and they know I'm happy.'

2 VOCABULARY Cause and result

a Correct the mistake in each sentence.
1. Smoking can lead in a lot of health problems.
   <u>Smoking can lead to a lot of health problems.</u>
2. No one knows what the affect was.
   _____
3. Shakespeare has had a big influence to the English language.
   _____
4. That's the main cause for the problem.
   _____
5. It could effect millions of people.
   _____
6. As a result from this, there is less money to spend.
   _____
7. The new law resulted of protests and demonstrations.
   _____
8. Generally, it's had a positive effect in people.
   _____

b Complete the text with the words in the box.

affect   as a result   ~~cause~~   effect   influence
is caused by   lead   result

What makes people unhappy? Some people think that the biggest [1] <u>cause</u> is stress, whether from work or the pressures of life. Certainly, lifestyle has a heavy [2]_____ on happiness. For example, a poor diet can [3]_____ your health and [4]_____ in illness and disease. There is also a view that unhappiness [5]_____ loneliness. Friends do have a positive [6]_____ on people's lives because friends provide support, entertainment and company. It's more complicated with family because relationships are often difficult and [7]_____ can [8]_____ to conflict and stress. This is clearly a difficult question to answer.

4B We weren't allowed to talk in class

1 GRAMMAR Modality review 1; Obligation and permission

a Complete the conversation with the responses in the box.

> I had to catch the 5:30 train.
> I'm tired during the day.
> No, I can work from home on Saturdays.
> No, I don't have to unless we have a deadline.
> ~~No, I had to get up at 5:00 this morning.~~
> Yes, I can find a seat on the train.
> Yes, the boss lets us have one day at home.
> You should speak to my boss!

JANE Are you feeling alright?
ALEX [1] No, I had to get up at 5:00 this morning.
JANE Why was that?
ALEX [2] _____
JANE Do you do this every morning?
ALEX [3] _____
JANE Is that the same for everyone?
ALEX [4] _____
JANE Are there any advantages of getting to work early?
ALEX [5] _____
JANE And the disadvantages?
ALEX [6] _____
JANE Do you need to work late as well?
ALEX [7] _____
JANE You need to ask for a pay rise.
ALEX [8] _____

b Underline the correct words to complete the sentences.
1. It's for girls only, so he *can / can't / has to* take part in the competition.
2. You really *can / ought to / don't have to* read this book about Jackie Chan. It's brilliant.
3. Louise *mustn't / doesn't have to / shouldn't* train hard because she is very talented.
4. You *mustn't / don't have to / are not allowed to* get nervous before the race.
5. The competition *was supposed / had / ought* to start at 7:00, but everyone was late.
6. Don't worry, you *mustn't / shouldn't / don't need to* train today.
7. My trainer made me *run / to run / running* ten kilometres.
8. During training we're not allowed *eat / to eat / eating* certain food.
9. Don't let them *beat / to beat / beating* you in the race!
10. They were *let / allowed to / forced to* train in the cold and rain, even though they didn't want to.

2 VOCABULARY Talking about difficulty

a Underline the correct adjectives for the pictures.

1. a(n) *arduous / strict* journey
2. *demanding / rigorous* testing 
3. *testing / strict* discipline 
4. a *tricky / punishing* training schedule 
5. *tough / punishing* standards 
6. a *tricky / gruelling* situation 

b Underline the correct words to complete the conversation.

KATE So what's it like to be a firefighter, William?
WILLIAM It's really [1] *straightforward / strict / tough*, much harder than I thought. The training is very [2] *rigorous / awkward / delicate* and the instructors really [3] *struggle / stretch / demand* us.
KATE But you've finished all the training?
WILLIAM Not yet. It's not so [4] *strict / demanding / straightforward* to become a firefighter. First, there's this [5] *arduous / straightforward / delicate* training schedule and then a [6] *gruelling / tricky / punishing* written test to do at the end.
KATE Well, you do like a [7] *struggle / punishment / challenge*! It sounds like a very [8] *rigorous / demanding / tricky* job.

c ▶4.2 Listen and check.

3 PRONUNCIATION Sound and spelling: u

a ▶4.3 Listen to the words in the box. How is the underlined letter *u* pronounced in each word? Complete the table with the words

> ~~umbrella~~   p<u>u</u>llover   <u>u</u>seless   s<u>u</u>gar   s<u>u</u>pper
> att<u>i</u>tude   res<u>u</u>lt   infl<u>u</u>ential   enth<u>u</u>siasm

Sound 1 /ʌ/ (e.g. c*u*p)	Sound 2 /ʊ/ (e.g. c*oo*k)	Sound 3 /uː/ or /juː/ (e.g. f*oo*d or c*u*be)
umbrella		

23

4C Everyday English
Thank you, you've saved my life

1 CONVERSATION SKILLS
Expressing careful disagreement

a Complete the table with the phrases.

> ~~I don't agree with you.~~
> Really, did you think so?
> That's just not true.
> Oh, I don't know.
> Maybe you're right, but …
> You can't really believe that.
> I know what you mean, but on the other hand …
> No way!
> I'm not sure about that.
> I'm afraid you're wrong there.

Careful disagreement	Direct disagreement
	I don't agree with you.

b Complete the conversation with the sentences in the box.

> I know what you mean, but on the other hand technology is so central.
> Really, do you think so?
> I'm not sure about that. They work very hard.
> ~~Oh, I don't know. Some things are improving.~~
> Maybe you're right, but teachers are not the real problem.

MARK Education is getting worse and worse in this country.
LILY ¹<u>Oh, I don't know. Some things are improving.</u>
MARK Like what? Teachers don't know what they are doing.
LILY ²_____
MARK Yes, but they need more training.
LILY ³_____
MARK True – kids just don't want to study.
LILY ⁴_____
MARK I do. They spend far too much time messing about on computers.
LILY ⁵_____
MARK Hang on, someone's texting me …

c ▶4.4 Listen and check.

2 PRONUNCIATION Contrastive stress

a ▶4.5 Listen to the exchanges. <u>Underline</u> the word in each response with the strongest stress.

1 **A** It was an absolutely terrible hotel! I never want to go there again.
  B Oh, I don't know. It wasn't that bad.
2 **A** I really didn't like that film. It was so boring!
  B Oh, I don't know. It wasn't that boring.
3 **A** I loved that restaurant. The menu was really original.
  B Oh, I don't know. It wasn't that original.
4 **A** Have you seen that new shop? It looks great!
  B Oh, I don't know. It doesn't look that great.
5 **A** I thought the meeting today was far too long.
  B Oh, I don't know. It wasn't that long.

4D Skills for Writing
I'm good at communicating with people

Do you want to learn new skills and live and work in a beautiful environment? Volunteer to work as a forest ranger in a variety of locations.

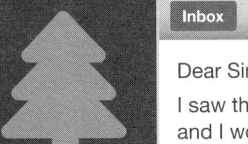

RESPONSIBILITIES
You will carry out work around the forest, protect the environment and provide help to visitors and the general public.

What we offer you
- free accommodation
- training and education
- the opportunity to learn new skills

QUALIFICATIONS
You care about the environment and you are a good team worker.
You have a basic knowledge of a subject related to the environment.
You have good oral and written communication skills in English.

Inbox

Dear Sir/Madam,

I saw the advertisement for volunteers to work as forest rangers and I would like to apply.

I am a student of environmental science in Milan and I have travelled to the UK many times, so my language skills are very strong. I am also a friendly and sociable person who enjoys working with people.

As a student, I am in an excellent position to explain the beauty of the forest to visitors and protect the forest from damage. I strongly believe that forests are essential for the world to survive and it is the work of rangers to make people aware of this.

In our studies we have field trips to forests to study their natural beauty. I also spend a lot of my free time outdoors exploring. I am sure this knowledge and enthusiasm would help me in this position.

I am confident that I can be an important part of your team. I am reliable and hardworking, so this challenge is ideal for me. When I finish university, I would like to work in this field, so this is a wonderful opportunity.

I am looking forward to hearing from you.

Yours faithfully,

Carla Rossini

---

1 READING

a Read the job advertisement and Carla's email. Then complete the summary with the words in the box.

| fluently | forests | outside | people |
| ranger (crossed out) | reliable | strong | student |

Carla wants to apply for a job as a ¹___ranger___. She is a ²_____ and speaks English ³_____. Carla loves spending time ⁴_____ in ⁵_____ and other interesting places. She likes to work with ⁶_____ and describes herself as ⁷_____. Carla sounds like a ⁸_____ candidate.

b Read the advertisement and the email again. Are the sentences true or false?
1 There are several places to work.
2 You don't need to find somewhere to live.
3 Carla has only been to the UK once.
4 She has finished her studies.
5 Carla thinks that the world will not survive without forests.
6 She has some practical experience.
7 Carla is worried about the responsibility.
8 In the future she wants to be a ranger.

2 WRITING SKILLS
Giving a positive impression

a Complete the sentences. Write one word in each gap.
1 I would ___like___ to apply to be a volunteer in the Winter Olympics.
2 I have always been interested _____ sport.
3 I would be more than happy to _____ up my free time.
4 I am in an excellent _____ to help athletes and visitors.
5 I _____ believe that sport brings people together.
6 I am looking _____ to hearing from you.

3 WRITING

a Read the advertisement and the plan. Then write an application email.

Do you want to be part of an international team and support the world's greatest sporting event? Become a volunteer in the Winter Olympics!

Responsibilities
There are a range of opportunities depending on your experience and skills, for example, preparing food for athletes, helping in the medical centre and interpreting.

What we offer you
- free accommodation
- tickets to events
- the opportunity to learn new skills

Qualifications
You are physically fit.
You have good oral and written communication skills in English.

✉ Apply for this job

★ Save to favourites

Plan
Paragraph 1: reason for writing
Paragraph 2: your background (work / education), your communication skills
Paragraph 3: your experience, personality and other skills, how these make you a good candidate
Paragraph 4: why you want to be a volunteer, your interest in sport / the Olympics
Paragraph 5: closing sentence

UNIT 4
Reading and listening extension

BLOG

Train journeys and unwritten rules
[posted by Paul, yesterday at 7:14 pm]

Well, I've just arrived home furious! Why? Something quite silly, really, but very annoying. As most of you reading probably know, I commute to work every day by train. Today, I was standing with a few other people by the train doors as the train pulled into the station, ready to get off. Now, what's supposed to happen is that people get off the train first, and then the people who are on the platform get on. It works better that way. It's the logical way to do it. But today, as soon as the doors opened, everyone on the platform started to get on and we had to kind of fight our way off. There was no advantage for the people on the platform to get on the train first – they still had to wait for everyone else to get off and it just created confusion, although I suppose they were worried about finding a seat on the train. While it was all happening, I got angry and ended up having an argument with someone getting on.

Anyway, it got me thinking. There's no rule anywhere that says that the people on the platform are supposed to wait and let the people on the train get off first. That's just what people do. It's an unwritten rule. So, what other unwritten rules can you think of? Do you ever see people breaking them? And if so, what do you do?

COMMENTS

Sam: yesterday at 7:43 pm
Exactly the same problem on the bus recently. Everyone tries to get on without letting anyone off first! It doesn't make sense – what's the hurry?

Irene: yesterday at 11:11 pm
Another unwritten rule? Waiting in a queue! There are some places, like clothes stores, where there are actually barriers that make you queue, but generally we just do it without thinking. And if someone jumps the queue? Generally I say nothing – at most I tend to give them a dirty look, but that's a waste of time because they're already in front of me in the queue and can't see my face!

Sara: today at 9:11 am
I suppose politely holding a door open for someone is another unwritten rule. It's funny because I think sometimes it would be easier for everyone not to – if the other person isn't directly behind you, you have to wait for them, and also they have to hurry so you're not waiting too long! But I always do it. If someone doesn't hold the door open for me, then I think they're rude.

Malc: today at 11:15 am
There's a rule that used to be unwritten but now it's actually written most of the time – tipping in a restaurant. In the past, you'd leave money if you thought the waiter or waitress was really good or you had a great time. Now unfortunately, most of the time they automatically add 10% or 15% to the bill and you have to tell them if you don't want to pay it. I preferred it the old way!

1 READING

a Read the blog post and comments. Tick (✓) the things which are <u>not</u> mentioned by the writer or in the comments.
   1 ☐ Behaviour on public transport
   2 ☐ Waiting in queues
   3 ☐ Doing something to be polite
   4 ☐ Regretting doing something rude
   5 ☐ Paying extra for something

b Read the blog and comments again. Write the names of the people.
   1 Which person mentions something they do that is pointless? _____
   2 Which person compares a past and present situation? _____
   3 Which person cannot understand a particular behaviour of other people? _____
   4 Which person describes a polite form of behaviour that may have a negative result? _____
   5 Which person suggests they may understand why rude behaviour took place? _____

c Read the blog and comments again. Are the sentences true or false?
   1 The original writer, Paul, was involved in a violent situation.
   2 Paul believes there needs to be a written rule to tell people to wait before getting on the train.
   3 Irene doesn't normally argue with queue jumpers.
   4 Sara doesn't expect people to hold the door open for her.
   5 Malc doesn't agree with restaurants automatically adding the tip to the bill.

d Write a paragraph about an 'unwritten rule' in your country or a country you know well. You should say:
   • what the rule is
   • whether you think the rule is necessary
   • what you or other people tend to do when the rule is broken.

26

2 LISTENING

a ▶4.6 Listen to some interviews with university graduates. How many are unhappy with their final results at university? Tick (✓) the correct answer.

1. ☐ one student
2. ☐ two students
3. ☐ three students
4. ☐ all four students

b Listen again and tick (✓) the correct answers.

1. What do we learn about Carl's summer?
   a. ☐ He studied a lot during this period.
   b. ☐ He had to buy a lot of books.
   c. ☐ He was very busy at work.
2. Why did Carl find his experience at university difficult?
   a. ☐ He had to pay a lot for the course.
   b. ☐ He has a young family to look after.
   c. ☐ He had to work and study at the same time.
3. Why did Samantha mention the fact she had three exams in two days?
   a. ☐ To show that this was really the only difficulty she had.
   b. ☐ Because she is unhappy with the university administration.
   c. ☐ To explain how little control you have over your timetable as a student.
4. Why didn't Luke get the final mark he wanted?
   a. ☐ He had a bad cold during the last two exams.
   b. ☐ His performance in his final two exams wasn't strong enough.
   c. ☐ He was seriously ill on the day of one exam.
5. Which of the following opinions does Luke express?
   a. ☐ He doesn't think that you should have to take an exam if you are seriously ill.
   b. ☐ He is sure he would have got the mark he wanted if he hadn't been ill.
   c. ☐ He thinks the university shouldn't consider illness only on the day of an exam.
6. Which of the following statements best matches something Jane says?
   a. ☐ You need to get a lot of sleep to succeed at university.
   b. ☐ It's harder to get a degree if you don't have friends or family who have studied at university.
   c. ☐ It's better to go to university before you're 40.
7. What do we learn about Jane's work situation?
   a. ☐ She hopes she will get a chance to progress more at work now that she's finished her course.
   b. ☐ She's found a new job since she finished her university course.
   c. ☐ She thinks it's going to be hard to find a job even though she now has a university degree.

c Write about an event that has had a big influence on your life. Use these questions to help you:
- What was the event?
- Why was it important for you?
- What was your life like before the event?
- How did your life change after the event?

Review and extension

1 GRAMMAR

Tick (✓) the correct sentences. Correct the wrong sentences.

1. ☐ My grandad use to work in a factory near Manchester.
   My grandad used to work in a factory near Manchester.
2. ☐ I would prefer to see my own doctor.
3. ☐ She used to living by herself now.
4. ☐ This can be the last time we come here.
5. ☐ I hope we could do this again some time.
6. ☐ If you want to apply, you should fill in this form.

2 VOCABULARY

Tick (✓) the correct sentences. Correct the wrong sentences.

1. ☐ Sunday is better cause I'm free then.
   Sunday is better because I'm free then.
2. ☐ I'm worried that it might effect my health.
3. ☐ It can lead to all sorts of problems.
4. ☐ My first teacher was very strickt.
5. ☐ She left because she felt she needed a new challenge.
6. ☐ Prisons are basically for punish criminals.

3 WORDPOWER *as*

Underline the correct words to complete the sentences.

1. The rules of the game are as *follows* / *a whole* – first, there must be at least five players.
2. It looks as *a matter of fact* / *if* we were all wrong.
3. There's a lot to do there as *far as* / *for* entertainment is concerned.
4. The competition was good for the country as *a whole* / *follows* – everyone benefited.
5. She's still on holiday as far as *I'm concerned* / *I know*.
6. The tickets are too expensive and as far as *I'm concerned* / *I know*, they're a waste of money.
7. More people live in the UK than in Spain. As *a whole* / *a matter of fact*, the population is 63 million.
8. Alice is lovely, but as *for* / *if* her husband – well, he's rather strange.

REVIEW YOUR PROGRESS

Look again at Review your progress on p.54 of the Student's Book. How well can you do these things now?
3 = very well   2 = well   1 = not so well

I CAN ...

discuss events that changed my life	☐
discuss and describe rules	☐
describe photos	☐
write an email to apply for work.	☐

27

5A You could live to be a hundred

1 GRAMMAR Future probability

a Underline the correct words to complete the conversation.

KATY Have you read this article, Josh? It says there's a good ¹*chance / doubt* our generation will live to be 150 years old!

JOSH Who knows, what it says ²*may / will* be true. But what evidence is there?

KATY Advances in medicine ³*might / will* certainly be a factor, and people ⁴*won't / couldn't* die from all sorts of diseases common today. Also, technology ⁵*will probably / probably will* make everyday life easier.

JOSH Fine, but I ⁶*don't suppose / doubt* if many people will want to live that long. It's ⁷*unlikely / sure* that it'll be much fun to be 150.

KATY The article says that we ⁸*may / will* well be able to work until that age. There's a good chance ⁹*of / that* machines ¹⁰*will / won't* do all the hard work, like washing and cleaning, so that we do easier tasks, like making phone calls.

JOSH Interesting. I'm ¹¹*probable / sure* there'll even be a special Olympics for people over 100!

KATY Yes, it's bound ¹²*to happen / happen*, so start training!

b ▶ 5.1 Listen and check.

c Tick (✓) the correct words to complete the sentences.

1 Pollution _____ well be even worse in the future if we don't start taking responsibility for it.
   a ✓ could   b ☐ will   c ☐ shall

2 I'm sure that it _____ happen in our lifetime.
   a ☐ may not   b ☐ mightn't   c ☐ won't

3 Online education _____ become more popular, but I doubt it.
   a ☐ might   b ☐ will   c ☐ can

4 The question is _____ we find a real solution to our energy problems?
   a ☐ may   b ☐ might   c ☐ will

5 Cinemas _____ go out of business in the next ten years.
   a ☐ probably will   b ☐ will probably
   c ☐ won't probably

6 It's unlikely _____ computers will replace teachers.
   a ☐ for   b ☐ if   c ☐ that

7 There's no _____ that they will stop printing books.
   a ☐ likely   b ☐ probability   c ☐ chance

8 I can't _____ that one day we will be able to choose the sex of our babies.
   a ☐ imagine   b ☐ suppose   c ☐ guess

9 Amanda is sure _____ do well in her exams next week.
   a ☐ to   b ☐ that   c ☐ of

10 Things at work are _____ to get better soon now we have a new manager.
   a ☐ possible   b ☐ bound   c ☐ probable

2 VOCABULARY Adjectives describing attitude

a Complete the words.

1 How r <u>e a l i s t i</u> c is it that we'll live to 150 years old? I mean will it actually happen?
2 Sam is always late handing in work. He's completely u_ r _ _ _ _ b _ e.
3 It was a t _ _ _ _ _ l _ _ s comment and he immediately felt sorry he'd said it.
4 Victoria is really a_ v _ _ _ r _ _ s. She just went on a trekking holiday in the Ecuadorian rainforest.
5 Wendy is quite s_ _p _ _ _ _ _ _ c , so you can tell her all your problems and she'll listen to you.
6 You can tell he's w_ _l -o _ _ _ _ _s _ d by looking at how tidy his desk is.

b Complete the sentences with the words in the box. There are four extra words you do not need.

adventurous ambitious cautious critical
disorganised irresponsible reliable ~~thoughtful~~
uncompetitive unrealistic unsympathetic

1 When he gets very <u>thoughtful</u> like this, it's like he's in a world of his own.
2 I've never known anyone so _____; you can never count on him.
3 It's dangerous out there; I guess it's better to be _____ and play safe.
4 Even if the place is a bit _____, we still know where everything is.
5 I may be _____ compared to everyone else, but I get there in the end.
6 That was a really _____ trip – you won't believe all the incredible things that happened.
7 The new waiter is obviously quite _____. I've never seen anyone work as hard as him.

3 PRONUNCIATION /θ/ and /ð/

a How are the underlined letters *th* pronounced in each word in the box? Complete the table with the words.

a<u>th</u>letic brea<u>th</u> brea<u>th</u>ing clo<u>th</u>es Ear<u>th</u> ei<u>th</u>er
lea<u>th</u>er leng<u>th</u> mon<u>th</u> <u>th</u>e ~~<u>th</u>ink~~ <u>th</u>ough

Sound 1 /θ/ (e.g. **th**ank)	Sound 2 /ð/ (e.g. **th**en)
think	

b ▶ 5.2 Listen and check.

5B I'll be settling into my accommodation

1 GRAMMAR Future perfect and future continuous

a Underline the correct words to complete the sentences.

1 Passengers, we will soon <u>be arriving</u> / have arrived at the base.
2 You can still help because they won't *have finished / be finishing* yet.
3 Will polar bears still *be living / have lived* in the Arctic in 50 years from now?
4 We'll *be feeding / have fed* the penguins at 2:30, so make sure you see that.
5 The team will *have completed / be completing* their project by 2025.
6 What will we *be achieving / have achieved* after we've spent all this money on research?
7 I don't think we'll *have driven / be driving* cars in 20 years' time.
8 Fleur will *be learning / have learned* a lot by the time she leaves Antarctica.
9 This time tomorrow, I'll *be getting / have got* ready to go.
10 Fleur will be glad to get back because she won't *be seeing / have seen* her friends for ages.

b Complete the text with the future continuous or future perfect forms of the verbs in the box.

change	complain	not cook	create	destroy
not eat	not fall	go	~~not live~~	replace	study
transport	turn	walk

Let's travel to the year 2049! We ¹ <u>won't be living</u> on Earth because pollution and wars ² _____ the old planet. Instead, planet Zeus will be our home. Giant space ships ³ _____ everyone and everything from Earth before it exploded in 2045. Zeus won't be a bad place to live and some things will go on as normal. Adults ⁴ _____ to work every morning. Children ⁵ _____ at school and old people ⁶ _____ about almost everything. Many things will be different, though. Because of the different atmosphere, our hair ⁷ _____ green – at least it ⁸ _____ out – and we ⁹ _____ about in space suits. Special tablets ¹⁰ _____ food and drink, so we ¹¹ _____ at all and we ¹² _____ out at restaurants. Yes, life ¹³ _____ quite a lot. Welcome to 2049, and the future we ¹⁴ _____ .

c ▶ 5.3 Listen and check.

2 VOCABULARY The natural world

a Match 1–8 with a–h to make sentences.

1 [f] Big companies don't seem to worry enough about the ecological
2 [ ] There was a spell of rough
3 [ ] There are people who think that climate
4 [ ] We make an effort to be environmentally
5 [ ] Just look at the river to see the effect of global
6 [ ] Protect the Earth's
7 [ ] We don't realise that we live in a fragile
8 [ ] I'm not sure that solar

a atmosphere by reducing greenhouse gases.
b change is some kind of myth.
c energy can fulfil all our needs.
d environment and everything is inter-connected.
e friendly, but it's not always practical.
f impact of what they do.
g warming on water levels.
h weather and we couldn't go out much.

b Complete the words.

1 Global w<u>arming</u> is changing animals' natural habitats.
2 Cities are trying to be more environmentally f_____. 
3 Obviously, s_____ energy is a cleaner alternative than oil and gas. 
4 Tourism can damage the desert's fragile e_____. 
5 The Earth's a_____ is being damaged by pollution. 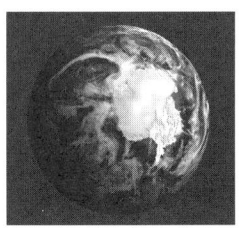
6 We can reduce our carbon f_____ by taking fewer flights. 
7 It would be crazy to go out to sea in this r_____ weather. 
8 Recent winters have been colder as a result of c_____ change. 
9 Just stop and think about the ecological i_____ of how we live. 

29

5C Everyday English
We're not making enough money

1 USEFUL LANGUAGE Discussing advantages and disadvantages

a Underline the correct prepositions to complete the text.

MAGDA You know, I'm seriously thinking ¹*at / of / on* taking this job in Paris.

ROMAN No wonder! One good thing ²*about / with / for* it is the higher salary. It's basically a promotion.

MAGDA True, but the trouble ³*by / for / with* that is more pressure and stress. A big disadvantage ⁴*by / of / for* the position I've been offered is that I'll have too much to do.

ROMAN Come on, one of the best things ⁵*about / with / of* you is how you respond to a challenge.

MAGDA I suppose so ... Another problem ⁶*at / from / with* this job offer is that I'll need to improve my French – and fast!

ROMAN No need to worry ⁷*for / at / about* that either. The advantage ⁸*for / of / at* living and working in a foreign country is that you learn the language quickly.

MAGDA You have an answer to everything!

ROMAN The only drawback ⁹*of / by / in* the job I can see is the size of the company. Do you really want to work in a company that big?

MAGDA If they pay me enough money, yes!

b ▶5.4 Listen and check.

2 CONVERSATION SKILLS Responding to an idea

a Complete the conversation with the responses in the box.

That's a great idea! You haven't made one for ages.
That's a possibility, although we might have to invite them in for a coffee or something.
Mm, I don't know about that. I'm not so keen on spicy food.
That's not a bad idea. They'd need to drive there, though.
Yes, that makes sense. I need the exercise!
It's an idea, I suppose. Where shall we go?
That might be worth a try and it's not far.

A How about eating out tonight for a change?
B ¹It's an idea, I suppose. Where shall we go?
A There's a new Thai place which has just opened.
B ²_____
A Well, there's the Italian just up the hill.
B ³_____
A Let's walk there, it's a lovely day.
B ⁴_____
A We could invite Amelia and Rob, too.
B ⁵_____
A Then they could give us a lift if we feel too lazy to walk back.
B ⁶_____
A So I've got an excuse to make one of your favourite lemon cakes.
B ⁷_____

b ▶5.5 Listen and check.

3 PRONUNCIATION Tone groups

a ▶5.6 Listen and underline the words which are stressed in the sentences.

1 The trouble is it could take a long time to get the money.
2 The good thing about it is we're not far away from the centre.
3 The problem is people are starting to talk about her.
4 The advantage is the price isn't very high.
5 The drawback is no one really knows what's going to happen.
6 The advantage is we can see a lot more of each other.
7 The trouble is I'm not sure I've got time to help him.
8 A definite disadvantage is it means selling the car.

30

5D Skills for Writing
The weather is getting more extreme

1 READING

a Read the essay and complete the summary with the words in the box.

| against | conclusion | crisis | essay |
| for | growth | manage | |

This [1] _essay_ discusses whether population [2]_____ is a problem. It considers arguments first [3]_____ and then [4]_____ the idea and comes to the [5]_____ that there won't be any major [6]_____ if we [7]_____ resources properly.

b Read the essay again. Are the sentences true or false?
1 Population growth is a new concern.
2 Food prices are rising.
3 The shortage of water is causing climate change.
4 There are ways of turning sea water into drinking water.
5 The real issue is how we share food and water.
6 The population will eventually stop growing.

People have always worried about population growth. It is a fact that the number of people on the planet is increasing very quickly, in some countries more than others. This puts a lot of pressure on the Earth's resources. But is population growth really leading to some kind of crisis?

Many people believe that we just cannot produce enough food to feed everyone. The increase in food prices is proof of this. Furthermore, clean drinking water is getting harder to find, a situation made worse by climate change.

However, not everyone agrees with these arguments. We could produce food much more efficiently with technology and in the same way we could treat sea water to produce an almost endless supply. Some people point out that our problem is distribution of resources, and this is something we can solve.

On balance, population growth is a concern, but there should be enough food and water for everyone if we become more efficient. My own view is that we can't do much about our increasing population, but we can make sure the way we produce and distribute resources is as effective and fair as possible.

2 WRITING SKILLS Reporting opinions

a Are the arguments for or against giving aid to developing countries? Tick (✓) the correct box.

	For	Against
1 Some of the aid is lost and stolen.		✓
2 Wealth needs to be shared around the world.		
3 We have a moral responsibility to help people in need.		
4 Giving aid makes developing countries dependent.		
5 We have problems to worry about in our own country.		
6 Developing countries could become important markets or partners.		
7 It will mean fewer problems with illegal immigration.		
8 There are always rich and poor countries – that's just how things are.		

3 WRITING

a Write an essay for and against the topic 'Richer countries should give aid to developing countries'.

Use the following structure:
- Introduction – state the problem
- Arguments for giving aid
- Arguments against giving aid
- Conclusion – summarise the main points and give your opinion.

31

UNIT 5
Reading and listening extension

1 READING

a Read an article about optimistic people. Tick (✓) the correct summary of the author's ideas.

1. ☐ It's usually impossible to be an optimist if you are not naturally positive.
2. ☐ Anyone can be optimistic if they choose to do the right things.
3. ☐ Highly optimistic people are more fun to be with.

b Read the article again. Match topics a–e with paragraphs 1–5.

a ☐ Choosing the right things to think about
b ☐ Having fantasies can help
c ☐ Keeping a record
d ☐ Rethinking your attitude to work
e ☐ Where you are, who you're with

c Read the article again. Are the sentences true or false?

1. Optimists are both healthier and more successful at work.
2. Optimists focus on the happiness that the money they earn can bring.
3. It's easier to think about bad things that have happened to you than good things.
4. The writer suggests that if you believe in something enough, you'll definitely achieve what you want.
5. The writer says that writing a diary can help you understand your negative thoughts better.
6. The article says that optimistic people are lucky because they are naturally very positive.

d Write a paragraph about staying positive. Remember to include:
- what makes you feel positive
- what makes you feel less positive
- what you do if you want to improve your mood.

THE *Five* SECRETS OF HIGHLY OPTIMISTIC PEOPLE

Everyone wants to be an optimist, but it's not always easy – most of us have to try hard to stay positive when life is getting us down. It's worth the effort, though, since optimists enjoy better health and even do better in their careers. Here are five things that optimists do that will help you look on the bright side, even when you're stuck in a traffic jam or forced to work on a Sunday.

The secret to optimism is that it doesn't just happen – highly optimistic people work hard to stay positive. If you want to do well in your career, improve your relationships and enjoy your life, it's time to give optimism a try.

1 Optimists are passionate about their work. Do you need to force yourself to go to work each morning? Optimists don't, because they jump out of bed excited to face the day. This is because optimists have chosen jobs and careers which they genuinely feel passionate about. If you can't remember the last time you enjoyed a day at work, it may be time to start looking for a new job. For optimists, work is more than just an opportunity to earn money. It's also an opportunity to learn, grow and do what they love.

2 Optimists focus on good things, even though it's not the easiest thing to do. According to Florida State University professor Roy F. Baumeister's article, 'Bad Is Stronger Than Good', it's much easier to focus on the rainy days than the sunny ones. In the paper, Baumeister says people are generally more upset about losing $50 than they are happy to gain $50. When you start to feel bad-tempered or depressed, think about something good from your day to balance out the negative emotions. Optimists make a choice to focus on the good in their life instead of thinking about the bad.

3 Optimists are more likely to be adventurous and ambitious. Believe in your dreams – and if you have big dreams, you might achieve better results. In 1997, researcher Gary McPherson studied child musicians, their goals and what happened to them later in life. He found that the child musicians who imagined themselves playing their instrument forever were more likely to become professional musicians in the future. So, while belief on its own isn't enough for success, a little dreaming certainly won't hurt.

4 Optimists keep a diary. As we've mentioned, it's very easy to focus on the negative events in our lives and ignore the positives. Keeping a diary can help you release negative energy and focus on positive emotions. During a few quiet moments in your morning or before bed, write a list of the positive moments from your day, or things you're trying to achieve in the future.

5 Optimists surround themselves with good feelings. If you surround yourself with supportive people and things you enjoy, you'll improve your mood and your day. The next time you lose concentration and start looking at videos of cats and dogs on the Internet, don't feel so bad about the time you wasted. Research has shown that spending a few moments doing something you enjoy will actually make you more productive.

2 LISTENING

a ▶5.7 Listen to a conversation between two friends, Andrew and Fran. Tick (✓) the things they talk about.

1. ☐ a new supermarket
2. ☐ packaging
3. ☐ air travel
4. ☐ food choices
5. ☐ technology
6. ☐ animal conservation

b Listen again and tick (✓) the correct answers.

1. What is unusual about the supermarket Fran mentions?
   a. ☐ It has very low prices compared to other supermarkets.
   b. ☐ It sells different kinds of things from most other supermarkets.
   c. ✓ The way it sells things is different from other supermarkets.

2. Why wouldn't Andrew want to use a supermarket like this?
   a. ☐ He thinks it would be too time-consuming to shop there.
   b. ☐ He doesn't want to have to use his car to get there.
   c. ☐ He thinks it's safer if products in the supermarket use packaging.

3. What problem does Fran not mention relating to the use of packaging?
   a. ☐ The pollution it causes when it is manufactured.
   b. ☐ The risk it causes to animals if they eat it.
   c. ☐ The fact that it is often not dealt with properly after it has been used.

4. What does Fran say about the idea of never using a car?
   a. ☐ It's probably impossible.
   b. ☐ It's difficult, but not impossible.
   c. ☐ Most people wouldn't agree to do it.

5. Which of the following statements is true about Andrew?
   a. ☐ He didn't know about the positive environmental impact of vegetarianism.
   b. ☐ He doesn't agree with people not eating meat.
   c. ☐ He is going to try to reduce the amount of meat he eats.

6. Which of the following statements best summarises Fran's views on the environment?
   a. ☐ We need to discuss what we can do to help the environment more often.
   b. ☐ People in general aren't doing enough to help the environment.
   c. ☐ People will probably start changing their behaviour when they realise how serious the situation is.

7. How hopeful is Fran about the chances of new technology solving environmental problems?
   a. ☐ very hopeful
   b. ☐ generally hopeful
   c. ☐ not very hopeful

c Write an email to a newspaper about a global problem that you are worried about. For example, 'Pollution is a major problem all over the world'. Remember to include:
- a short description of the problem
- why the problem worries you
- a possible solution to the problem
- why the problem might be difficult to solve.

Review and extension

1 GRAMMAR

Tick (✓) the correct sentences. Correct the wrong sentences.

1. ☐ Please write as soon as possible to me.
   Please write to me as soon as possible.
2. ☐ She probably has been waiting for this news all week.
3. ☐ Your trip to Antarctica won't certainly disappoint you.
4. ☐ It's not likely that she will persuade her parents.
5. ☐ What will we doing this time tomorrow?
6. ☐ We hope that the problem will have been solved.

2 VOCABULARY

Tick (✓) the correct sentences. Correct the wrong sentences.

1. ☐ We need someone responsable for this job.
   We need someone responsible for this job.
2. ☐ I always thought Tom was relyable until this latest incident.
3. ☐ I prefer to talk to Ann because she is more sympathetic.
4. ☐ If your desk is always tidy, you're probably organised well.
5. ☐ Pollution has led to the climate change in many areas.
6. ☐ Most things we do leave some kind of carbon footprint.

3 WORDPOWER side

Complete the sentences with the expressions in the box.

both sides   from side to side   nice side
~~side by side~~   to one side

1. Developed countries need to work _side by side_ to help the developing parts of the world.
2. Lisa seems a bit cold sometimes, but she definitely has her _____.
3. In this essay, you need to present _____ of the argument.
4. I was so scared – the boat was rocking _____ in the high winds.
5. The teacher took the child _____ and told her not to do it again.

REVIEW YOUR PROGRESS

Look again at Review your progress on p.66 of the Student's Book. How well can you do these things now?
3 = very well   2 = well   1 = not so well

I CAN ...

discuss possible future events	☐
prepare for a job interview	☐
discuss advantages and disadvantages	☐
write an argument for and against an idea.	☐

Vox pop video

Unit 1: Outstanding people

1a ◀ What are your hobbies?

a Watch video 1a. Match 1–6 with a–f to make sentences.

1 [b] Willemien likes   a watching sport.
2 [ ] Richard likes   b making music.
3 [ ] Hannah likes   c designing clothes.
4 [ ] Maddy likes   d playing music.
5 [ ] Heather likes   e drawing.
6 [ ] Maureen likes   f performing.

1b ◀ Which hobby would you like to try?

b Watch video 1b. <u>Underline</u> the correct words to complete the sentences.

1 Willemien *has never been / <u>used to go</u>* running.
2 Richard's hobby would involve *horses / travelling*.
3 Hannah wants to do *something with a friend / a water sport*.
4 Maddy would *not be / be* worried about how well she does this new hobby.
5 Maureen wants to try something that *is old fashioned / people think is impossible*.
6 Heather thinks she will try painting after she *does the housework / has finished working*.

1c ◀ How successful are you when you take up new activities?

c Watch video 1c and tick (✓) the correct answers.

1 Willemien has a _____ % success rate.
  a [ ] 0
  b [✓] 50
  c [ ] 100
2 Richard only takes up activities which he _____.
  a [ ] wants to do
  b [ ] will be good at
  c [ ] needs to do
3 Hannah would probably be good at _____.
  a [ ] tennis
  b [ ] photography
  c [ ] dancing
4 When she tries something new, Maddy often _____.
  a [ ] needs help
  b [ ] fails
  c [ ] loses interest
5 Heather has no problem with _____.
  a [ ] motivation
  b [ ] time
  c [ ] work

Unit 2: Survival

2a ◀ Which animal are you most scared of?

a Watch video 2a. <u>Underline</u> the correct words to complete the sentences.

1 Lauren has a very *unusual / <u>common</u>* fear.
2 Matt is not so scared of cows *on their own / in groups*.
3 Anna is afraid of animals which *can harm her / are wild*.
4 Martina *could have died / didn't really need to worry*.

2b ◀ What are some dangerous animals in a country you've visited?

b Watch video 2b and tick (✓) the correct answers.

1 Lauren was in danger because _____.
  a [✓] of her shoes
  b [ ] she was alone
  c [ ] she was on a mountain
2 Matt was worried about snakes because he was staying _____.
  a [ ] in a hotel
  b [ ] in a tent
  c [ ] on a boat
3 Anna was surprised that the local people _____.
  a [ ] helped her
  b [ ] weren't afraid
  c [ ] had no special method
4 Martina was afraid of this animal because _____.
  a [ ] of a disease it spread
  b [ ] her friends were scared of it
  c [ ] she was living in a foreign country
5 What happened showed that Martina's fear was _____.
  a [ ] reasonable
  b [ ] silly
  c [ ] selfish

Vox pop video

2c◀ If you got too close to a lion, what would you do?

c Watch video 2c. Match 1–5 with a–e to make sentences.
1 [e] Lauren
2 [ ] With a lion, Matt
3 [ ] With a shark, Matt
4 [ ] Anna
5 [ ] With a shark, Martina

a might attack the animal.
b wouldn't be able to scream.
c would lose consciousness.
d doesn't think climbing a tree would be effective.
e thinks it depends where it happened.

Unit 3: Talent

3a◀ Can you tell me about a popular sport and why people like it?

a Watch video 3a and tick (✓) the correct answers.
1 Eugenia talks about _____ marathons.
   a [ ] running
   b [ ] winning
   c [✓] watching
2 Eugenia thinks the best thing about marathons is that _____.
   a [ ] the pace is fast
   b [ ] they are open to everyone
   c [ ] you can run on the roads
3 James thinks that rugby is _____ football.
   a [ ] more complicated than
   b [ ] difficult to compare to
   c [ ] basically the same as
4 Guy thinks Formula 1 is _____.
   a [ ] dangerous
   b [ ] the most popular sport
   c [ ] full of surprises
5 Guy likes the fact that Formula 1 _____.
   a [ ] races last two days
   b [ ] goes over a longer period
   c [ ] drivers need good qualifications

3b◀ Are there any sports or activities you've been doing for a long time?

b Watch video 3b. Underline the correct words to complete the sentences.
1 Eugenia was good / bad / average at sport at school.
2 Eugenia didn't finish the marathon / run the marathon quickly.
3 James does athletics / plays football at university.
4 Guy thinks that talent / dedication is more important for success in sport.

3c◀ What do you think makes a successful athlete or sports person?

c Watch video 3c and tick (✓) the correct answers.
1 Eugenia thinks the most important thing is to _____.
   a [ ] have natural talent
   b [ ] do a range of sports
   c [✓] start young
2 When Eugenia was a girl, she wasn't very interested in _____.
   a [ ] music
   b [ ] sport
   c [ ] anything
3 James thinks success in sport is to do with _____.
   a [ ] how you think
   b [ ] how fit and strong you are
   c [ ] how you think and how strong you are
4 Guy thinks there are _____ factors involved.
   a [ ] lots of
   b [ ] not many
   c [ ] one or two
5 Guy is the only person to talk about _____.
   a [ ] training
   b [ ] diet
   c [ ] what sports people think about

Unit 4: Life lessons

4a◀ How would you spend the money if you suddenly had £1,000,000?

a Watch video 4a. Match 1–4 with a–d to make sentences.
1 [a] Ollie
2 [ ] Chris
3 [ ] John
4 [ ] Margaret

a names three things to spend money on.
b talks about a business opportunity.
c would spend the money on other people first.
d hasn't thought much about this before.

4b◀ How would having a lot of money change your life?

b Watch video 4b and tick (✓) the correct answers.
1 Ollie would feel _____.
   a [✓] more secure
   b [ ] lazier
   c [ ] less motivated
2 Chris would _____.
   a [ ] give up work
   b [ ] not work as hard
   c [ ] have more breaks
3 John thinks _____ would change.
   a [ ] everything
   b [ ] nothing
   c [ ] few things

65

4 Margaret likes _____.
   a ☐ saving up to buy something nice
   b ☐ spending a lot of money
   c ☐ the responsibility of having a lot of money

5 The only person to see a negative side to this question is _____.
   a ☐ Ollie
   b ☐ John
   c ☐ Margaret

4c◀ Do you think winning a lot of money would have a positive or a negative effect?

c Watch video 4c. <u>Underline</u> the correct words to complete the sentences.

1 Ollie concentrates on the *positive* / *negative* consequences.
2 Ollie would choose a job which was *well paid* / *enjoyable*.
3 At the moment, Chris feels *satisfied* / *dissatisfied*.
4 At first, John would feel he didn't *want* / *deserve* the money.
5 Margaret would *give the money away* / *make it a positive experience*.

Unit 5: Chance

5a◀ Would you rather live somewhere really hot or really cold?

a Watch video 5a and tick (✓) the correct answers.

1 Anna _____ of wearing jumpers.
   a ✓ doesn't like the idea
   b ☐ understands the benefits
   c ☐ doesn't see the point

2 Anna and Matt both _____ about clothes.
   a ☐ agree
   b ☐ talk
   c ☐ complain

3 Matt feels _____ in hot conditions.
   a ☐ relaxed
   b ☐ ill
   c ☐ uncomfortable

4 Maibritt would prefer somewhere _____.
   a ☐ cold
   b ☐ neither cold nor hot
   c ☐ hot

5 Martina mentions California as an example of a place where _____.
   a ☐ it gets too hot
   b ☐ the weather doesn't change much
   c ☐ the weather makes her uncomfortable

5b◀ Have you ever experienced extreme weather?

b Watch video 5b. Match 1–4 with a–d to make sentences.

1 [c] Anna has experienced
2 ☐ Matt has experienced
3 ☐ Maibritt has experienced
4 ☐ Martina has experienced

a being unprepared for extreme weather.
b travelling from a hot place to a cold one.
c nothing extraordinary.
d a feeling of helplessness.

5c◀ What do you know about Antarctica?

c Watch video 5c. <u>Underline</u> the correct words to complete the sentences.

1 Anna wouldn't live in Antarctica because there <u>aren't many people</u> / *are too many dangerous animals*.
2 Matt had *higher* / *lower* expectations of Antarctica before he spoke to someone who worked there.
3 Unlike Anna and Matt, Maibritt mentions *animal life* / *industry* / *the weather* in Antarctica.
4 Maibritt would live there for a few *weeks* / *months*.
5 What Martina knows about Antarctica comes from *the media* / *personal experience*.
6 Martina *can* / *can't* imagine being there.

This page is intentionally left blank

Audioscripts

Unit 1

▶ 1.1

The other day I was walking down the street when I saw Sam Carter, you know, the famous film director. I was really excited because he has been one of my favourite directors for ages and I watch his films all the time. 'What is he doing here?' I thought to myself. There was only one way to find out. Sam was going into a café, but I stopped him before he got inside and said, 'Hi, Sam!' He smiled at me and we started to talk outside. Me and Sam Carter! He always looks so serious in photos, but he's a really friendly guy. In the end, Sam invited me for a coffee. Then he told me why he was in town. His film company were making a new film and they have lots of new faces in it, just ordinary people, but they need some more. 'How about you?' Sam asked. 'Have you watched any of my films? Do you want to be in one?' I was so shocked I dropped my cup on the floor! The hot coffee went all over Sam; he screamed and ran outside. I lost my big chance!

▶ 1.2

/e/: desert, helpful, identity, sensitive, slept
/ɪ/: desire, prizes, revise
/ɜː/: concerned, dessert, prefer, service

▶ 1.3

FABIO Hi, there. Have you got five minutes?
GABRIELLA Sure, what did you want to talk to me about?
F Well, I'm doing a triathlon next month. Didn't you read my post?
G No, I haven't seen it. A triathlon, wow! What for? It sounds really tough!
F It's not easy, yeah, swimming, cycling, then running.
G Which of those is the most difficult?
F All of them! Er, weren't you a good swimmer once?
G Yeah, once. What are you looking at me like that for?
F Do you think you could coach me?
G I don't know whether I've got enough time. Can I think about it and phone you later?
F No problem. That's great, I'll swim a lot faster with your help.
G Who knows? You might win!

▶ 1.4

You don't need to get a very expensive camera. These have a lot of functions you just don't need. Do you understand what I mean?
But whatever camera you buy, read the instructions carefully. Make sure you know what your camera can do. Have you got that?
When you take a photo, the most important thing is the light. Basically, the more light, the better, so choose the right time of the day and place. Do you get the idea?
Always remember to keep still. If the camera moves about, you get a bad photo.
Another thing to remember is to take your time. Only real professionals can take good photos in a hurry. Is that clear? Do you want me to explain any of this again?

▶ 1.5

1 I must go and see her soon.
2 The nurse said I must eat less bread.
3 We've got to have more help.
4 Sorry, you can't take one with you.
5 Haven't any of the people arrived?
6 Sarah said she didn't do the homework.
7 Claudia has been there, hasn't she?
8 The shop might open again.
9 We can't use our phones here.
10 Children mustn't play ball games.

▶ 1.6

MICHAEL What are you reading?
SARAH An article about this guy … Frane … Selak.
M Who's that?
S He's a man from Croatia … They've called him the unluckiest man in the world. It looks like he's had an incredible life.
M Incredible, how?
S Well … It started in the 1960s. He says he was on a train that came off the tracks and crashed into a river – 17 people died, but he survived!
M Lucky.
S He did break his arm, though. Anyway, the next year he was flying on a small plane, which also crashed. The incredible thing was that as it was about to crash, one of the doors opened – the article says it had a fault – and he was sucked out. He landed safely but nobody on the plane survived!
M That's amazing!
S I know. Then a few years later, he was in a bus accident. There was heavy rain and the bus driver lost control on the wet roads and crashed into a river. He survived, although four people drowned. Then he was in a car that caught fire while he was driving it on the motorway. He managed to get out with seconds to spare before the fuel tank exploded.
M Wow. I don't think I ever want to travel with this guy …
S Yeah, but that's not all … He got hit by a bus in 1995.
M But he was OK?
S Of course. And then the year after, he had another car crash. He was driving on a road in the mountains and he had to turn out of the way of a lorry coming in the other direction. So then his car went off the edge of the mountain and when it hit the bottom, it exploded. But Selak was OK because he'd managed to jump out just before it went over the edge. He was found holding onto a tree near the side of the road.
M That's just amazing.
S Yeah.
M But I don't know whether he's unlucky or extremely lucky.
S Well, the story's not finished yet. Apparently in 2003, he won the Croatian lottery. With the first ticket he'd ever bought.
M No way!
S That's what it says! So in the end, he's definitely lucky, not unlucky!
M Or maybe a mix of both.
S Yeah, maybe.
M Do you think it's true, all that? Can all these things really happen to one person?
S I don't know. I don't think everyone believes it. And it says there's no record of any plane crash in Croatia in the 1960s.
M Mmm.
S So I don't know. What do you think?
M Well, it's a fascinating story, so I want to believe it's true. But who knows?
S Yeah.
M What did he do with the lottery money, by the way?
S Well, first he bought himself a luxury home, that kind of thing. But then he decided to sell it and give most of the money away to friends and family because he thought that money couldn't buy happiness.
M Well, it could all be true then. Anyone who would give away all their lottery winnings must be a really good person, so they wouldn't make up a story like that. I think that's quite inspiring.

Unit 2

▶ 2.1

One evening some years ago, I was thinking about what to do when my friend Janice phoned. Janice was in a good mood because she had finished all her exams and she was free now. She came round and we decided to go for a walk. We hadn't gone very far when we saw something very unusual inside the old building near the market. Years earlier the place burnt down. No one knew how the fire had started, but ever since then the place had been empty. Anyway, in one of the windows we saw a face, the face of a young girl. She obviously had been crying because there were still tears on her face. It was getting dark by then, but we could still see her quite clearly. 'Did you see that?' I whispered to Janice. We had never been in this building before and felt a bit scared, but we went inside to find the girl. She was wearing some really old clothes, they were dirty and smelt of smoke. 'I didn't get out.' she said, crying again. 'I was too late!' We looked at each other and ran all the way home. The place is now a restaurant and all our friends wonder why Janice and I will never go there with them!

▶ 2.2

1 We'd been swimming in the sea.
2 The fishing had been fun and I wanted to try it again.
3 I'm not sure what's been decided.
4 What had they been doing on the journey?
5 He's been told to rest at home.
6 Tim had been learning to ride a bike.
7 She'd never been climbing in her life.
8 Her husband's been worrying about her.
9 The expedition had been my idea at first.
10 The TV people had been trying to interview him.

▶ 2.3

MARIO Hi, Silvia. Are you coming camping with us?
SILVIA If you still want me to, sure.
M Great. It should be good fun unless the weather gets bad.
S As long as we get a couple of days of decent weather, I don't mind. What do I need to take?
M The usual stuff. When I get home, I'll text you the list I've made just in case. You don't need to worry about food though. I've packed enough provided you like pasta. That's the easiest thing to make.
S Fine. In case we run out of pasta, I'll take some tins and rice.
M Good idea. If you want, bring some cards. We could play at night.
S I'll do that provided I don't forget. Text me tomorrow as soon as you get up.
M OK. Remember to buy pepper spray because we might see bears.
S If I see a bear, I'll run all the way home!

▶ 2.4

MIKE It's a beautiful day!
LUCY It's lovely, isn't it? Why don't we go to the beach?
M Yes, let's do that, shall we?
L We could drive but let's walk, we need the exercise.
M We do, don't we? I'll get my things.
L Last time you forgot your towel.
M I didn't have it with me, did I, so I borrowed yours. Anyway, let's go.
…
L That was great, wasn't it? I feel really hungry now.
M Me too. This place looks good.
L Yeah, we've been here before, haven't we? It does really good pizza.
M That's right. Oh, I haven't got my wallet. You couldn't lend me some money, could you?
L First a towel, then your wallet, you never remember anything.
M Well, we're friends, aren't we? Let's go inside.

▶ 2.5

1 A You're so good at singing.
  B Do you think so?
2 A Your hair is amazing!
  B I'm glad you like it.
3 A You really managed to get it just right.
  B Guess it's not bad.
4 A The colour is just perfect.
  B It's not bad, is it?
5 A It's so tasty!
  B It's alright.
6 A That was a lovely present!
  B I'm glad you like it.

70

Audioscripts

2.6
1 It was a great idea, wasn't it?
2 You don't know where Oxford Street is, do you?
3 That's obvious, isn't it?
4 They just didn't understand, did they?
5 He hasn't finished university yet, has he?
6 I'm not on the team, am I?
7 They will be able to do it, won't they?
8 You've been there before, haven't you?
9 She's forgotten all about it, hasn't she?
10 She's not going to agree, is she?

2.7
ANNOUNCER A woman reported missing over a month ago has been found safe. Alicia Lone, who works as an assistant chef, was expected home shortly after 9 pm. Her family were not initially concerned, as she had recently got involved with a sports club and often went there after work, before returning home. But when she still hadn't returned by early next morning, they contacted the police. Here's Michael Sanderson with the full report.

REPORTER When Alicia Lone went missing last month, it seemed a complete mystery. Police knew she had left work by car after her shift finished at 8:15 pm, but after that, there were no signs of her at all. But last Saturday, the mystery was solved – Lone was found alive inside her car, under over a metre of snow, where she had managed to survive for 15 days. Police say there was no problem with her car and that it seems she got into trouble when she decided, because of the heavy snow, to take a different route. But she didn't get very far – her car was found two kilometres from the main road. Police say she stopped soon after turning because the road was so bad, but was unable to turn back. She then spent a night in the car expecting to be able to get home the next day, but the snow got heavier and her car got totally stuck. Earlier, I spoke to Police Sergeant Granger, who gave us further details.

POLICE OFFICER We've only been able to speak very briefly to Lone at the hospital so we don't know the full story yet. But it seems she turned up that road to try and avoid some of the snow on the main road, but obviously she didn't get anywhere and became stuck. Very few cars travel around this area during this winter period unless there's some special reason, so she wasn't able to get anyone's attention to ask for help. So nobody saw her until yesterday, when a road maintenance crew went up there to check on the state of the road and saw the car under all the snow. When they found her, she was basically asleep. We could see she'd been eating in the car, that she had had some food in there, and she'd also been drinking melted snow. But it's incredible that she was able to survive with so little, really.

R Did they give you any idea at the hospital *how* she survived?

PO Well when she was found, her body temperature was very low and they think that because of the cold weather her body just kind of went to sleep, like some animals do in winter. She couldn't speak or walk when we found her. So the doctors say her body basically went to sleep, so she didn't need much food or water. But she was sure lucky.

R And do they think she's going to be OK?

PO They think so, yes – she's going to make a full recovery. She has a few problems now but she should get over them fine.

R So, it's a story with a happy ending, fortunately. We'll give you more news on Lone's condition as soon as we get it.

Unit 3

3.1
When I was at school, I didn't think I was good at anything. The other kids picked things up really quickly, but I didn't and everyone looked down on me as some kind of loser. The only thing that interested me was cars and I spent ages in the garage with my mum's old car looking into how it worked. My mum wasn't into cars at all though and she was tired of me going on about them all the time. Anyway, one day there was a school trip. We set off by coach and were going down the road when the coach suddenly stopped. I thought we had run out of petrol, but the driver told us there was an engine problem and he would have to call the garage. I went to see for myself and quickly figured out what to do: I just needed to put back a cable. After ten minutes, the coach was on the road again. After that, everyone looked up to me and I realised there was something I could do well. When I left school, I set up my own car repair business and now I'm doing really well.

3.2
MARIANA Have you heard of this writer Daniel Kalder?
LOUIS Yes, I read *Strange Telescopes* some time ago. It's a brilliant book.
M I agree. Kalder has got this ability to make a serious statement but make you laugh at the same time.
L It really is outstanding. I just wish I had some talent for writing.
M Kalder is successful because he's spent so many years improving his style. That kind of hard work is exceptional.
L True. I don't think many people have heard of Kalder yet, but he has the potential to be a really well-known writer.
M He is very skilled at what he does, so good luck to him.

3.3
Samantha Hill has just broken a new world record! Yesterday in Manchester she ran 100 metres backwards in 16.5 seconds. Samantha is only 17, but she has already beaten all the best runners in the world. She started retro-running – running backwards – when she was 14 as a bit of fun, but soon she was winning lots of competitions and now she is the best in the world. We spoke to the new world-record holder. 'It's amazing! I've been training since January for this and I've tried three times to get this world record, but today was the day. It doesn't even have a trainer – I've been looking for one for the past few years, but no one has contacted me yet. Sorry ... I'm still very emotional. Excuse me ...' We could see she had been crying. Samantha then ran away – forwards – with tears running down her cheeks.

3.4
Everyone thinks that professional sportspeople get paid a lot of money to compete, but this is not always true. The top athletes in smaller sports like handball, mountain running and women's cricket don't earn much money. Such sports are very competitive and the athletes train hard, but even if they represent their country, they often can't make a living from their sport. Unfortunately, victory in championships and new world records very often don't mean money, especially if the sport isn't popular on TV. But maybe this doesn't matter if the athletes enjoy what they do and spectators are happy to watch them perform and cheer for them. Money isn't everything, after all.

3.5
ELENA I know you like athletics, but do you ever take part in competitions?
DIMA Sometimes – in fact I'm going to compete in the national championships next weekend.
E So you're almost a professional athlete then?
D Not really, it's hardly a profession but I do a lot of training and I'm hoping for a good performance. There'll be a lot of strong competitors and I'll have to perform really well on the day.
E So victory might be yours then and we'll welcome the victorious champion home?
D Don't laugh, I might win!

3.6
1 game	came	6 save	safe
2 beach	peach	7 pie	buy
3 ferry	very	8 pig	pick
4 simple	symbol	9 pack	back
5 girl	curl	10 have a	have to

3.7
TINA Mark, I've been going through my cupboards and I've found some old photos from school. Do you want to look at them?
MARK Yeah, of course!
T Right, well, here they are. There are quite a lot ... Look at this one – do you remember her? Martina?
M Oh yes, Martina ... I do. She was brilliant at maths, and all those kinds of subjects, wasn't she?
T Yeah. I wonder what happened to her. Probably became an economist or something.
M Yeah, I reckon. Anyway, I bet she's really successful, whatever she's doing.
T Oh, and here's one with you in it.
M Yeah, but who's that with me? I don't recognise her.
T That's Julia. Don't you remember her?
M Oh yeah, Julia, of course. She was really talented at sports, wasn't she?
T Yeah, tennis especially, I think.
M Well, I haven't seen her for years anyway.
T No. I know that she lives in Madrid now.
M Really?
T Yeah, she's been living there a while. I don't know what she's doing there though.
M I didn't like her much, to be honest. She was always a bit too ... competitive.
T Yeah, I know what you mean. She wasn't exactly my favourite person either. We both represented the school at athletics, but she was always so arrogant. Like she thought she was better than us. And she was always going on about tennis!
M I wouldn't say she was arrogant, to be honest. Just too competitive for me!
T Hmm, look at this one. It's me, you, and Mr Edwards.
M The best teacher ever!
T Hmm, I'm not sure about that.
M Come on! I thought he was exceptional. He was the only one that made me really feel I had any ability. You know what I was like at school. But he really seemed to believe in me.
T Well, I suppose what I liked was that he made us try out new things. But anyway … have a look at this one.
M Oh, that's Sarah.
T Yeah. Didn't you fall out with her once? At a party or something?
M More than once, I think. We didn't get on – in fact, nobody at school got on with her.
T Right, let's move on quickly then! Here, look – it's our whole class, after a French lesson, isn't it?
M Yeah, look, there's the French teacher.
T Mrs Taylor.
M Yep. That classroom doesn't bring back too many happy memories, I have to say.
T But you have a talent for languages. You speak French really well now, and Spanish.
M Yeah, but the lessons at school weren't for me. I'd say that Mrs Taylor was skilled at teaching grammar, but we never did any kind of speaking practice, did we? I can only actually speak French because I've been to France so often, and spoken to real French people.
T Mmm. Ah well, here's the last one. A school trip, but I don't know where we were.
M No, nor do I. That just looks like a field in the middle of nowhere! I used to love the school trips, though.
T Yeah, they were fun. And sometimes we even learned something!
M Sometimes, yeah. But most of the time it was just good to get out of school for a day!

Unit 4

4.1
Richard Morgan lives on a boat on a canal in London. His life used to be very different a few months ago. Richard left university in 2005 and got a great job in a law firm. It was interesting and well paid, but a very hard job. Richard used to work 12 to 14 hours a day and sometimes he would sleep at the office because it was so late. Richard realised that this kind of life was killing him. 'I was used to spending all my time at work, it was normal for me, that was the frightening thing,' Richard says. On Sundays Richard would go for a walk down the canal and he always enjoyed this. So one day, when he had had enough, he decided to change his life completely.

71

He gave up his job, bought a boat and said goodbye to his stressful life as a lawyer. 'It was a big contrast, I still haven't got used to the ducks waking me up, but it's a great life,' he says. 'My family and friends were shocked at first, but now they are used to visiting me on my boat and they know I'm happy.'

▶ 4.2

KATE So what's it like to be a firefighter, William?
WILLIAM It's really tough, much harder than I thought. The training is very rigorous and the instructors really stretch us.
K But you've finished all the training?
W Not yet. It's not so straightforward to become a firefighter. First, there's this arduous training schedule and then a tricky written test to do at the end.
K Well, you do like a challenge! It sounds like a very demanding job.

▶ 4.3

1 umbrella
2 pullover
3 useless
4 sugar
5 supper
6 attitude
7 result
8 influential
9 enthusiasm

▶ 4.4

MARK Education is getting worse and worse in this country.
LILY Oh, I don't know. Some things are improving.
M Like what? Teachers don't know what they are doing.
L I'm not sure about that. They work very hard.
M Yes, but they need more training.
L Maybe you're right, but teachers are not the real problem.
M True – kids just don't want to study.
L Really, do you think so?
M I do. They spend far too much time messing about on computers.
L I know what you mean, but on the other hand technology is so central.
M Hang on, someone's texting me …

▶ 4.5

1 **A** It was an absolutely terrible hotel! I never want to go there again.
   B Oh, I don't know. It wasn't that bad.
2 **A** I really didn't like that film. It was so boring!
   B Oh, I don't know. It wasn't that boring.
3 **A** I loved that restaurant. The menu was really original.
   B Oh, I don't know. It wasn't that original.
4 **A** Have you seen that new shop? It looks great!
   B Oh, I don't know. It doesn't look that great.
5 **A** I thought the meeting today was far too long.
   B Oh, I don't know. It wasn't that long.

▶ 4.6

REPORTER I'm here on the grounds of the University of South Norwood, on a day that many of the students here will remember for a long time – graduation day. I took the chance to speak to some of them today about this – you could maybe call it a life-changing day.
OK, so I'm here with Carl. How are you feeling today?
CARL Pretty happy! It's not been easy. I had to work really hard this summer, a lot of revision, a lot of time spent in the library or in my room with a pile of books in front of me. It was all pretty gruelling really.
R Was it worth it?
C Oh, yeah, definitely. I feel great today. All the hard work paid off, I suppose. It's really been a struggle at times – I'm a full-time student, or I was, but I also had to work in a restaurant for 20 hours a week to support my studies. So it was a challenge sometimes. But today, being here with my family and getting my diploma – it's great, and it's why I put all that effort in.
R Great, well, congratulations!
C Thank you.
R So, Samantha, are you happy today?
SAMANTHA Of course! It means I've finished university now and I can go and find a job.

R So how has it been? It must have been a lot of work for you to get through.
S Well, yeah, I suppose. It's been tricky sometimes, but it's never been a struggle. I found most parts of my course quite straightforward. I always did quite well in my exams, so it wasn't a big problem really. The only thing was that I had to do my last three exams in two days – that was quite demanding. But in the end, you just do it – you're forced to really, there's no choice.
R Enjoy your day.
S Thanks.
R OK, so we're going to speak to Luke. How are you feeling?
LUKE OK, I suppose. Yeah, pretty good.
R You're not happy that you're graduating today?
L Yeah, I am happy. But I'm a bit disappointed as well. I didn't get the grade I was hoping for, so today, well I'm happy, but I'm also a little bit … sad, I suppose.
R Sorry to hear that. Do you want to tell us what went wrong?
L I don't know really. In my last two exams, I just didn't get very good marks, and that influenced my final grade for my whole degree. I had a really bad cold in the week before those last two exams, so I think that affected me a bit. But unless you're seriously ill on the day of the exam itself, the university doesn't take things like that into account. I don't think it's right because it probably had an effect on my performance in those two exams.
R Well, I hope you enjoy your day despite your disappointment.
L Thanks.
R So, Jane, how are you feeling right now?
JANE I feel great! And relieved! It means I can relax a bit.
R What kinds of things will you remember about your time at university?
J Mainly being tired, I think! It's been a pretty punishing time. As you can probably tell, I'm a bit older than most of the students graduating today. I was 40 when I decided to go to university. None of my friends had ever gone to university, nobody in my family. So that really stretched me, really challenged me. But that's also why I wanted to do it.
R And what's the future for you now? Have you found a job yet?
J Well, I already had a job – I never gave it up. But hopefully, having a degree will open up a few more opportunities for me at work. I was a bit stuck before, I think.
R Thanks, and best of luck.
J Thanks.

Unit 5

▶ 5.1

KATY Have you read this article, Josh? It says there's a good chance our generation will live to be 150 years old!
JOSH Who knows, what it says may be true. But what evidence is there?
K Advances in medicine will certainly be a factor, and people won't die from all sorts of diseases common today. Also, technology will probably make everyday life easier.
J Fine, but I doubt if many people will want to live that long. It's unlikely that it'll be much fun to be 150.
K The article says that we may well be able to work until that age. There's a good chance that machines will do all the hard work, like washing and cleaning, so that we do easier tasks, like making phone calls.
J Interesting. I'm sure there'll even be a special Olympics for people over 100!
K Yes, it's bound to happen, so start training!

▶ 5.2

1 think
2 athletic
3 breath
4 Earth
5 length
6 month
7 the
8 breathing
9 clothes
10 either
11 leather
12 though

▶ 5.3

Let's travel to the year 2049! We won't be living on Earth because pollution and wars will have destroyed the old planet. Instead, planet Zeus will be our home. Giant space ships will have transported everyone and everything from Earth before it exploded in 2045. Zeus won't be a bad place to live and some things will go on as normal. Adults will be going to work every morning. Children will be studying at school and old people will be complaining about almost everything. Many things will be different, though. Because of the different atmosphere, our hair will have turned green – at least it won't have fallen out – and we will be walking about in space suits. Special tablets will have replaced food and drink, so we won't be cooking at all and we won't be eating out at restaurants. Yes, life will have changed quite a lot. Welcome to 2049, and the future we will have created.

▶ 5.4

MAGDA You know, I'm seriously thinking of taking this job in Paris.
ROMAN No wonder! One good thing about it is the higher salary. It's basically a promotion.
M True, but the trouble with that is more pressure and stress. A big disadvantage of the position I've been offered is that I'll have too much to do.
R Come on, one of the best things about you is how you respond to a challenge.
M I suppose so ... Another problem with this job offer is that I'll need to improve my French – and fast!
R No need to worry about that either. The advantage of living and working in a foreign country is that you learn the language quickly.
M You have an answer to everything!
R The only drawback of the job I can see is the size of the company. Do you really want to work in a company that big?
M If they pay me enough money, yes!

▶ 5.5

A How about eating out tonight for a change?
B It's an idea, I suppose. Where shall we go?
A There's a new Thai place which has just opened.
B Mm, I don't know about that. I'm not so keen on spicy food.
A Well, there's the Italian just up the hill.
B That might be worth a try and it's not far.
A Let's walk there, it's a lovely day.
B Yes, that makes sense. I need the exercise!
A We could invite Amelia and Rob, too.
B That's not a bad idea. They'd need to drive there, though.
A Then they could give us a lift if we feel too lazy to walk back.
B That's a possibility, although we might have to invite them in for a coffee or something.
A So I've got an excuse to make one of your favourite lemon cakes.
B That's a great idea! You haven't made one for ages.

▶ 5.6

1 The trouble is it could take a long time to get the money.
2 The good thing about it is we're not far away from the centre.
3 The problem is people are starting to talk about her.
4 The advantage is the price isn't very high.
5 The drawback is no one really knows what's going to happen.
6 The advantage is we can see a lot more of each other.
7 The trouble is I'm not sure I've got time to help him.
8 A definite disadvantage is it means selling the car.

▶ 5.7

ANDREW What's that you're reading on the Internet, Fran?
FRAN It's just a news story. It's about a supermarket chain. It has most of the products that a normal supermarket has, but it doesn't sell anything with packaging – so nothing's sealed in plastic, not fruit, not vegetables, not even meat or eggs.
A Really? How does that work?
F Well, you just take along your own bags, or boxes, or whatever.

Audioscripts

A Oh, I see ... Isn't that a bit complicated?
F Or you can actually get bags there. But then you bring them back and use them again and again.
A Well, I suppose it sounds like a good idea. But I don't think I'll be going to a supermarket like that by choice.
F Why?
A Well, when I do the shopping I just want to get everything done quickly. I don't want to have to worry about bringing my own boxes or packing things myself.
F But it's much more environmentally friendly!
A Sure, I imagine it is, but I'm too busy for that kind of thing. And anyway, I already do quite a lot. I'm aware that we have to think about global warming, so I don't use the car too much, I throw litter in the bin, I turn the tap off when I'm brushing my teeth, that kind of thing.
F I really don't think that taking some extra bags to the supermarket is going to take you that much time! Just think of all the damage that's caused by plastic packaging. Producing it pollutes the Earth's atmosphere and that's the kind of thing that causes climate change.
A Well ...
F But it's not just that – it has a big impact in general. A lot of packaging ends up in the sea, in rivers ...
A I know. You're probably right. I suppose I'm probably just a bit lazy.
F Well, I know it's not easy. But there are lots of things I think we could all do to reduce our carbon footprint ...
A Like what?
F Well, only taking public transport, for example. Never using the car.
A Not easy.
F I know, but there's a difference between 'not easy' and 'impossible'. Or we could all become vegetarian.
A Does that help the environment?
F Yes, because producing meat actually uses a lot of energy and water, much more than producing vegetables.
A Does it? Oh. I'd no idea.
F And it takes up more space, too. More land, I mean, to farm all those big cows ...
A Well, I guess that could be a good reason to cut down on meat. But do you really think people are going to be happy to change their lifestyles like this?
F No, that's my point. We could all do more, but we don't. We just talk about what we should do.
A Personally, I think there's a chance that technology will save us. You know, if we're able to come up with technology that doesn't harm the environment, like electric cars, factories that don't pollute the air, really efficient machines that don't use much energy ...
F Yeah, there's always that hope, but I think we'll have destroyed the planet before we manage to come up with smart enough technology.
A I suppose we'll see. I'm not as pessimistic as you, though.
F Well, one thing's for sure – if we don't start to deal with the problem, then people on this planet will be paying for it for a long time.

Answer key

Unit 1
1A
1

a 2 has been 3 is he doing 4 was going 5 looks 6 invited 7 were making 8 have 9 Have you watched 10 dropped

c 2 have, met 3 do, do 4 wrote 5 were coming 6 remember 7 didn't have 8 hasn't finished 9 are, getting 10 think

2

a 2 unsympathetic 3 inspiring 4 passionate 5 arrogant 6 motivated

b Across: 6 stubborn 8 optimistic
Down: 2 ambitious 3 determined 4 sensitive 5 respected 7 naive

3

a /e/: desert, helpful, identity, sensitive, slept
/ɪ/: desire, prizes, revise
/ɜː/: dessert, prefer, service

1B
1

a 2 what did 3 Didn't 4 What for? 5 Which 6 weren't 7 that for 8 you could 9 whether 10 Can 11 knows

c 2 Why is she going to do this?
3 Who doesn't need to register for the competition?
4 Why aren't they giving us our tickets?
5 Which of the challenges would you like to do?
6 What is the most difficult thing you have ever done?
7 What did we do all this hard training for?
8 What happened at the end of the game?
9 Do you think we have a chance of winning?
10 Who designed your website?

2

a 2 try out 3 give up 4 keep it up 5 manage to 6 keep to

b 2 successfully complete 3 keep to 4 work out 5 manage to 6 give up 7 keep it up 8 try out 9 make an effort

1C
1

a 2 c 3 b 4 a 5 c 6 b 7 b 8 c

2

a 4, 6, 2, 1, 5, 3

3

a Final /t/: 2, 5, 8, 9

1D
1

a True: 2, 5; False: 1, 3, 4, 6

b 2 b 3 b 4 c 5 a 6 c

2

a 2 Bad 3 Bad 4 Good 5 Good 6 Good 7 Good 8 Good

3

a Suggested answer

I live in a small town but I use my car to get to work and do the shopping because it's easier. I walk short distances, usually when my husband has the car, but I never cycle, so naturally this was a new experience for me!

Both walking and cycling are great exercise and surprisingly I really enjoyed the week because I saw lots of interesting things that I never usually notice. Quite a few other people were walking and cycling too, so it was quite sociable. I also saved a lot of money because petrol is so expensive.

Inevitably, there were some problems. I needed more time to get to work, and one day it rained and that wasn't much fun on my bike. Unfortunately, cycling can be dangerous even in small towns because of all the traffic.

It was an interesting experience, but I think in modern life we do need to make use of cars and public transport because they are so convenient. We could probably use them less and this would be good for our health and the environment.

Reading and listening extension
1

a 3

b 2 a 3 b 4 c 5 a 6 a

2

a 2, 3, 7, 1, 4, 5, 6

b 2 c 3 a 4 b 5 c 6 c 7 b 8 a

Review and extension
1

2 ✓
3 I think I've decided what to do.
4 Did you ever hear from her again afterwards?
5 ✓
6 I don't know Tom. What's he like?
7 Why didn't you tell me?
8 ✓

2

2 Don't mention it to Laura. She's quite sensitive about it.
3 The Mayor is very respected in this town.
4 The President gave a passionate speech about crime.
5 ✓
6 ✓

3

2 b 3 c 4 e 5 d 6 f

Unit 2
2A
1

a 2 was speaking 3 had left 4 set 5 had been 6 were you doing 7 bought 8 had broken 9 were you waiting 10 made

b 2 had finished 3 came 4 hadn't gone 5 burnt / had burnt 6 had started 7 had been crying 8 was getting 9 Did you see 10 had never been 11 went 12 was wearing 13 didn't get 14 ran

2

a 2 rid 3 hold 4 swept 5 point 6 attention 7 away 8 involved

b 2 get through 3 get the feeling 4 get anywhere 5 get into trouble 6 get on my nerves

3

'had': 1, 2, 4, 6, 7, 9, 10

2B
1

a 2 unless 3 As long as 4 When 5 provided 6 In case 7 If 8 provided 9 as soon as 10 If

c 2 c 3 h 4 a 5 f 6 d 7 g 8 e

78

Answer key

2

a

A	E	N	V	I	R	O	N	M	E	N	T	E	U	L
K	N	C	R	H	B	E	X	U	D	D	O	X	K	E
X	D	T	S	G	T	I	C	U	L	E	T	C	E	L
S	A	D	S	N	P	C	L	N	Y	P	B	E	K	M
U	N	Q	E	T	B	S	R	I	A	R	N	P	Y	J
C	G	L	M	R	A	M	A	O	T	O	T	T	X	K
O	E	X	T	T	S	N	R	O	R	T	A	I	J	Z
C	R	E	A	T	U	R	E	Q	K	E	G	O	S	L
S	E	B	R	I	L	L	I	A	N	C	L	N	H	B
F	D	K	I	H	L	E	D	G	N	T	D	A	P	L
U	F	L	A	U	C	C	N	S	P	E	C	I	E	S
L	P	J	H	N	F	Y	Q	T	D	D	G	A	S	R
B	U	V	J	T	J	Z	Q	K	E	I	B	B	B	C
Y	Z	Z	I	I	R	M	P	H	A	B	I	T	A	T
S	K	T	S	X	A	Z	D	I	J	G	B	W	D	X

b 2 creatures   3 risk   4 extinct   5 survive   6 hunt   7 environment   8 habitat

2C

1
a 2 shall   3 don't   4 did   5 wasn't   6 haven't   7 could   8 aren't

2
a 2 b   3 a   4 b   5 a   6 c

3
a Asking a question: 2, 5, 7, 10
Checking information: 3, 4, 6, 8, 9

2D

1
a 1 Getting into the sport   2 Training   3 What you need   4 On the day

b True: 1, 3, 4, 6, 8; False: 2, 5, 7

2
a c

3
a Suggested answer

Preparation
1 The best time to go is in the autumn. You can find more mushrooms in the morning, when there are fewer people around.
2 Mushrooms grow everywhere, but forests are the best place to find them. They grow near trees, so look carefully there.
3 It can be cool in a forest, so wear some warm clothes. You'll need strong shoes or boots.
4 Check the weather forecast before you go.

In the forest
5 Be careful. There may be dangerous animals, but the biggest risk is simple accidents like falling over.
6 You can't eat every mushroom. Go with someone experienced and never pick mushrooms you don't know. There are internet applications to check mushrooms.
7 Remember where you are going, use stones to mark your way if necessary. If you are lost, keep calm and plan how to get back.
8 Forests are beautiful places, so don't drop any litter or damage anything.

At home
9 Mushrooms don't last very long, so eat them at once or put them in the freezer.
10 There are many ways to cook mushrooms, for example in soups and pies. Enjoy your tasty meal and start planning your next trip to the forest!

Reading and listening extension

1
a 1, 3, 5, 6
b 1 d   2 c   3 a   4 b
c True: 1, 3, 5, 7; False: 2, 4, 6, 8

2
a 2
b 2 a   3 b   4 c   5 b   6 a   7 c

Review and extension

1
2 ✓
3 I met Maria three years ago, when I was a student.
4 She had been waiting for a chance and finally she got one.
5 ✓
6 I'll watch it if it's on TV.

2
2 ✓
3 ✓
4 People could do more to protect the environment.
5 Every year, hundreds of animal species just disappear.
6 The Siberian tiger could soon become extinct.

3
2 face the fact   3 say it to my face   4 can't face   5 face a difficult choice
6 face the music

Unit 3

3A

1
a 2 down on   3 it out   4 into   5 on about   6 off   7 of   8 out   9 up to me
10 up

c 2 Try your hardest and don't let us down.
3 I've fallen out with Tony and we're not friends.
4 You can't get away with mistakes like that.
5 Go and figure it out for yourself.
6 Why don't you just try it out?
7 Michelle made it up to impress him.
8 You need to believe in what you're doing.
9 Can anyone come up with a better idea?
10 French is difficult, but I soon picked it up.

2
a 2 ability   3 outstanding   4 talent   5 successful   6 exceptional
7 potential   8 skilled

c 2 Olympic athletes are all exceptional in their field.
3 She's quite successful at what she does.
4 I became quite skilled at the game.
5 The ability to run long distances is important.
6 Lesley is brilliant at most ball sports.
7 He has the potential to be world champion one day.
8 Carl Lewis was outstanding at the long jump.

3B

1
a 2 They won   3 did you think   4 have just arrived   5 I was running
6 has been doing   7 completed   8 I've been running   9 played
10 been learning

b 2 ran   3 has already beaten   4 started   5 was winning   6 've been training
7 've tried   8 've been looking   9 has contacted

2
a 2 referee   3 cheer   4 spectators   5 represent   6 pitch

b 2 compete   3 athletes   4 competitive   5 train   6 represent   7 victory
8 championships   9 records   10 cheer

3
a 2 compe<u>ti</u>tions   3 com<u>pete</u>   4 <u>cham</u>pionships   5 pro<u>fess</u>ional   6 <u>ath</u>lete
7 pro<u>fess</u>ion   8 <u>train</u>ing   9 per<u>form</u>ance   10 com<u>pet</u>itors
11 per<u>form</u>   12 <u>vic</u>tory   13 vic<u>tor</u>ious

79

3C

1

a
2 Another thing to remember is the price.
3 I think maybe we should stay at home.
4 Don't you think it's a good idea to ask?
5 How does it sound if we watch a film on Sunday?
6 But don't you agree that it'd be easier to eat out?

b
2 Anyway, as I was saying, Tessa needs to decide.
3 Another idea might be to go the day before.
4 Just going back to what I was saying before.
5 I thought maybe we could invite Simon.
6 Of course, we could always check on the Internet.
7 But don't you agree that it'd be better to ask first? / But don't you agree that it would be better to ask first?
8 So, to get back to Martin and his problems.

2

a
2 beach V   peach U
3 ferry U   very V
4 simple U   symbol V
5 girl V   curl U
6 save V   safe U
7 pie U   buy V
8 pig V   pick U
9 pack U   back V
10 have a V have to U

3D

1

a a 4 b 3 c 5 d 1 e 2

b 2 b 3 c 4 a 5 b 6 c 7 a

2

a 2 most 3 least 4 decrease 5 50 6 5

3

a Suggested answer

Sport is a very important part of life and apart from actively taking part, many people enjoy following sports championships and events throughout the year. However, they can choose how they prefer to do this.

The bar chart compares five ways of following sport today and fifteen years ago. The results in the graph show their relative popularity in percentages, not whether we are actually watching more sport.

You can see that there are obvious changes in the graph. In fact, the Internet seems to have completely changed our habits of following sport.

As you can see, the most noticeable increase is in the use of the Internet, while there's a significant decrease in watching TV and reading newspapers. Perhaps this is because the Internet offers instant news all the time and it is more convenient and cheaper than the alternatives.

These results shouldn't surprise anyone, as they are a reflection of the modern world where technology has changed so much of how we live. This trend may continue into the future or perhaps some new medium may appear.

Review and listening extension

1

a 1, 2, 4

b 2 a 3 a 4 b 5 a 6 c 7 b 8 c

2

a 1 d 2 c 3 b 4 a 5 e

b 2 Tina 3 Mark 4 Mark 5 Mark 6 Both Mark and Tina

Review and extension

1

2 ✓
3 It's warm, take your jumper off.
4 We're looking for a new secretary at the moment.
5 ✓
6 Sheila has just been told about it and needs time to think.
7 Don't worry. I've already sent the letter.
8 I've been waiting for you for ages!
9 ✓
10 I don't know. I haven't decided yet.

2

2 It's not possible to get there by public transport.
3 No one doubts her ability to get to the very top.
4 It was another fantastic performance by the Kenyan.
5 ✓
6 ✓
7 What did the audience think of the film?
8 And the footballers are just coming out on to the pitch.

3

2 If you don't know it, look it up online.
3 She thought about it and decided not to bring the matter up.
4 I used it all up yesterday, so I went and bought some more.
5 We looked at the bill and added it up again.
6 I went running with Sarah, but I couldn't keep up with her.
7 I started to learn Spanish and picked it up quite quickly.
8 He works so hard and I've always looked up to him.

Unit 4

4A

1

a 2 used to 3 wouldn't 4 lived 5 used to 6 wasn't 7 used to work 8 got used to 9 wasn't used to 10 get

b 2 left 3 used to 4 would sleep 5 realised 6 was used to 7 would go 8 decided 9 got used to 10 are used to visiting

2

a
2 No one knows what the effect was.
3 Shakespeare has had a big influence on the English language.
4 That's the main cause of the problem.
5 It could affect millions of people.
6 As a result of this, there is less money to spend.
7 The new law resulted in protests and demonstrations.
8 Generally, it's had a positive effect on people.

b 2 influence 3 affect 4 result 5 is caused by 6 effect 7 as a result 8 lead

4B

1

a
2 I had to catch the 5:30 train.
3 No, I can work from home on Saturdays.
4 Yes, the boss lets us have one day at home.
5 Yes, I can find a seat on the train.
6 I'm tired during the day.
7 No, I don't have to unless we have a deadline.
8 You should speak to my boss!

b 2 ought to 3 doesn't have to 4 mustn't 5 was supposed 6 don't need to 7 run 8 to eat 9 beat 10 forced to

2

a 2 rigorous 3 strict 4 punishing 5 tough 6 tricky

b 2 rigorous 3 stretch 4 straightforward 5 arduous 6 tricky 7 challenge 8 demanding

3

a /ʌ/: supper, result
/ʊ/: pullover, sugar
/uː/ or /juː/: useless, attitude, influential, enthusiasm

4C

1

a Careful disagreement
Really, did you think so?
Oh, I don't know.
Maybe you're right, but …
I know what you mean, but on the other hand …
I'm not sure about that.

Direct disagreement
That's just not true.
You can't really believe that.
No way!
I'm afraid you're wrong there.

b 2 I'm not sure about that. They work very hard.
3 Maybe you're right, but teachers are not the real problem.
4 Really, do you think so?
5 I know what you mean, but on the other hand technology is so central.

# Answer key

2

a The strongest stress in each response is on the word 'that'.

4D

1

a 2 student 3 fluently 4 outside 5 forests 6 people 7 reliable 8 strong

b True: 1, 2, 5, 6, 8; False: 3, 4, 7

2

a 2 in 3 give 4 position 5 strongly 6 forward

3

a Suggested answer

Dear Sir/Madam,

I read your advertisement on the Internet and I would like to apply to be a volunteer in the Winter Olympics.

I am a student of economics in Granada. I am a good communicator and speak several languages: my native language is Spanish, I know English to B2 level and B1 French. In addition, I am friendly and hardworking and love new challenges.

As someone very interested in sport myself – I am a keen skier and snowboarder – I believe that I am in an excellent position to help athletes and visitors with any problems they have. I am flexible and ready to take on any task. I have never been a volunteer before but I would be more than happy to give up my free time.

Every four years I watch the Winter Olympics on TV and it has always been my dream to attend and help in this amazing event. I strongly believe that sport brings people together and the Olympics are very important. Volunteers are an essential part of the Olympics and I am sure that I can make a valuable contribution.

Thank you for considering my application. I am looking forward to hearing from you.

Reading and listening extension

1

a 4

b 1 Irene 2 Malc 3 Sam 4 Sara 5 Paul

c True: 3, 5; False: 1, 2, 4

2

a 1

b 1 a 2 c 3 a 4 b 5 c 6 b 7 a

Review and extension

1

2 ✓
3 She is used to living by herself now.
4 This could be the last time we come here.
5 I hope we can do this again some time.
6 ✓

2

2 I'm worried that it might affect my health.
3 ✓
4 My first teacher was very strict.
5 ✓
6 Prisons are basically for punishing criminals.

3

2 if 3 far as 4 a whole 5 I know 6 I'm concerned 7 a matter of fact 8 for

Unit 5

5A

1

a 2 may 3 will 4 won't 5 will probably 6 doubt 7 unlikely 8 may 9 that 10 will 11 sure 12 to happen

c 2 c 3 a 4 c 5 b 6 c 7 c 8 a 9 a 10 b

2

a 2 unreliable 3 thoughtless 4 adventurous 5 sympathetic 6 well-organised

b 2 irresponsible 3 cautious 4 disorganised 5 uncompetitive 6 adventurous 7 ambitious

3

a /θ/: athletic, breath, Earth, length, month
/ð/: the, breathing, clothes, either, leather, though

5B

1

a 2 have finished 3 be living 4 be feeding 5 have completed 6 have achieved 7 be driving 8 have learned 9 be getting 10 have seen

b 2 will have destroyed 3 will have transported 4 will be going 5 will be studying 6 will be complaining 7 will have turned 8 won't have fallen 9 will be walking 10 will have replaced 11 won't be cooking 12 won't be eating 13 will have changed 14 will have created

2

a 2 h 3 b 4 e 5 g 6 a 7 d 8 c

b 2 friendly 3 solar 4 environment 5 atmosphere 6 footprint 7 rough 8 climate 9 impact

5C

1

a 2 about 3 with 4 of 5 about 6 with 7 about 8 of 9 of

2

a 2 Mm, I don't know about that. I'm not so keen on spicy food.
3 That might be worth a try and it's not far.
4 Yes, that makes sense. I need the exercise!
5 That's not a bad idea. They'd need to drive there, though.
6 That's a possibility, although we might have to invite them in for a coffee or something.
7 That's a great idea! You haven't made one for ages.

3

a 2 The <u>good</u> thing about it <u>is</u> we're not far away from the centre.
3 The <u>problem is</u> people are starting to talk about her.
4 The <u>advantage is</u> the price isn't very high.
5 The <u>drawback is</u> no one really knows what's going to happen.
6 The <u>advantage is</u> we can see a lot more of each other.
7 The <u>trouble is</u> I'm not sure I've got time to help him.
8 A <u>definite disadvantage</u> is it means selling the car.

5D

1

a 2 growth 3 against 4 for 5 conclusion 6 crisis 7 manage

b True: 2, 4, 5; False: 1, 3, 6

2

a For: 2, 3, 6, 7; Against: 4, 5, 8

3

a Suggested answer

There are many countries around the world where people live in difficult circumstances and struggle just to survive. The question is whether it is the responsibility of richer countries to give them aid, and if this actually produces any results.

Many people believe that we have a moral responsibility to help poorer people. It is not fair that where you are born determines your standard of living. Everyone should have an equal chance, but this is only possible if wealth is shared around the world.

However, there is an argument that giving aid just makes developing countries dependent on richer ones and stops them finding their own solutions. Furthermore, internal politics and even corruption can mean aid never reaches the people who need it. In some situations, then, aid is wasted and actually has a harmful effect.

On balance, it seems that helping other people is our responsibility, but we must think before we act. My own view is that we should try to find reliable charities and make an effort to help poorer countries. Saying that aid doesn't reach people is not an excuse.

Reading and listening extension

1

a 2

b a 2   b 3   c 4   d 1   e 5

c True: 1, 3; False: 2, 4, 5, 6

2

a 1, 2, 4, 5

b 2 a   3 b   4 b   5 a   6 b   7 c

Review and extension

1

2 She has probably been waiting for this news all week.
3 Your trip to Antarctica certainly won't disappoint you. / Your trip to Antarctica will certainly not disappoint you.
4 ✓
5 What will we be doing this time tomorrow?
6 ✓

2

2 I always thought Tom was reliable until this latest incident.
3 ✓
4 If your desk is always tidy, you're probably well organised.
5 Pollution has led to climate change in many areas.
6 ✓

3

2 nice side   3 both sides   4 from side to side   5 to one side

Video exercises

Unit 1

a 2 a   3 e   4 f   5 d   6 c

b 2 horses   3 a water sport   4 be   5 is old fashioned   6 has finished working

c 2 a   3 b   4 c   5 a

Unit 2

a 2 on their own   3 can harm her   4 didn't really need to worry

b 2 b   3 c   4 a   5 a

c 2 c   3 a   4 d   5 b

Unit 3

a 2 b   3 a   4 c   5 b

b 2 run the marathon quickly   3 plays football   4 dedication

c 2 b   3 c   4 a   5 b

Unit 4

a 2 b   3 d   4 c

b 2 c   3 c   4 a   5 c

c 2 well paid   3 satisfied   4 deserve   5 make it a positive experience

Unit 5

a 2 b   3 c   4 b   5 b

b 2 a   3 d   4 b

c 2 higher   3 industry   4 weeks   5 the media   6 can

Acknowledgements

The authors and publishers acknowledge the following sources of copyright material and are grateful for the permissions granted. While every effort has been made, it has not always been possible to identify the sources of all the material used, or to trace all copyright holders. If any omissions are brought to our notice, we will be happy to include the appropriate acknowledgements on reprinting.

The publisher has used its best endeavours to ensure that the URLs for external websites referred to in this book are correct and active at the time of going to press. However, the publisher has no responsibility for the websites and can make no guarantee that a site will remain live or that the content is or will remain appropriate.

The publishers are grateful to the following for permission to reproduce copyright photographs and material:

Key: L = left, C = centre, R = right, T = top, B = bottom

p.4(TR): Shutterstock/Auremar; p.5(1): Shutterstock/Goran Bogicevic; p.5(2): Getty Images/Mike Harrington; p.5(3): Alamy/Tom Parkes; p.5(4): Alamy/Mac Pix; p.5(5): Alamy/Image Source Salsa; p.5(6): Shutterstock/Natasha Breen; p.6(TR): Shutterstock/Maria Danilkina; p.6(BL): Shutterstock/Orletskyyyy; p.7(BR): Shutterstock/Warren Goldswain; p.8(BL): Shutterstock/Yakub88; p.9(TL): Shutterstock/Tyler Olson; p.11(BR): Shutterstock/Peter Wollinga; p.12(BL): Shutterstock/Tatiana Popova; p.13(B): Alamy/Eitan Simanor; p.14(CL): Shutterstock/Mogens Trolle; p.14(BR): Shutterstock/Enciktat; p.14(C): Shutterstock/Erni; p.14(BL): Shutterstock/James Van Den Broek; p.15(TL): Shutterstock/Salajean; p.16(TR): Shutterstock/Iculig; p.17(TL): Getty Images/MLB Photos; p.20(B): Alamy/PCN Photography; p.21(TL): Shutterstock/Mangostock; p.22(B): Shutterstock/Shahid Ali Khan; p.25(BR): Shutterstock/Vito Zgonc; p.26(C): Shutterstock/Connel; p.27(TL): Shutterstock/Rawpixel; p.28(T): iStockphoto/Mlenny; p.29(CL): Alamy/Robert Harding Picture Library Ltd/Geoff Renner; p.29(1): Alamy/Design Pics/Ernest Manewal; p.29(2): Shutterstock/CoolKengzz; p.29(3): Shutterstock/Johnny Habell; p.29(4): Shutterstock/Keith Wheatley; p.29(5): iStockphoto/MarcelC; p.29(6): Shutterstock/OliverSved; p.29(7): Alamy/Keith Morris News; p.29(8): Alamy/Ellen McKnight; p.29(9): Shutterstock/Huguette Roe; p.30(B): Shutterstock/Gurgen Bakhshetsyan; p.31(T): Shutterstock/Blvdone; p.31(BR): Corbis/Per-Anders Pettersson; p.32: Shutterstock/Ollyy; p.33(TL): Shutterstock/Kzenon.

Video stills by Rob Maidment and Sharp Focus Productions: p.18, p.24.

Filming in King's College by kind permission of the Provost and Scholars of King's College, Cambridge.

Illustrations by David Semple p.23; Vicky Woodgate p.10.